Seven League Boots

by
Richard Halliburton

The Long Riders' Guild Press
www.thelongridersguild.com
ISBN No: 1-59048-081-3

D1475598

To the Reader:

The editors and publishers of The Long Riders' Guild Press faced significant technical and financial difficulties in bringing this and the other titles in the Equestrian Travel Classics collection to the light of day.

Though the authors represented in this international series envisioned their stories being shared for generations to come, all too often that was not the case. Sadly, many of the books now being published by The Long Riders' Guild Press were discovered gracing the bookshelves of rare book dealers, adorned with princely prices that placed them out of financial reach of the common reader. The remainder were found lying neglected on the scrap heap of history, their once-proud stories forgotten, their once-glorious covers stained by the toil of time and a host of indifferent previous owners.

However The Long Riders' Guild Press passionately believes that this book, and its literary sisters, remain of global interest and importance. We stand committed, therefore, to bringing our readers the best copy of these classics at the most affordable price. The copy which you now hold may have small blemishes originating from the master text.

We apologize in advance for any defects of this nature.

Portrait of the author painted in Addis Ababa by an Ethiopian artist.

Books by

RICHARD HALLIBURTON

∾

THE ROYAL ROAD TO ROMANCE
THE GLORIOUS ADVENTURE
NEW WORLDS TO CONQUER
THE FLYING CARPET
SEVEN LEAGUE BOOTS

CONTENTS

CHAPTER		PAGE
	INTRODUCTION: SEVEN LEAGUE BOOTS	13
I	DEVIL'S ISLAND—IN AMERICA	21
II	EIGHT VOLUNTEERS FOR DEATH	34
III	A BATTLE AND A CAT	47
IV	HIS MAJESTY THE DISHWASHER	59
V	THE BLACK KING'S CASTLE	71
VI	THE BONES OF COLUMBUS	79
VII	HOW TO BUY AN ELEPHANT	91
	THE MASSACRE OF THE ROMANOFFS	
VIII	1. *The Assassin*	100
IX	2. *The Victims*	110
X	3. *The Death House*	120
XI	4. *Slaughter*	139
XII	5. *Postscript*	145
XIII	THE WHEAT AND THE EMERALDS	156
XIV	MRS. LENIN	167
XV	THE HUNDRED HAPPIEST CHILDREN IN THE WORLD	176
XVI	STRAIGHT TALK FROM RUSSIA	182
XVII	THE OLDEST MAN IN THE WORLD	199
XVIII	THE LAST OF THE CRUSADERS	208
XIX	OUT OF RUSSIA	220
XX	THE SULTANA OF TURKEY—FROM MARTINQUE	229

CONTENTS—*concluded*

CHAPTER		PAGE
XXI	No Woman's Land	245
XXII	The Involuntary Monk	255
XXIII	The City of the Minotaur	271
XXIV	The Deadliest Sport in History	285
XXV	Horror Island	291
XXVI	Scarlet Sister Salome	303
XXVII	Hadji Halliburton	318
XXVIII	The Giant	333
XXIX	The Rhinoceros Express	349
XXX	The King of Kings	362
XXXI	In the Tracks of Hannibal	376
XXXII	Uphill	386
XXXIII	Half-way to Heaven	401
XXXIV	The Elefantessa	409

INTRODUCTION

SEVEN LEAGUE BOOTS

ONE midsummer night, not long ago, a motor-powered fishing boat put out to sea from the harbor of a small port on the Gulf of Mexico. There were no waves, no wind. Upon the unruffled waters of the Gulf the planets caught glimpses of themselves, and the stars strewed their images in the helmsman's path.

The fishing boat had a crew of two. I was the only passenger. With a ten-hour voyage ahead, I tried, using my suitcase for a pillow, to make myself comfortable on the deck.

But there was no comfort. The engine was too close, the deck too hard. So I lay awake, face up to the stars, listening to the splashing water at the prow—and thinking:

The last three days—what eventful days they had been for me! Three days ago I had been sitting, just a little bored perhaps, in my house on the Pacific coast, looking out across the blue channel that separated me from Catalina Island twenty miles away. Beyond Catalina lay Hawaii, and beyond that Borneo, and still further Bali. . . . I had been to Hawaii, and Borneo, and Bali . . . but never, I reflected, to Catalina. Some afternoon I ought to make this popular little trip.

Anything to break the spell of an idle California summer. . . . .

And now, seventy-two hours later, I found myself three thousand miles away, leaping off from the southern tip of Florida, westward into the middle of the Gulf of Mexico—found myself catapulted suddenly out of my lazy life by a commission that promised violent activity, perpetual change of scene, and the constant shock of novelty for months to come.

I'm afraid I smiled a little to myself when I thought of it . . . for this was the sort of opportunity every writer, surely once in his life, has dreamed about. I had been commissioned to go anywhere in the world I wished, and write about whatever pleased me. If I wanted to fly to Zululand and write about that— very good. If I wanted to call on the Queen of Bulgaria and write about *that*—also very good. My only orders were to move fast, visit strange places, try to meet whomever I thought interesting and important—and to start at once.

Such a commission was so beautiful I felt it was almost immoral.

Nevertheless, three nights after this invitation had dropped into my lap, I was sailing aboard the fishing boat toward my first "strange place."

Back in California, I'd read the published letters of Dr. Samuel Mudd to his wife.* Dr. Mudd (misleadingly unheroic name!) was the physician who set the

---

* See *The Life of Dr. Samuel A. Mudd, containing Letters from Fort Jefferson,* edited by his daughter, Nettie Mudd; Neale Publishing House, 1906

broken leg of John Wilkes Booth after the murder of
Lincoln and suffered, in consequence, what many believe was a tragic miscarriage of justice. He was sentenced to life imprisonment in Fort Jefferson, that incredible Federal sea-fortress on the Dry Tortugas, the
outwardmost of the Florida keys. Dreyfus himself
could not have told a more tragic and bitter story than
Dr. Mudd, nor was Dreyfus' prison in French Guiana
ever more terrible than Fort Jefferson. Of all the
points of historical interest I had yet to see in America,
this seemed most worthy of a journey.

And so, launched upon my new quest, I left California, reached Florida, and headed for Fort Jefferson,
sixty miles out in the Gulf from Key West.

But after Fort Jefferson——? Because of the pressure of time I'd had no opportunity to re-examine the
map of the world and chart my year ahead. Where was
I going next—now that I could go anywhere?

A flood of answers met these questions:

Cuba, certainly. Through a pleasant friendship with
Admiral Richmond Pearson Hobson,* I had developed
a great desire to know more about the Spanish-American War. Hobson had made me eager to visit Santiago, at the east end of the island, where he had sunk
the *Merrimac,* and where the Spanish warships, in the
famous naval battle that followed, were driven in flames
upon the shore.

And I was resolved to travel to Haiti and climb the
Bonnet à l'Évêque, the mountain soaring three thousand
feet above Cap Haitien, from the summit of which the
ruins of King Christophe's Citadel, one of the wonders
of the world, still command the Black Republic.

---

*Died 1937.

I knew the astonishing story of the rediscovery of Columbus' bones only a generation ago, in a church in the city of Santo Domingo. At this same church the bones are still to be seen, incased in the original leaden casket. Santo Domingo was another place I must explore.

A biography of Hannibal and the chapters on the Punic Wars in Livy's *History of Rome* had given me the idea of retracing Hannibal's elephant-march across the Alps, aboard an elephant of my own, the next time I got to Europe—just as a sporting adventure.

And Russia! I was particularly interested in the tragic end of the Romanoffs. On the map I had found Ekaterinburg, the city in Siberia where the Czar and his family were massacred, and I had made it one of my travel goals.

And Abyssinia! Now was my chance to reach this marvelous and romantic land.

Several times, in years past, I had just missed getting to Mount Athos, that fantastic community in northern Greece where no woman, or any female animal or fowl, has been allowed for centuries. I would include Athos on my tour.

I wanted to return to Palestine and explore the hilltop, overhanging the Dead Sea, where one finds the site of the palace in which Salome danced for the head of John the Baptist.

Arabia Deserta and the explorations of Sir Richard Burton had rekindled my lifelong desire to visit Mecca.

Undisturbed for six months, I had had little else to do but read books about the foreign world . . . hungry, each time I closed one, to see for myself the countries and the people that lived in its pages.

And now suddenly had come the command to go and see them all, to possess myself of a pair of seven league boots and stride across the map, from nation to nation, from continent to continent, straightway to these beckoning goals, to these islands of desire.

At dawn, one of the fishermen roused me, and suggested that I look to the west. There, three miles away, across the pale gray water, I saw, through the early morning haze, the sinister, scowling walls of Fort Jefferson rising, like a sea-monster with a hundred eyes, right out of the waves.

SEVEN LEAGUE BOOTS

Seven League Boots

CHAPTER I

DEVIL'S ISLAND—IN AMERICA

In all the history of America there is no story stranger than the story of Fort Jefferson.

And its strangest feature is that, until just yesterday, no one knew this story—or at least no one remembered it.

Yet of the score or so of forts that safeguard our coasts, Jefferson has had the most troubled and tragic past. Without once engaging in a warlike action, it has seen enough agony to supply a war. In times of peace, it has killed enough men to people a city. The money it cost must have staggered the Treasury. During an entire decade, when it served as a prison, it had the most sinister renown of any spot in the United States. It was our own Devil's Island, filled with traitors, political offenders, spies. The most notorious miscarriage of justice in our records had Fort Jefferson for the scene of its fulfilment.

But during the three decades preceding 1930, not one person in ten thousand, visiting Fortress Monroe or Fort Sumter or Fort McHenry, even so much as knew that Fort Jefferson existed.

While it is difficult to understand how we could have forgotten the history of this astonishing place, it is wholly impossible to understand why the sheer size of the structure has not made it a celebrated monument and kept it in the public eye.

Built by the Federal Government from 1846 to 1860, on one of the coral keys of the Dry Tortugas, the fort remains the largest mass of unreinforced masonry ever raised by Americans. Four hundred guns were lifted to its battlements. Fifty million bricks, brought thirteen hundred miles from Philadelphia, were used to build its walls. No other American fort was ever erected at such fantastic cost.

Nor did any other fort ever turn out to be such a colossal folly. This titanic project, planned for heroic deeds, was carried to completion only to serve, for a while, the most wretched ends, then be abandoned, and allowed to become a vast and desolate derelict whose very name has only recently been rescued from complete oblivion.

But the mystery of its abandonment is not as great as the mystery of its building. Who ordered it built? Who chose the lost little island—barren, waterless, hurricane-swept—for its site? Who supplied the mountains of material and the army of workmen for this stupendous white elephant?

Nobody knows. Some forgotten file in the government archives may hold the secret, but there are almost no public records. Fort Jefferson is just there, blocking out the horizon with its grim and inscrutable presence, giving shelter only to the ghosts of prisoners who perished there by the hundreds, and to the sea birds that have come in to take possession of this vastest ruin in all America.

Visualize, if you can, a huge fort such as this, isolated in the sea with scarcely another human trace from horizon to horizon. Now cover it with half a century of rust and decay, and strew it with the wreckage left by a score of hurricanes—and you will see the sight that greeted me at dawn on the day my fishing boat carried me out into the Gulf of Mexico.

I knew in advance, more or less, what I was to find. But I was still not prepared to come upon so foreign-looking a structure within the boundaries of my own country. It was difficult to believe that this could possibly be part of Monroe County, Florida, U.S.A. . . . perhaps I'd drifted off my course to one of the twelfth-century Crusadic strongholds in Syria, or upon some Norman keep from which William the Conqueror set sail for England. Bastion and battlement, salient towers, crenellations, ramparts—all anchored immovably to the coral key, and all surrounded by a moat and a break-water wall that wars perpetually with the waves.

The reason the government chose this location for a fort, in 1846, is obvious. At that time one of the greatest trade routes for American shipping lay through the Straits of Florida and right past the Dry Tortugas, islands which command (as a glance at the map will show) the northern entrance to the Gulf of Mexico. The military authorities in President Polk's administration decided that this rich avenue of trade must be protected by the greatest of forts—against the Spaniards in Cuba, or any enemy who might come from over the Atlantic. It would dominate the entire Gulf region.

So a super-fortress was designed, apparently in secrecy. And despite the fearful obstacles which the situation offered, the foundations were laid, deep down in the coral rock, at the very edge of the sea. Just above the waves two huge stories of brick arose, built around a fifteen-acre parade ground, solid-faced on the seaward side except for the cannon-ports, but opening into galleries and alcoves toward the court. On the roof were placed the heaviest artillery, bomb-proof shelters and powder magazines, all protected behind masonry barricades.

Almost invariably, in the construction of other castles and forts, stone and earthworks are extensively used. But Fort Jefferson is a mountain of solid brickwork— brick pillars twenty feet in diameter, brick walls ten feet thick, avenues of ponderous brick arches staunch enough to support a thousand tons of brick ramparts and to uphold fifteen-foot, fifteen-inch guns, the very firing of which must have shaken the entire coral key.

And remember, all these bricks, along with tons upon tons of general supplies, had to be brought by sea all the way from Delaware Bay and the Hudson River.

Before setting foot in this strange sea-castle, I had my boat sail completely around the walls. No matter from which side one approaches the fort, it turns a stern, forbidding face. Each of the six sides is five hundred feet long, fifty high and fifty thick. At each of the six corners a huge squat tower bulges out, from which the tower-garrison could rake the wall and moat. From each wall three rows of guns, seventy to a side, once glared down so menacingly that few enemies ever dared come in range of them. Most of the guns are gone, stolen by Cubans for scrap iron, but the biggest ones still remain on the topmost ramparts and reveal clearly what a Gibraltar of defiant strength Fort Jefferson once was.

My fishermen landed me at the crumbling iron dock. This leads to the moat of still water thirty feet wide, separated from the sea itself by a six-foot wall. Across this moat is a wooden bridge, which gives access to the castle's only entrance. In former times a drawbridge was raised and lowered here, but that is gone. Across the top of the portal, carved in the granite facing of the arch, is the ironic name ARCADIA.

Alone, into this frowning and deserted place, I found my way. Within, the view is anything but Arcadian. One comes upon the parade ground, a thousand feet across, strewn, choked, with the most appalling wreckage. In 1898, at the beginning of the Spanish-American War, Fort Jefferson, because of its proximity to Cuba, was temporarily re-occupied. New and elaborate three-story barracks for officers and men were erected on the parade ground, and for a brief period inhabited. But the terrible hurricane of 1919 shook these buildings, long deserted and dilapidated, in its teeth, and strewed their wreckage all over the great court. The weeds and cactus thickets then seized upon these hillocks of debris, and soon a miniature jungle spread across the ruins.

But the original fort is undisturbed, except for the missing guns and the trifling damage done by looters. Down its endless corridors of arched and groined brick rooms I walked, noting that each room enclosed a single gun emplacement, which commanded the sea through a port. Signs of prison occupation were all about— names, drawings, comments, scratched and painted on the walls. And dates: 1852, 1865, 1898. There is no plaster, no wood, no glass—just brick.

By means of worn spiral stairs, I climbed to the ramparts overhanging the moat. Here the enormous cannon, the fallen giants, are strewn about, dismounted and half buried in the sand. For three-fifths of a mile I made the circuit of these battlements. Always the moat was below, fifty feet beneath the parapet. In the old days this moat was stocked with sharks. These man-eaters kept enemies out—and prisoners in.

At the time of my visit, there was not another human being in sight. My boatmen had put out to sea again to fish. Was the stillness then so noticeable, so disconcerting? Far from it. A constant, a strident, a nerve-shattering noise filled the air: the screaming of a million sea birds.

These birds swarm around the fort, in flocks, in clouds, terns and noddies flying swiftly overhead and down into the shallow sea to dive upon the schools of minnows which darken the water with their countless multitudes. The birds do not live within the fort itself, but on a small island, Bird Key, a government preserve, a hundred yards away. When later I visited the islet I could scarcely walk for the thousands of eggs and chicks strewn across the sand. The birds have never learned to be afraid of men. I stroked the neck of a mother noddy sitting upon her single egg. She closed her eyes and purred like a kitten. I walked through a flock of terns that carpeted the beach. They wouldn't even move out of my way.

But tame as both species are, they keep up their screaming day and night. One would have to shout to be heard above the tumult. The air, the land, the sea, vibrate with darting frantic wings and petulant piercing cries. One becomes dizzy and deafened after a few minutes' visit to this whirling world of shrieking birds. Fort Jefferson is a good friend to all these creatures. To it, as to a beacon light, the terns and noddies steer their course each spring. They will not nest elsewhere. They are safe here, and they know it, protected by the grim walls and the tumbled cannon of Fort Jefferson.

As I continued my exploration of the ramparts and battlements, a hot wind from the Gulf beat against my head. I could look out over the water and see ten thousand whitecaps dancing in the sun. And the wind and the waves made me think of the tropical hurricanes that have so frequently swept across this region.

What a fearful battle such a storm must bring about. One hundred and twenty miles out from the mainland, the fort, shunned and desolate, has to face the full fury of the tempest.

Imagine the Gulf, hurricane-driven, raging in the lightning-split darkness against this citadel in the sea. The six-foot brick frame at the outer edge of the moat only serves to trip the giant rollers. They dash across the moat, and fling themselves with a roar against the fortress' walls, sending their bursting spray up over the cannon on the battlements. And the ally of the waves—the wind—racing past at a hundred miles an hour, tears at the huge unyielding blockhouse, determined to blast it from the coral key.

The outer walls themselves face the onslaught unperturbed as granite cliffs. But inside the court, the storm seizes the wrecked barracks, and flings flying timbers, bits of roofs, bricks, furniture, tree-tops, cactus plants, weeds, into a wild maelstrom that beats against the imprisoning inner walls. The wreckage falls to the ground, and is seized again and flung again and shattered again for the hundredth time.

And the terns and the noddies—what happens to them when the hurricanes blow? Do they stay on and struggle with the storm, or do they sense the approach of doom and hurry from its path?

Perhaps no man can tell, for when the barometer drops and the skies blacken, every fisherman or trader runs for his life away from this shallow, reef-strewn, harborless chain of coral islets. The hulks of a hundred ships, from fishing boats to Atlantic liners, lying in pieces on the ocean floor and visible through the clear water, remind seafarers of the deadliness of Fort Jefferson and its neighborhood when these tropic twisters strike the Gulf.

And so, year after year, the fort fights its wild battles in utter loneliness. The wind howls and the waves crash against its sides, and the garrison of ghosts flees, panic-stricken, back into the deepest dungeon. Only when the sea is calm again can one approach the battlefield and view the desolation. One finds the wreckage in the parade ground smashed to smaller bits than before, every tree and bush uprooted, bodies of dead terns in the corners of the court, dead fish floating in the moat where they have fallen after being hurled by the waves against the walls.

For eighty years Fort Jefferson has withstood every assault. But like the very rock which water wears away, the fort's defenses are breaking down. On two of the six sides, the storms have driven great holes in the moat's outer rim, and filled the moat with sand. On these sides the great fortress is now left unprotected—the front-line trench is gone. How many years more can the brick walls themselves, solid and massive though they are, hold back the relentless sea?

It was not the hurricanes, however, that caused the government to abandon this military monster. Scarcely was it finished when the builders realized that for all practical purposes it was going to be a complete failure. For two reasons: the Straits of Florida here are a hundred miles wide, while the fort's largest guns could not command even a tenth of that distance; and there was no harbor nearer than Key West where supporting naval ships could anchor. Terrifyingly armed though it was, it could dominate only a small radius of shallow sea, so that hostile men-of-war could, and did, pass safely by, well out of range even when they were in sight.

Useless as a fort, perhaps—but as a prison Fort Jefferson was, theoretically, ideal. And from 1860 to 1870, the Federal Government, beset with more political and military enemies than during any other period of its history, had need of just such a penal island, escape-proof and isolated.

So, along with the six hundred soldiers in the garrison, all kinds of Federal prisoners (numbering at times more than a thousand) were sent to fill up the great vaulted compartments of the fort. Escape, with the shark-filled moat to face, and the open sea, was almost impossible. Yet to remain was nearly as dangerous, for within the prison there lurked an unrecognized enemy—the mosquito. In the rain-water cisterns beneath the fort, these villainous insects bred, and scattered their terrible yellow-fever germs. Fort Jefferson stands today as a monument to yellow fever. Not the Confederates, nor the Spaniards, nor the hurricanes, ever daunted the garrison or caused the loss of a single life. But the mosquito annihilated thousands of prisoners and guards alike, turned the fort into a pestilential death-trap, and finally drove the few survivors back to Florida.

Into this morgue, in July, 1865, one of the most tragic figures in American history was delivered—Dr. Samuel Mudd.

On April fifteenth of that year, at four o'clock in the morning, two men rode up on horseback to Dr. Mudd's house in southern Maryland, thirty miles below Washington. One of the men had a broken leg and was suffering intensely. Dr. Mudd skilfully set the leg and bound it in splints. Being a kindly, hospitable man as well as a good doctor, he persuaded his patient to rest the remainder of the night in the guest-room. The next morning the two travelers, having paid their bill, rode away.

Because of this merciful act, Dr. Mudd was subsequently arrested and charged with being an accomplice in the most monstrous of crimes, the murder of Abraham Lincoln. The traveler with the broken leg was John Wilkes Booth. He had broken it five hours before, as he leaped from the President's box onto the stage of Ford's Theater, after firing the fatal shot. Escaping despite his accident into Maryland, he sought frantically for a doctor, and found one.

Dr. Mudd insisted, indignantly and consistently, that he knew nothing of the conspiracy. For him the suffering patient, heavily disguised, was just one more anonymous case, which he had treated professionally as was his duty. But the military prosecution, vengeful beyond all reason and looking for victims, guilty or not, to throw to the mob, made a sacrifice of Dr. Mudd. He was sentenced to life imprisonment in Fort Jefferson.

Arriving at this even then notorious place, Dr. Mudd was singled out for especially harsh discipline. He was kept chained in his cell and guarded by blacks.

Two years of this he endured, then once more the yellow fever struck. As usual, everyone went down before it. A most graphic account of this plague of 1867 is given by Dr. Mudd himself in his letters to his wife— letters mailed from the prison. He reported that the disease spread so quickly that the afflicted died faster than they could be buried. Bird Key was turned into a cemetery. There the noddies built their nests in coffins uncovered by the waves, and the terns laid their eggs among the corpses and the skeletons. At one time, every officer in the place was stricken. Nobody knew the cause of the epidemic, nobody knew the cure. Everybody lived in terror, wondering if he were going to be the next victim of the scourge.

Discipline and guard duty were abandoned, for the guards were all dead or dying. The fort doctor perished—one doctor with a thousand delirious patients— and Dr. Mudd, chained in the depths of his cell, volunteered to replace him, and was accepted.

Day and night he worked. He had the gun ports bricked up "to keep out the miasma from the moat," not knowing he was only keeping the mosquitoes in. The mosquitoes finally overtook Dr. Mudd himself, but he did not die. He lived, and as soon as possible returned to his ministrations.

By the time the pestilence had passed, Dr. Mudd had become a hero among those few who survived. They prepared a long petition requesting his liberation, and sent it to Washington. But Washington had not yet recovered from its misdirected fury. Instead of liberty, the authorities sent back orders for the courageous and self-sacrificing doctor to be put back into his cell and his chains.

Is it to be wondered that his next letter to his wife was a bitter cry of complete despair?

Meanwhile, Mrs. Mudd had been as tireless in her efforts to liberate her husband from his prison, as he had been in his efforts to relieve the sick inside it. And in 1869 she succeeded.

The doctor, back in his Maryland home, lived another thirteen years, more or less an invalid, but serving to the last whoever called at his door.

I had read this tragic story before my visit to the Dry Tortugas.* How grimly real it seemed, now that the actual setting was around me. I found the Doctor's cell; the portholes he had bricked up; and I spent half the afternoon deciphering the inscriptions scrawled on the walls, wondering if some of them were not the only epitaphs of prisoners whose fate was no less tragic than that of Dr. Mudd.

---

* A fascinating account of Fort Jefferson and Bird Key is given by George Allan England in *Isles of Romance*, published by The Century Co., 1929.

When darkness made it dangerous to continue my wanderings about the corridors, where hidden openings might drop me into the cisterns below, I mounted again to the ramparts faintly luminous beneath the stars.

How many ghosts the starlight evoked as the shadows crept across the ruins. . . . I could not persuade myself that Fort Jefferson, where so much suffering has been endured, where so many have died in anguish, is not a haunted place. The night-flying, night-crying terns were still darting about the walls. But at night their cries sounded subdued and distressful, like the complaints of slaves dragging cannon to the battlements, like the far-off moans of convicts dying in their subterranean cells. What eerie things one can imagine when watching and listening, alone, in the nighttime, on this island of the dead.

Suddenly a mosquito drifted past my ear, whining its murderous little song—the song of death that killed Fort Jefferson.

This was reality . . . the tiny assassins still ruled the domain they had conquered. Shivering, I retreated through the blackness, down the spiral steps, along the black arches, across the shining moat, away from the portals of Arcadia, and told my fishermen, waiting in their boat, to turn their prow toward Florida and take me back to the land of living men.

CHAPTER II

"To RICHMOND PEARSON HOBSON—the Congressional Medal of Honor, for extraordinary heroism."

"To Richmond Pearson Hobson—advancement to the rank of Rear Admiral, in acknowledgment of his great service in sinking the *Merrimac* at Santiago de Cuba in the war with Spain."

The generation of Americans who were young in 1898 will remember this heroic naval officer as long as they live. And with good reason, for Hobson's exploit at Santiago is one of the finest examples of discipline, courage and patriotism in the annals of America.

It has been my privilege since I was a boy in school to be able to claim the friendship of Admiral Hobson. On several occasions he has allowed me to examine his charts, maps and photographs dealing with the *Merrimac* sinking; and he has borne patiently and answered generously the innumerable questions I've asked him about the last hours of the famous ship.

One of the results of this association was the desire it aroused in me to go to Cuba and make a pilgrimage to the *Merrimac's* grave. Now was my opportunity.

From Fort Jefferson, Santiago was not very far away . . . a hop across the Straits of Florida to Havana, then a run of four hundred miles through the heart of the island to the eastern end.

Santiago lies on the southern coast, six miles from the open sea, at the innermost corner of the most perfect harbor in the West Indies. The bottleneck entrance is scarcely wide enough for two ships to pass, but inside there is room for all the shipping of the world.

The entrance is guarded on each side by two high sentinel-like promontories of rock. On the right side, looking from the ocean, the Spaniards in the sixteenth century built, four hundred feet above the shore, a formidable fortress and called it Morro Castle, after a similar fort guarding the harbor at Havana.

Even before war was declared between Spain and the United States, the Spaniards at Santiago, fighting the rebellious Cubans, had increased the defenses until there were one hundred cannon behind the walls and along the terraces of Morro Castle, and behind hidden earthworks on the opposite slope. The military authorities had every right to feel that no battleship could force its way in and survive the cross-fire of these massed batteries.

On reaching Santiago it was easy enough for me to hire a launch and, with one of Admiral Hobson's charts aboard and a crew that knew every inch of the harbor, go straight to the exact spot where the *Merrimac* sank— a spot in the narrows leading into the inner basin.

The water here is about thirty-five feet deep, but so clear that with a water-glass I could discern the demolished hulk. In order to clear the channel, the Americans on their capture of Santiago dynamited the sunken ship and split the hull down the center, so that today the two halves lie on their sides, partly embedded, with their ribs exposed,

Desiring a closer view I dived overboard and held on to a heavily weighted rope which my boatmen lowered through the water. Not being accustomed to the pressure I was able to descend only some eighteen feet. But this reduced the distance to the closest part of the hulk to about twelve feet, and enabled me to note the barnacles crusted on the iron fragments and the fish swimming in and out among the ribs.

This, then, was where the gallant ship went down. But what of that agonized last voyage, through the darkness, that brought her, tortured and mangled, to this place? From what point had she started, and what had happened on the way?

From the topmost tower of Morro Castle, I knew I would be able to survey the *Merrimac's* entire course. So I beached my boat and climbed the steep trail that led to the fortifications. Here, seated on a prostrate Spanish cannon, four hundred feet above the sea, I could observe the entire sweep of ocean beyond, and channel below, and harbor behind. From this commanding position I could reconstruct all that took place on that fateful night nearly four decades ago.

Immediately upon declaration of war between Spain and America, in April, 1898, Admiral Cervera, Spain's foremost naval commander, with four speedy armored cruisers and two torpedo boats, sailed from Cadiz, headed westward across the Atlantic, eluded the American fleet, and reached Santiago. Single file, the ships steamed into the channel below me, to be greeted by the booming of the gun I sat on and the cheering of the garrison.

The American fleet, consisting of five battleships and

two cruisers, learned of this move and rushed to block-ade the entrance. From my tower every ship, both the American outside and the Spanish inside, would have been in clear view.

Admiral Sampson, aboard the flagship *New York*, immediately saw that there was no hope of forcing the entrance and going after the Spaniards within the har-bor, for no hostile battleship could possibly run the deadly gantlet of the Morro Castle guns.

But he also knew that the channel leading into the harbor was so narrow that a three-hundred-foot ship, sunk athwart, would bottle it up completely, and pre-vent the exit of the Spanish fleet. Naval Constructor Hobson, then twenty-seven years old, likewise aboard the *New York*, insisted he could carry out this daring plan, though he knew it would probably mean—because of the hundred guns that would be trained upon him—his death, and the death of every man accompanying him. Nevertheless Sampson decided that Hobson should make the attempt.

Being a naval engineer, Hobson knew exactly what to do.

He chose the *Merrimac* (a coal collier named after the celebrated Civil War ironclad), because she was long enough—three hundred and thirty feet—to close the channel when properly sunk, and because she was strong enough (he hoped) to withstand, for the few minutes necessary, the concentrated hail of shells that would be poured into her as she approached and passed the deadly batteries.

The general plan was very simple. At night, in the moonlight, Hobson would steer his ship straight at the entrance, and down the channel to the narrowest point. That point, clearly visible from my tower, just to the right of the base of the Morro bluff, was some fifteen hundred feet in from the mouth. Here he would drop his anchors, and then sink the *Merrimac* by means of eight torpedoes lashed alongside, twelve feet below the water-line. Any one of the torpedoes should tear a hole in the hull of the ship big enough to scuttle it.

In case a miracle did happen, and anyone survived the sinking, there was to be a lifeboat towed behind.

Now for a crew.

Who would volunteer?

The regular crew of the *Merrimac* numbered sixty-four. There was no reason to take—and kill—them all. In fact Hobson made his plans so that only seven men besides himself would be necessary.

From the *Merrimac's* own crew there were *sixty-four volunteers*. Of these Hobson chose four—Phillips, a machinist, thirty-two years old; Kelly, a watertender, twenty-nine; Clausen, a cockswain, twenty-eight; and young Deignan, twenty-one, a quartermaster. Hobson told these four exactly what they must expect: that they would be the point-blank target for a hundred guns and would in all probability be blown to pieces. Did they—before it was too late—wish to be excused?

Most certainly not!

Three more were needed. The *Iowa*, commanded by "Fighting Bob" Evans, was asked to contribute one volunteer. Every single man—over six hundred—stepped forward, and begged to be allowed to serve on the *Merrimac*. Evans finally chose a thirty-year-old seaman named Murphy.

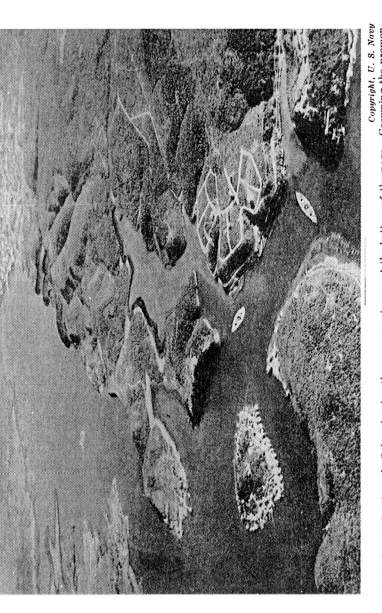

The harbor of Santiago de Cuba, showing the narrow entrance at the bottom of the page. Crowning the promontory at the right of the entrance is Morro Castle. The white ship just beyond the Castle indicates the point where Hobson intended to sink the *Merrimac*. The second white ship indicates the point where it actually sank.

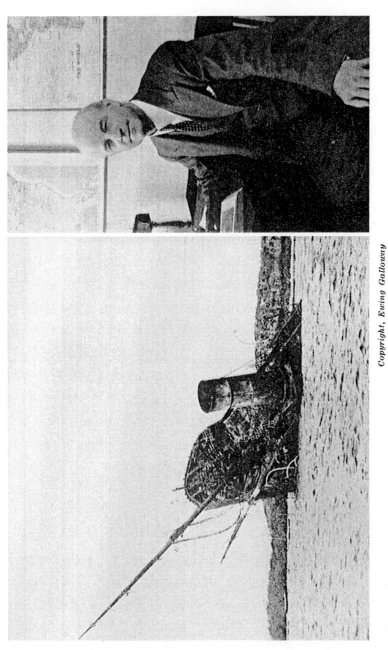

The wreck of the *Merrimac*, photographed shortly after she was sunk in the entrance to Santiago Harbor.

Rear Admiral Richmond Pearson Hobson.

From the *New York* (every man on this ship had likewise volunteered) Hobson selected Charette, thirty-three, an expert gunner's mate familiar with torpedoes, and Montague, thirty-one, the chief master-at-arms.

The crew was now complete.

Hobson was to stand on the bridge and signal his men by means of ropes attached to their wrists. He anticipated there would be such a roar of exploding shells that he would not be able to shout his commands.

Murphy was to lie on the fo'castle head and cut the lashings of the forward anchor when the narrowest point of the channel was reached. At the same time he must set off torpedo No. 1, at the extreme bow.

Charette, at the forward hatch, was to fire No. 2 and No. 3.

Deignan, the baby of the crew, but the well-chosen quartermaster, after putting the helm hard aport to swing the ship across the channel, was to go down from the wheelhouse and explode No. 4.

Clausen at No. 5.

Phillips in the engine room, and Kelly in the boiler room, on a signal from the bridge were to stop the engine, knock the sea-cocks wide open and come on deck. Phillips was then to fire No. 6 and No. 7, Kelly No. 8.

Montague was to wait aft, ax in hand, ready to drop the stern anchor.

By midnight the *Merrimac* had crept within two miles of the Morro. The Spanish garrison, watching from my battlement, saw her dim shadow moving along. But they were accustomed to these night maneuverings. Hobson planned to sink his ship at four o'clock in the morning—the moon would then be setting—and be gone when the time came to escape in the rowboat. If the rowboat were smashed, and they had to swim, they were to try to meet in a sea-cave, directly below the castle, the cave into which I could hear the waves booming at this very moment.

Half-past three. With no lights showing anywhere, the last of the regular crew departed in a launch. The eight men left aboard stripped off their jackets and put on their life-preservers. They intended to save their lives if they could.

The *Merrimac,* a black wraith on the shining sea, began to move in toward the gash in the black hills of the shore, rapidly gaining speed. Straight down the path of moonlight she steamed—straight toward these Spanish guns—straight toward her fiery doom.

I tried to picture her, headed for the entrance below me. I tried to picture the tenseness of the crew. What a great moment for boy Deignan, steering his immortal ship right through the dragon's jaws. Twenty-one! How his eyes must have shone! How his heart must have pounded from exultation and glory!

And Phillips and Kelly below, waiting with straining ears for the signal to stop the engine. . . .

And the other four, crouching, ready to pounce on their anchors and torpedo keys when they have the word. . . .

And Hobson, on the bridge, nerves taut, but self-possessed as steel machinery.

These men see Morro Castle drawing higher in the sky. Ship and shore are now only five hundred yards apart—four hundred. The Spanish sentinels pacing my battlement must certainly be alarmed. The ship is no longer just suspicious—it is obviously about to try to force the entrance, and coming on at full speed.

Aboard her the crew is wondering: When will those Spanish devils open fire—when—when? This dangling on the edge of doom . . .

Two hundred yards—one hundred . . .

Flash! A gun roars right at the water's edge, from an almost invisible Spanish picket boat. Flash! Flash! Viperish streaks of fire, *straight at the Merrimac's rudder.* Whir! Clang! A shell strikes steel. The Spanish gunners rush out from their shelters. The entire Morro slope awakens with a blazing roar simultaneously with the batteries opposite. Two volcanoes of flame burst from the two hillsides.

The oncoming *Merrimac,* staggering under the rain of screaming and exploding shells, is passing below, so close to the Morro slope that the garrison is firing at her bridge with pistols.

Hobson gives the signal to Phillips. He stops the engine. Kelly opens the sea connections, and geysers of water flood the engine room.

While the seven-thousand-ton ship is still driving on under its own momentum, the two men below race up the ladder and take their posts by the torpedo batteries.

By now the frenzy of firing and the blazing powder from five score Spanish guns are lighting up the night. The hills shake and spout fire. And the Spanish cruisers, anchored inside, behind that round little island a half-mile deeper in the channel, let go their biggest guns with a roar that splits the firmament. The *Merrimac* is enclosed in flames. Shells shriek through her, leaving huge holes in the steel plates; shells explode inside, flinging up her decks with an insane crash; shrapnel sweeps the bridge and fo'castle—who could hope to live through such a murderous assault?

Captain Evans aboard the *Iowa,* out there on the moonlit ocean, watches until the *Merrimac* is shut from his view. For him it is "a most dreadful sight—what hell must look like with the lid off." Convinced that Hobson and his men have gone forever, he looks away.

But Hobson and his men are not, by a series of miracles, gone forever—not yet. They are actually getting past the Morro, and though burned, dazed and shell-shocked by the hurricane of fire, not one of them is out of the fight.

But the *Merrimac* itself is mangled and dying. One moment more and she will be in a position in which Hobson *wants* her to die.

"Hard aport," he yells to Deignan through the roar of the bombardment.

Deignan obeys, but there is no response from the ship.

"Hard aport, I say," in desperation.

"The helm *is* hard aport, sir, and lashed!"

The steering gear has been shot away!

And the *Merrimac* is still moving on, six knots an hour, down the flaming channel.

The anchors! Hobson gives the signal to Murphy. There is a blow from the ax—and the bow-anchor falls.

And one second afterward, as planned, torpedo No. 1 goes off with a blast that out-roars the Spanish shells.

Charette, waiting a lifetime in the last ten minutes, tries to set off No. 2 and No. 3.

Dead silence. His two firing switches have been blown to bits.

Deignan leaps down from the bridge to fire No. 4. There isn't a shred of a connection left.

Only Clausen's No. 5 goes off.

Phillips and Kelly, aft, find a great hole in the deck where their firing switches had once been.

And worse. Not only has the stern-anchor lashing been blasted away, but the anchor as well. And in a moment more the chain holding the anchor at the bow is likewise shot in two.

The *Merrimac* has lost every means of control, has become a helpless hulk. She has sunk into the water almost to the level of her deck, but is still maddeningly buoyant, drifting with the incoming tide farther and farther up the ever-widening channel, straight toward those spouting Spanish battleships waiting behind Smith Island.

She's grounded. A fresh avalanche of shells is hurled at her from a battery not two hundred feet away. But Hobson's heart leaps up. His daring thrust is not yet parried. His ship is settling, and may block the passage after all, there by Estrella Point.

But in another moment the cursed tide lifts her, and down the channel she drifts once more, still pursued by the storm of shells.

A mine goes off! The *Merrimac* receives the full shock of the blast. She is lifted upward ten feet, quivers and, groaning, sinks back again. Hobson prays that her back is broken. Such is not the case. The water-filled compartments have prevented.

As for the *Merrimac's* tormented crew, they seem invulnerable, crouching together on the shattered deck waiting for the next shell to annihilate them all.

Already their ship is fifteen hundred feet past the narrowest point. But her course is almost run. She is sinking fast. And two Spanish battleships now lie in wait. As she staggers helplessly past, her forward deck awash, four torpedoes are shot into her submerged bow from a distance less than her own length. The explosions hurl up a column of blinding light and twisted steel. This is the *coup de grace.*

The *Merrimac* plunges down by the bow in a roaring cauldron of bursting boilers, shells, mines, torpedoes, of escaping steam and flames—in a place where the channel is nearly five hundred feet wide.

The eight Americans, wounded and stunned but still miraculously alive, are thrown off the deck as the ship, in sinking, turns on her side. The rowboat has long since been smashed, but the wreckage of a life-raft is in reach. All eight cling to this raft, with just their faces exposed above the water that is still churned by shells.

But the firing is now ceasing, and the moon is dipping behind the hills. In complete darkness nobody makes a move. The Americans know they cannot swim against the tide, back down the channel and out to sea. Shaking with cold they hold onto their raft for four endless hours, hoping that when they are taken prisoners at dawn it will be by some responsible Spanish officer.

It is eight o'clock before an armed Spanish launch draws cautiously alongside. It finds the *Merrimac's* men, literally almost dead—first the flames, and now the freezing. They are taken aboard by a fine-looking elderly Spanish naval officer. He expresses keen admiration for the Americans' bravery, and asks their commander for his name and rank:

"Richmond Pearson Hobson, Ship-Constructor, U.S. Navy," was the reply. "And may I ask," he added, "the same question of you who have taken us prisoners?"

"I am Pascual Cervera y Topete, Admiral of the Spanish Fleet."

From my perch on top the Morro I had been able to follow, in my mind's eye, every move of Hobson's desperate adventure. And now, still in the Morro, I was close to the aftermath, for Hobson was brought to this fortress and imprisoned in the cell directly beneath the battlement to which I had climbed to watch the *Merrimac* go by. After visiting that cell, I feel sure that Hobson will not soon forget his detention there—its dreariness, its age, its spiders. But there is another reason too, for here it was that Charette said to him: "I have come, sir, to present the compliments of the *Merrimac's* crew, and to say that we would do it all over again—for you."

Hobson's exploit has been called a "heroic failure." Hobson himself wept bitter tears of disappointment when, after all the hell he and his men had gone through, he failed in his main objective.

But subsequent events proved that for the American cause, the *Merrimac* had been sunk in the best possible place, for it still so nearly closed the channel that the blockaded Spanish ships did not dare try to escape at night—their original intention. And even by day, at the time of their final sortie, they had to come to a dead stop in order to shave past the sunken hulk— a fatal move, for it gave the Americans waiting outside just the time needed to get up steam, man their guns and go racing to the complete destruction of the Spaniards and the quick ending of the war. Except for the *Merrimac,* all the Spanish vessels, with their superior speed, might have escaped.

Each one of the *Merrimac's* crew was given, immediately, the Congressional Medal of Honor; and the same medal was given to Hobson later when officers became eligible for the award. Of the immortal eight, four are still alive, all of whom are now between sixty and seventy years old. Deignan, the boy quartermaster, was the first to go—in 1906.

As for Hobson himself, a special act of Congress, in 1934, authorized his appointment and retirement in the grade of Rear Admiral "in acknowledgment of his great service in sinking the *Merrimac*—one of the most gallant acts of bravery and self-sacrifice ever known in any Navy in the history of the world."

CHAPTER III

A BATTLE AND A CAT

THE most joyously acclaimed Fourth of July in American history was that of 1898.

In comparison, the original Fourth in 1776 was a very mild affair, for few people then knew that such a document as the Declaration of Independence had been signed.

The news of Gettysburg and Vicksburg, arriving on the Fourth in 1863, thrilled half the nation, and plunged the other half in gloom.

But on the great day in '98 the entire population of America went half-crazy with excitement because, early that morning, the newspapers announced that, on the day before, a great and long-awaited naval battle had been fought between the Spanish and American fleets off Santiago de Cuba, in which every Spanish ship had been destroyed and Admiral Cervera himself had been taken prisoner.

There was certainly good reason for rejoicing. This decisive victory practically ended the Spanish-American War.

Interesting as the international consequences of this engagement were, even more interesting, to me, is the battle itself. The American Navy had not given us as dramatic a story since the *Monitor* fought the *Merrimac*

(the original *Merrimac*) at Hampton Roads in '62—
nor ever one with as much grimly eloquent evidence to
verify it. We can go today and see the wrecks of the
Spanish ships still piled up on the southern coast of
Cuba, right where they were burned to death on that
fateful morning.

To examine them closely, to get this further acquaintance with the reality of the now dim and far-off Spanish War, on the day after my visit to Morro Castle I
once more hired my launch and set out for the scene of
the sea-battle.

Throughout the entire month of June, 1898, Cervera
with his four fast armed cruisers had been bottled up in
Santiago Harbor by the American fleet. The Americans waiting outside were becoming increasingly impatient. But they did not dare try to force their way
into Cervera's lair. The terrific fire that Hobson had
drawn from the 'Spanish batteries made clear to Admiral Sampson what would be the fate of any ship that
attempted to pass the fortifications.

Cervera, on the other hand, found himself in a
dilemma that was daily becoming more uncomfortable.
The American Army had invested Santiago from the
landward side, and the city was on the point of surrender. If it fell, and the Spanish ships had not withdrawn, they would be captured without firing a shot.

But could they withdraw? Cervera had previously
planned to wait for a dark and rainy night, and then,
with all lights out, make a sudden sortie from the harbor,
dash through the American battle line, order his ships
to scatter, and hope that some of them at least would
get away.

But Hobson had upset *that* plan with his cursed *Merrimac*. The hulk, though it did not block the channel entirely, still lay in wait to rip the bottom out of any ship steering ten feet off its course. To try to rush past in the darkness would be to invite sure disaster.

And yet, to try to escape by day would be just as fatal. Cruising up and down in a semicircle before the entrance of the harbor, never sleeping, were five first-class and (for those days) extremely powerful American battleships, the *Iowa, Oregon, Indiana, Texas* and *Massachusetts*, and the heavy cruisers *Brooklyn* and *New York*. Together they carried twenty-four twelve-inch guns. Against this formidable array the Spaniards had only four cruisers, the *Vizcaya, Cristobal Colon, Almirante Oquendo* and the *Maria Teresa*, the flagship.

Cervera knew what to expect from a clash between such unequal forces. By cable he explained his hopeless position to the ministers in Madrid and suggested that he be allowed to scuttle his ships right where they were and surrender his crews. He declared that if the War Ministry forced him to try to run the American blockade it could result only in a horrible and useless slaughter of his men.

But the ministers, safe from the twelve-inch guns, had reputations at stake. To sink the fleet without a fight, when the American Army took Santiago, would drive *them* from office. They curtly ordered Cervera to be brave and make a break for liberty. Maybe one of the ships might escape in the confusion.

So Cervera, helpless and resigned, prepared to perish. But he chose his hour well. The *Massachusetts* had departed for Guantánamo Bay to coal. And the *New York,* with Admiral Sampson aboard, was eight miles to the east conferring with the Army. Also it was Sunday. About nine o'clock all the American crews, so Cervera believed, would be "at church."

Now was the time!

The Spaniards got up steam and moved down the harbor. But as they approached the entrance, just as they had anticipated, they had to come almost to a standstill in order to slide past the *Merrimac*—in full view of the Americans.

The Americans *were* at church. But somebody wasn't paying much attention to his prayers, for he noticed the leading Spanish ship trying to work past the sunken hulk two thousand feet up in the channel, and gave the alarm.

There was pandemonium for a moment . . . little or no pressure in the boilers . . . the flagship and the Admiral almost out of sight. This confusion, however, did not last long. The American crews knew their duties, and leaped to do them. In five minutes the smokestacks were spouting forth dense clouds of smoke and the guns began to take their deadly aim.

The *Maria Teresa,* leading the Spanish line, was the first to meet the American onslaught. To escape, she turned sharply to starboard and hugged the coast, steaming with all the desperate speed her boilers could provide.

In the launch in which I was retracing the battle-route, having once more passed the hulk of the *Merrimac* and reached the open sea, I likewise headed west along the spectacular southern shore of Cuba, in the track of the flying flagship.

On board, Admiral Cervera, having cleared his decks for action, ordered a bugle call from the bridge, the signal to begin firing—the signal, wrote her Captain later, that the history of four centuries of Spain's greatness was ended.

But Cervera meant to go on, game to the end. The *Teresa's* guns roared forth, but missed their mark. The *Iowa* and *Texas* roared back, with appalling results. One of the *Iowa's* twelve-inch shells tore through a gun room on the *Teresa* and killed sixty men. Another set her on fire. A third destroyed the water-supply pipes. In a few minutes she was a mass of towering flames. In vain did the officers threaten the tortured and blistered gunners, for it was soon impossible to fight. The guns were being blown from their foundations. Nearly half the crew were dead. Crazed by the conflagration and the insupportable pain, the *Teresa* had veered straight in to the shore, struck the rocks and exploded.

Having come up in my launch, I landed at this spot on the beach where the flagship had grounded—seven miles west of Morro Castle.

It was here that Cervera, half-suffocated from smoke, jumped overboard, to be followed by as many of his men as were still alive. The risk of being drowned was better than the certainty of being burned to death. Two sailors pulled Cervera onto a raft and towed him to shore.

But though I knew that this was the exact place where the *Teresa* hit the beach, there is not the smallest fragment of the hulk left to verify the fact. Today the hulk is five hundred miles away. The astonishing story of how it managed to travel so far I'll presently relate.

Back in my launch, and on down the mountainous coast. After a ride of less than a mile I found the *Oquendo* which had followed the flagship in the line of battle. As in the case of the *Teresa,* the first American shells set ablaze her wooden decks and cabins. She rolled and staggered under the avalanche of steel. But all the time she was continuing to fire what guns could still be worked or still had crews to work them, until the draft made by her own motion turned her into an inferno.

Half hidden in flames, she too lunged for the shore. A hundred of her crew were dead. The fire swept away her royal flag. Her Captain shot himself.

For all these years the *Oquendo* has lain there. For a decade the whole superstructure of her burned and twisted hulk remained entirely clear of the waves. But about 1908, Cubans dynamited her for scrap metal, and storms have helped the wreck to dig a grave for itself in the sand. Today only the two heavy-battery turrets extend above water, sticking their single eleven-inch guns reproachfully at the sky.

I climbed up on one of these guns from the launch and looked down at the demolished hull, clearly visible though submerged. And I recalled extracts from a vivid description of the *Oquendo* I had recently read in an old copy of *Harper's Weekly,* written the day after the destruction, by a reporter who was on hand:

"Smoke still pours from the hulk even though the surf surges back and forth through the huge gashes in her side. . . . The scorched paint hangs in folds. Guns are knocked about in every wry position, and the tackle streams down in wild disorder. . . . Piled about the guns, half-concealed in the curling smoke, are charred and mutilated bodies that have begun to decompose. . . . The masts have fallen. The exploding magazines have torn great holes in her decks. . . . There are fifty dead Spaniards beneath the forward turret, killed by one shell. But the metal there is still too hot to admit investigation. Even so, American sailors are swarming over her, looking for souvenirs. One sailor has a hat full of melted money—another a bottle of Spanish wine." *

Of all this the storms have left but little trace. A few more years and perhaps even the two guns and the turrets, the last above-water evidence of a once proud ship, will vanish.

The *Vizcaya* and the *Colon* had likewise come out of the harbor behind the *Teresa*. The *Colon,* the fastest of the Spanish ships, began to forge ahead of her pursuers. But the *Vizcaya* was not so fortunate. Blown to pieces and in flames, she also soon turned toward shore, fifteen miles from Santiago.

Still in my launch I easily found the *Vizcaya's* grave, for her one turret and gun, extending like the *Oquendo's* above water, can be seen a mile away. As I jumped from the launch to the rust-encrusted side of the turret, a sea-swallow flew out of the gun's stark muzzle. I crawled up the gun to examine it and found, inside the mouth, a nest with three chicks just learning to fly.

The *Vizcaya,* commanded by Captain Eulate, was

---

* Quoted by permission of Harper & Brothers, publishers.

well known in America, for she had come to New York with a show of defiant courtesy when the *Maine* was sent to Havana. But that visit had gained her no privilege in the battle. She received the worst punishment of any Spanish ship. Her gunners, too, were all killed (but not until one of her shells had decapitated a seaman on the *Brooklyn,* the only American casualty). Of her crew of five hundred and fifty, over two hundred perished.

Eulate himself reached shore, badly wounded and covered with blood, with some three hundred and fifty of the crew. Captain Evans of the *Iowa* sent out his boats to pick them up. As Eulate was brought aboard he unbuckled his sword, kissed the hilt and presented it to Evans as a token of surrender. But the American Captain handed it back, saying Eulate had fought four ships and deserved to keep it. Just before being escorted below to have his wounds dressed, Eulate turned toward the wreck of his ship, now a wild-burning furnace on the rocks, saluted and exclaimed, "Adios, *Vizcaya.*" At that moment as if by prearrangement the *Vizcaya* exploded with an earth-shaking roar, sending up a flaming geyser of steel and burning decks and mangled bodies.

Shortly after, Cervera himself, in his dripping uniform, was brought aboard the *Iowa.* On seeing him the American crew burst into spontaneous cheering for the brave old Admiral.

Meanwhile the *Colon* was fifty miles away. But the *Brooklyn,* the speed-queen of the American fleet, was forty-eight. It had become a contest of boilers rather than guns. The Spanish officers, determined to keep

ahead at any cost, pushed back into the stokehole the
firemen and engineers who, unable to endure the horrible
heat, were trying to escape on deck. Even this did not
suffice. The *Colon's* coal gave out just when she was on
the verge of escape. It is reported that in an insane
fury over this new disaster, the officers, as they headed
for the beach, poured coal-oil on the stokehole hatch
and ignited it, so that no man came alive out of that hell
under the water-line.

When the bow of the *Colon* struck the rocks, her stern
was still in seventy-five feet of water. Consequently
when wreckers tried to salvage her she turned over and
sank completely out of sight. And there on the bottom
of the ocean, fifty miles down the coast of Cuba, the
Cristobal Colon remains today.

Of the four hulks only the *Teresa's* has not been
accounted for in my story.

When the *Teresa* exploded on the beach, Cervera and
every living member of the crew, as I have explained,
swam to shore—every living member of the crew but
one, Cervera's cat. In the panic she was forgotten and
left behind.

And a fortnight later she was found still alive by
Hobson himself, who had come aboard to salvage the
flagship. Hobson gave her food and water, and she
accompanied him everywhere as he went about his job.

Afloat once more after weeks of patching and pumping
(afloat, though nothing but a corpse of a cruiser), the
Teresa was towed out to sea by the repair ship
Vulcan, and then on around the eastern end of Cuba
and north toward the navy-yard at Charleston.

But a hurricane arose off the Bahamas, and the Cap-

tain of the *Vulcan,* in Hobson's absence, became terrified that the seven-thousand-ton hulk he was towing
would sink and pull him down with it.   In fact, in the
stormy darkness he *saw* her sinking and ordered her
temporary crew to abandon her at once.   Before casting off, the crew tried to rescue the cat.   She refused to
be rescued, and ran up the mast.   So without her they
moved hurriedly to the *Vulcan,* cut the hawser and
struggled on through the storm unencumbered.

Reaching Charleston the Captain reported the total
loss of the *Teresa*—and the cat.

But four days later an American freighter, likewise
steaming off the Bahamas, saw a hideously charred,
shell-ravaged battleship drifting along, apparently deserted.   The officer on watch first thought he was seeing
a ghost.   Then he looked at her name:

Maria Teresa.

She had sunk only in the terrified imagination of the
Vulcan's Captain.

The freighter, via the Navy Department, rushed a
report of the find to Hobson who had gone on ahead
to America.   Naturally, having devoted so much time
and effort to raising the *Teresa,* he felt indignant that
the *Vulcan* had been so lacking in courage and so ineffectual as to have abandoned, in a moment of panic,
a still valuable ship.   Hobson was also angry that they
had left the companionable cat on board to die.   Feeling that quick action was necessary he took passage on
the wrecking ship himself and steamed back at full
speed in the hope of finding the *Teresa* in time.

They did find her, but not in time.   The currents had

carried the hulk fifty miles to the west, and the waves had dropped her on a coral reef, breaking her back completely, just off the shore of one of the Bahamas.

Hobson, approaching from the sea, realized there was absolutely no hope of salvaging the *Teresa* now, for the two halves of the ship had fallen apart.

But the cat.

Young Lieutenant Simms was sent to search the twice-dead derelict, and told not to come back without the animal.

Simms was gone a long time. He found that the cat was still alive, having been taken from the ship by the island's Negro natives and given to their chief, who in turn had given it to his little daughter. The child adored the cat and, not knowing or caring about its marvelous history, would not part with it for anything. Simms offered her five dollars—ten dollars. He finally offered her fifteen dollars, a fortune in the remote Bahamas. This was more than her father could resist. He took the famous puss from the weeping child and gave it over to Simms, who brought it back to Hobson in triumph.

But the story of the cat is by no means ended. Hardly had the *Vulcan* set sail again when the barometer began to drop and ominous clouds to gather in the sky . . . another storm for sure.

The Captain of the *Vulcan* swore it was the cat. She was a witch, a demon and a curse. She had been aboard the *Teresa* at Santiago, and see what happened. The ship was wrecked and one hundred and fifty of the crew were killed. The cat had lived two weeks with no water, and no food except, he hinted, corpses. On the way to

Charleston with the cat still on the helpless *Teresa,* the hurricane had almost sunk them both. He had cut the *Teresa* loose because he *saw* her sinking.

True, she hadn't sunk, but she had gone to pieces on the reef.

And now that cat was back—and look at the barometer! The Captain swore he'd never get the *Vulcan* home with such a jinx aboard. And he seized her to throw her into the sea.

But Hobson leaped to the cat's defense.

"If anybody goes overboard," he said to the Captain, "it should be you. This cat has given us all an extraordinary example of fidelity. She clung to her ship when everybody else deserted it. She stood guard alone for two weeks while the sea swept over the hulk. She helped me raise the *Teresa,* and would have got her all the way to Charleston, if *you* hadn't lost your nerve and set the cruiser adrift. Even adrift, all through the hurricane, that cat knew exactly where to go. Do you know the name of the coral key to which that brave little Captain laid her course? Look at your chart. *It's Cat Island!"*

Hobson took the "witch" into his own arms and fed her apple-pie; and the wind went down, and the barometer went up, and nobody went overboard. In the summer twilight the two of them climbed to the top deck, where Hobson found a canvas chair. And there the heroine of the *Teresa* curled up on the lap of the hero of the *Merrimac,* and together they watched the moon rise out of the sea.

CHAPTER IV

HIS MAJESTY THE DISHWASHER

FOR two hours, from the airplane in which I traveled, I had been watching three hundred miles of tropical scenery unfold below. We had taken off from Santiago, circled over the hill-framed harbor, climbed high above Morro Castle and sailed on down the coast of Cuba in the opposite direction from the scene of the naval battle. We flew over Guantánamo Bay, the greatest American naval station in the West Indies, sighted a few warships at anchor, rushed on past to the eastern tip of Cuba and saw before us a hundred miles of open water—the Windward Passage between Cuba and Haiti, the passage through which the *Vulcan* had towed the hulk of the *Maria Teresa*.

Before long the Haitian mountains, floating in the sky, appeared ahead. And then we found the coast of the long narrow peninsula that extends westward toward Cuba, and for another hundred miles followed the procession of romantic little offshore islets set in a pale green sea, little bays splashed with ten shades of blue, and the endless lines of royal palms leaning out to greet the great white waves rolling in from the Caribbean.

Changing to a smaller plane at Port-au-Prince, the capital of the Black Republic, I was carried on north through the interior of the island, hoping that the single motor of our ship would not fail, for in the wild confusion of jungled canyons and cloud-topped summits below, there was nothing to land on but the tops of trees.

The northern coast now appeared in the dim distance. Twenty miles back from it, right in our path, the pilot pointed out to me a peculiar peak that stood forth bold and isolated—a peak marked on my map Le Bonnet à l'Évêque, the Bishop's Bonnet.

This peak was my destination, for on its pinnacle, three thousand feet above the valley, soared the ruins of one of the most spectacular castles on earth—the Citadel of Christophe, the Black King of Haiti.

Christophe has been dead more than a hundred years, but this incredible Citadel still stands guard over what was once his kingdom, to remind the world that the man who built it was a giant, a genius, a tyrant and the most masterful Negro in history.

The name Haiti, to most people, suggests merely the western half of a backward island in the West Indies, populated by primitive Africans addicted to voodoo worship, and once policed by the U. S. Marines. Yet during the latter part of the eighteenth century, as a French colony, Haiti was one of the richest countries in the world. By 1785 the French were operating several thousand sugar and coffee plantations, worked by half a million slaves. The chief metropolis, Cap Haitien on the north coast, rarely saw less than a hundred ships in the harbor. Compared with it, New York was only a modest little port of secondary importance whose merchants, when they came to Haiti, were always astonished at the brilliance and richness of the social life. From Paris the planters imported the most beautiful and luxurious furnishings money could buy for their palm-shaded châteaux. Commerce and industry came to be so highly developed and so profitable that the revenues from this one colony provided the greatest single source of income for the French Government.

This was the scene in which a Negro slave, Henry Christophe, one hundred per cent black, rose to a position of dictatorial power not matched in the Western hemisphere by anyone, black or white, before or since.

Christophe was born in 1767 of slave parents, so one legend tells, on the West Indian island of St. Kitts. Taken to Haiti as a boy, he became a waiter and dishwasher at a public bar. But such a menial job was not to hold him forever. He was too strong, too tall, too intelligent, and much too unruly. A slave rebellion, vengeful and determined, ignited the island when Henry was twenty-seven, and he promptly gave up washing dishes to join the insurrection against the French masters. His natural ability to command was soon recognized, so that before the long and bloody conflict was ended, Christophe was a "General." And his generalship, as much as anything, brought about the victories by which the slaves completely wrested the island from French control.*

But France was not to be disposed of so easily. Napoleon was in power and declared he had no intention

---

* For the facts of Christophe's life, and for the history of Haiti at this period, I am especially indebted to the English historian, W. W. Harvey, whose book, *Sketches of Hayti from the Expulsion of the French to the Death of Christophe*, is the all-important source for anyone writing on these subjects.

of losing his richest colony to a mob of savages. In 1802 he dispatched eighty ships and an advance contingent of twenty-two thousand veteran soldiers to regain Haiti from the slaves, placing General LeClerc, one of his most successful officers, in command. The General was accompanied by his beautiful young wife, none other than Pauline Bonaparte, Napoleon's favorite sister. No one expected a real war.

But after three years of the most vicious fighting, fifty thousand French soldiers lay dead from battle and disease. LeClerc himself contracted yellow fever and died—and Pauline fled back to France. A British fleet, likewise warring with Napoleon, blockaded the harbor. To this fleet the despairing French surrendered, and were carried off to European prisons.

Napoleon had been utterly and permanently expelled. Scarcely a white man remained alive in Haiti.

Christophe's ambition soared. Another ex-slave, Jean Jacques Dessalines, thanks to his unrivaled ability in murder and slaughter, had become Emperor, with Christophe next in command. But Christophe had visions of *himself* as dictator. And his visions were all realized when, in 1806, Dessalines having been assassinated, he was able to seize complete mastery.

The new ruler's civil administration turned out to be no less remarkable than his military leadership. He could not read or write; he knew nothing of politics or science; but he did know that his black followers must be controlled with an iron hand if they were to maintain their hard-earned freedom.

So he had himself crowned King Henry I. Now he

could, and did, have discipline. He began to force his ex-slave subjects with lash and bayonet, to work, to build, to produce, to obey. Mussolini and Stalin, a hundred and twenty-five years later, were to seem like weak sisters compared to this towering black tyrant. Anybody caught loafing in King Henry's country was shot. No one could escape from serving his relentless ambition to rehabilitate the ravaged country, to give it self-respect and security and pride.

As for the pride, he set them a grand example. Being a royal personage now, he wanted a suitable dwelling to proclaim his majesty. So he began to build, twenty miles inland from Cap Haitien, a château whose lavish beauty was not equaled this side of Europe. When it was finished, it contained fifty rooms, with a magnificent façade approached by a double staircase where sentries stood guard. The rooms inside and the gardens outside shone with royal splendor. Christophe called it Sans Souci.

With a Versailles of his own, the King next tried to organize a court similar to that of Louis XVI. He created a "nobility" with princes and barons, and ladies-in-waiting for Marie-Louise, his Queen. All the Negro love of showy spectacle and bright colors burst like fireworks in this Haitian court. Napoleon and Josephine never saw such scarlet uniforms, so much gold braid, such fancy plumes, as the black nobles and their black consorts wore in the black King's throne room. A few whites were permitted to join the court. Christophe's health was guarded by a Scotch doctor, and two American maiden ladies came from Philadelphia to teach the two Princesses, Améthyste and Athénaire, the graces of polite society, including poetry, the harp and the straightening of kinky hair.

This court was not just an empty show, but the visible symbol of a rich and well-disciplined monarchy. In its best days under France, Haiti had never known such prosperity as the masterful ex-slave gave it. His notion of the public welfare, however, was sometimes a little unusual. For example, when it became obvious that Haiti would need an increased population to work the cane-fields, Christophe decided to inflate the birth-rate. In one provincial town, he ordered all the women, young and old, to assemble in the public square before the church. On assembling, those already married were excused, leaving only maidens. The Royal Guards were then commanded to advance and seize, each for himself, the handiest virgin—regardless of the number of obligations he might already have at home.

But for Christophe, prosperity and fecundity were not enough. He wanted security too, and race-consciousness. His people had no tradition, no heroes. They were just animals being driven. He would give them a national symbol to respect, a national monument that would get into the blood of every citizen, for with their own blood and brawn they themselves should build it—an impregnable fortress on the summit of the Bonnet à l'Évêque, three thousand feet above Sans Souci, placed so as to lord it over the plain and the town and the bay. It would be invulnerable to attack; stronger than Napoleon, or the voodoo enchantments, or the devil himself—something incomparable in *any* land, something to make the world, and all the hated white men in it, stare with astonishment and admiration.

So Christophe dreamed, and so his dream came to pass in brick and stone.

French architects drew the original plans and in fact began to lay the foundations. But the work had hardly started when they were expelled. Christophe, being determined to make the fortress into a monument to himself, greatly enlarged the design and changed the details to his own taste. The overpowering grandeur of this grim, contemptuous Citadel bears the stamp of his spirit alone. The north bastion, a vast prow of sheer cannoncrowned wall a hundred and thirty feet high, jutting arrogantly toward the harbor where Napoleon's army had landed and departed, toward France and all white domination, might be his own huge black fist.

With his genius for organization, Christophe marshalled his nation's forces as for war. Thirty thousand people were driven, like the slaves of Pharaoh, to work on the walls. Day and night they toiled, not just men alone but women as well. The women carried eight tenpound bricks or an equivalent weight of cannon balls on each ascent from the valley three thousand feet below. Barrels of lime and gunpowder, crude machinery, and cannon, cannon by the score, heavy as the sandstone blocks of Cheops' pyramid, had to be dragged, amid groans and sweat and agony, to the summit. The ascending and descending slaves made two continuous lines each six miles long, an army of reluctant black ants. And all along the way were drivers with whips to speed the laggards.

Christophe himself became obsessed with the work.

He stormed up and down the steep trail shouting orders, threatening his masons. It is said he even shot to death numbers of his cannon-sled crews to encourage those remaining to move faster.

Twelve months went by. Two thousand laborers had perished (ten times as many more were yet to die), but only the foundations were in place. Christophe demanded more slaves, more speed, more victims, more bricks. The Citadel *must be finished* before the French came back.

And so the years succeeded one another, with the forced labor never ending on the peak. The walls rose to greater and greater—to unbelievable—heights, continuing the upward sweep of the mountain side, walls strong and cruel as Christophe's heart. And crowning them were battlements for the great bronze guns. Christophe already had the three hundred which Le-Clerc had left behind, but he wanted thrice three hundred. So every ship that sailed to Europe sailed back with cannon and cannon-balls, to be dragged by whip-lashed blacks up into the clouds.

Eight years passed. Napoleon had been five years a prisoner on St. Helena. Christophe was fifty-three, but he was still in power, and still his castle-madness grew. To command the strongest fortress on earth had become his dominant obsession. It is said that when he learned another fortress, called Gibraltar, was stronger, he executed the architect who had dared to plan the Citadel on a smaller scale.

Even so, by 1820 the end of the endless labor was in sight, and Christophe redoubled his merciless efforts to bring his castle to completion. His tyranny became demonic. In paroxysms of impatience, he would beat his ministers with his riding whip and order his generals to work on the walls like ordinary slaves. The number of laborers who died from brutality or exhaustion reached new and dreadful totals. The slightest hint of insubordination brought down his murderous wrath. Suspecting the fidelity of a company of Citadel guards, he lined them up, so one story goes, on the highest battlement and commanded them to march forward, right over the edge of the hundred-and-thirty-foot wall. And so iron-fisted was Christophe's discipline that they obeyed, to be dashed to pieces on the rocky mountain side below.

One thing alone could give the builders release from Christophe's bloody tyranny. As John Vandercook tells so well in his splendid biography of Christophe, *Black Majesty,** the King was a devout churchgoer and regularly took a recess from his shootings and lashings to attend Mass. Early one morning in the summer of 1820, he was kneeling before the altar, praying to be forgiven for having executed a traitorous priest. Suddenly he saw, or thought he saw, standing before him, the ghost of the priest himself. Horrified, with a stifled shriek, Christophe fell gasping to the floor, half his body paralyzed.

The fateful news of King Henry's stroke spread across Haiti with the wind and the tom-tom telegraph. Christophe was the State, the Law, the heart-beat and the will-power of the nation. If he slipped, the whole tyranny-built structure crumpled. He knew, and Haiti knew.

---

* Published by Harper & Brothers.

Consequently, paralyzed or not, he must maintain front. He had his soldiers drawn up before the palace, and prepared himself, by means of a supreme effort, to mount his horse and ride before them, to show his army, to show himself, that he was still Christophe. But his effort was to no avail. His legs would not obey. Clutching at his saddle, he collapsed, and lay helpless in the dust.

Among those who saw him fall there was no pity for the King, only rejoicing thàt this despot who had driven them so mercilessly was stricken and defenseless. The packs of his revengeful subjects began to close in on the wounded lion. In a few days more the army, released from its brutal discipline, was swept by the wildfire of rebellion. On hearing this good news the thousands of slave-laborers, struggling with their cannon up the trail to the Citadel, dropped their hateful burdens with shouts of joy and rushed down the mountain side, brandishing clubs and bricks and trowels, to swell the forces of destruction.

The yelling and exultant mobs were pounding on the very gates of the château. Christophe had seen other victims torn to pieces under his own orders, by just such mobs as these. He knew what to expect. Better go painlessly and decently—and quickly, before the door was broken down. Alone in his bedroom, he took from its case his favorite weapon, a silver-mounted pistol given him by an English admiral. With it went a supply of bullets. He fired one straight into his heart.

In an effort to preserve the King's body from the rioters, the Queen, with Améthyste and Athénaire and one faithful mulatto companion, hurriedly lifted the corpse onto a litter and, escaping from a rear door of the château, started off with their heavy burden to climb to the Citadel, where Marie-Louise hoped to be able to bury her husband.

With the savage shouts and the flames of Sans Souci behind them, the pitiful cortège struggled upward. They passed cannon and cannon-balls, bricks and stone, abandoned in the middle of the path by the suddenly liberated slaves. But there was no time to take notice of this—the mobs were already in hot pursuit, shouting for the Black King's head. Desperate and almost spent, the three women and one man reached the Citadel's towering prow just ahead of the rebels. They stumbled through the entrance, across the inner moat and bridge, along the first cannon-gallery, into the great court. The gravel underfoot in the courtyard was hard as stone. There was no opportunity to dig a grave—the rebels were running headlong through the lower gates. Then Marie-Louise noticed a huge vat of liquid lime, left there by the runaway plasterers. Into this white and all-consuming bath the black corpse of Christophe was dropped, and pushed downward until it disappeared.

The bullet that killed Christophe killed his kingdom too, which without him collapsed like a stuck balloon and was annexed by a rival neighbor. In the anarchy that followed, Marie-Louise and her daughters escaped to Europe, but the Crown Prince was murdered. The dukes and duchesses took off their shoes again and went back to work in the fields of cane. Haiti returned to its primitive African ways and soon forgot that it was once the proudest land in the Americas.

As for the Citadel, from the day of the King's death until now it has remained intact, but abandoned, an unfinished nightmare, fearfully shunned by the black men of Haiti. Only the jungle has dared creep up to inhabit it—one of the most marvelous monuments in the world.

An incredible story? Yes, until you have seen with your own eyes the great fortress which is evidence of its truth. Perhaps I myself half disbelieved until I looked down from the airplane upon the Bonnet à l'Évêque and saw the enormous lichen-covered walls swelling up from the peak-top, saw the one-hundred-and-thirty-foot prow thrusting toward the sea, saw the foothills, three thousand feet beneath, where the Black King wrought his empire. I could not doubt the story then. The Citadel was *there,* to be entered, admired, explored. Having beheld it I became eager to do all three.

And so next day, down to earth again, I set out from the little hotel at Cap Haitien to climb the Bishop's Bonnet, knowing that I had before me a profoundly moving experience.

CHAPTER V

THE BLACK KING'S CASTLE

My MOTORCAR bumped along a wretched Haitian road that seemed to lead deeper and deeper into primitive Africa. Past groups of crude mud houses crumbling in the heat, past gross-faced barelegged black women shuffling along the side path with burdens upon their heads, past innumerable half-wild pigs and piccaninnies, through a land that had succumbed to dilapidation, shiftlessness and weeds. With each one of the twenty miles from Cap Haitien I had become less hopeful that there could be anything beautiful in such a decayed and backward country.

And then, rising graceful and cool right out of this squalor, the ruins of a superb French château loomed up at the end of the road.

Had I at that moment met Marie Antoinette walking along with the black Haitian women, I couldn't have been more surprised. Here was a palace, abandoned and falling, but designed unmistakably in the purest French Renaissance tradition, and far more majestic than the most extravagant reports had led me to expect. For this was Sans Souci of which I had heard, the palace Christophe had built for himself in 1812.

For a decade this imposing residence housed the

Black Monarch's grandiloquent court of dusky dukes and duchesses. And then for one final tragic week it was the scene of murder and destruction, and suffered with the royal family the vengeance of the mob which came to exterminate the monarchy. Gutted by flames, roofless, exposed to tropical wind and rain for over a century, it is still magnificent. The harmonious lines, the sweep of the grand staircase, the whole effect softened by the green vines that trail from the weathered walls, made me agree with the poet who said, "More beautiful than beauty—are its ruins."

And as I stood before this château, which would have been notable in any country, I remembered that it had been built in the jungle and regally occupied by an illiterate black ex-dishwasher who had once served in a public bar.

From room to room of this stately ruin I walked, trying to picture the scenes it had witnessed. Here Christophe held his court beside his ex-slave Queen, and received the dark-skinned Comte de Limonade and the Duchesse de Marmelade, without once smiling at their names. Here the white maiden ladies from Philadelphia taught Christophe's daughters, Améthyste and Athénaire, to play the harp. Here in the courtyard above the great fountain, Christophe reviewed his troops. Here in this bedroom, paralyzed and faced with assassination, he fired into his heart the bullet that ended his reign of terror.

But I knew that this palace was only a prelude to the *great* work, the Citadel waiting three thousand feet above.

Continuing on beyond the formal gardens, I found

the path that led to it. Up this path for eight years the thousands of slaves had struggled with bricks and cannon. Up this path Christophe strode countless times, driving forward his slave-laborers, lashing one, shooting another; and here vengeance pursued him as his wife and children, frantic with fear and sobbing with despair, strove to drag his corpse to safety.

The trail, mounting and twisting, tunneled through the dense jungle. I climbed steadily for two hours and finally reached a clearing near the mountain top. And there, still farther above me, I saw the Citadel's colossal prow rearing haughtily from the summit of the peak.

The day before, I had looked down at it from the air. That view was extraordinary; but now, looking upward from below, I felt the full impact of its forbidding bulk. No wonder the Haitian natives leave it strictly alone, this evil reminder of the tyranny their ancestors endured. No wonder Christophe had to squander the wealth and energy of his nation in the creation of such a refuge.

I reached the entrance. A hundred and thirty feet of wall rose sheer above me. The ponderous gates, still on their hinges, allowed me to pass inside. The ramps and steps were dark and damp. Bats flew about in the dimness. The doorways from room to room were like tunnels, for Christophe had taken no chances with the walls and partitions of his fort. A ten-foot thickness of such master masonry would have held up the Pyramids. So he made them twenty and thirty feet, vowing they must outlast the ages. And outlast the ages I have no doubt they will.

And cannon! Surely such a collection of cannon is to be found nowhere else on earth. There must be six hundred rusty muzzle-loaders, some lined up on wooden carriages, some strewn about like wind-blown straws. There are monster mortars with fifteen-inch bores, and green, richly embossed bronze guns, seized when Napoleon's expedition was defeated in its three-year effort to regain the French colony of Haiti from Christophe's army of rebellious slaves. These guns, marked with the date and place of forging, bear German, English and Austrian marks as well as French. Many of them were captured by Napoleon at Lodi and Marengo, before his veteran troops lost them in turn to the Negroes at Cap Haitien. The largest heap of these cannon is, by accident, in the cellar of the great bastion. This part of the Citadel contained four heavily fortified galleries, but the gallery floors were of wood, which has rotted and allowed all the ordnance to tumble helter-skelter to the ground.

If I was astonished by the cannon, I was doubly astonished by the accumulation of cannon balls. Tons upon tons of these projectiles lie piled up in metal hillocks everywhere, enough to feed the guns for weeks of continuous firing. Just outside the gates I found a space thirty feet square packed solid with a mound of four-inch shot nearly four feet high—over eighty thousand in one place. That there are at least a million more of all sizes in and about the Citadel, is not an extravagant estimate. And all have been lifted three thousand feet to their resting place by women, who balanced the heavy burden in baskets on their head.

No matter where the eye falls within the fortress, one sees evidence—on the parapet, in the galleries, in long rows, in grass-grown heaps—of the fact that Christophe was driven by an obsession for more and more guns and ammunition. He amassed them throughout fourteen back-breaking years with a hunger amounting to a mania, as if by sheer quantity he could attain godlike security and hold his power. Since fate overtook him before his refuge was entirely completed, not one gun in twenty is mounted, and ironically enough, not a single shot from all this vast arsenal was ever fired. The stores of gunpowder are there, too, enough to insure an ample supply during the longest siege. Spilling out of the barrels stored in dark stone cellars, the powder has never been disturbed; but the dampness of a century has taken the life out of it. Fortunately, none of Christophe's many enemies chose to touch a match to this tremendous store when it was still fresh, for the explosion would have blown the Citadel completely off the mountain.

Vaulted stairs led to the courtyard. At one end of it rose the private quarters of the King, a separate building standing apart and built with considerable refinement and grace, somewhat in the manner of Sans Souci. But this apartment felt the concentrated fury of the destroying mobs which, rushing in behind Christophe's fleeing corpse-bearers, soon reduced it to bare and broken walls. At the other end, multi-storied galleries and barracks blocked out the sky, enough to shelter five thousand men. And beneath these barracks were rows of dungeons which Christophe kept filled, as they were completed, with those of his victims for whom he thought shooting too merciful.

In the center of the courtyard I found a loaf-shaped mound of solidified plaster, twenty feet long and higher than a man. Beside it is an undistinguished stucco tomb inscribed in French: "Here Lies King Henry Christophe—1767: 1820—Whose Motto Was 'I Rise From My Ashes.'" Alas, there were no ashes. The tomb contains only chunks of the plaster mound, for this mound, on the day of Christophe's suicide, was the vat of liquid quicklime in which his family, too close-pressed by the pursuing rebels to dig a grave, flung his corpse. Soon nothing remained of the body but the brass buttons on his uniform and the bullet in his heart.

So occupied was I in noting the cannon and the courtyard, it took me all afternoon to reach the battlements. Several times I had stopped to examine shallow excavations in the walls and floors, dug there by treasure hunters searching for the millions of dollars' worth of gold which Christophe is supposed to have buried secretly somewhere in the Citadel. As yet no one has found anything, but then no one has known where to begin to dig in such a mountain of masonry, and consequently the searches have been only half-hearted, in spite of the prize.

Climbing to the highest rampart, I could look down at the world three thousand feet below. The audacious skyrocketing walls of the Citadel fell sheer a hundred feet or more on every side, and joined the mountain top as solidly as a tree rises from its roots. Now I could appreciate for the first time the giant size of the fortress—five hundred by three hundred feet—and grasp its full beauty. For beautiful it is, in a cruel, powerful way. The walls, once grimly gray, are ablaze with bright orange lichen which has spread across the stones, and upon this burning color the sunset must fall with splendor. Until the arrival of the U. S. Marines the entire Citadel was a hanging garden of trees and shrubs, almost merging with the jungle which had reached up to take possession the moment it was abandoned. But the Marines cleared the courts and battlements of a hundred years' growth of vegetation, and little else was necessary to restore it to the original condition.

If only for its commanding position, Christophe must have loved this site well, since from it he could survey a large part of his kingdom. Through his telescope he could see, twenty miles away, Cap Haitien's harbor filled with a forest of ships. But when I looked I found only a fishing smack or two, beached in the mud. Where Christophe beheld rich plantations and broad fields of cane, producing at that time enough sugar for the world, I could see only a wilderness of brush and trees. But what Christophe heard, rising clearly from the lowlands, I too could hear the same as he: the rhythmic chanting of the black Haitian villagers, and the incessant all-pervading throbbing of the drums. The physical aspects of Haiti have changed since Christophe's time, but its fundamental self not at all. In everything but geography, it is still African.

Since mid-morning the sun had been obscured, and now, as I stood just before nightfall on top of the prodigious prow and looked out upon King Henry's land, a heavy black mist gathered and filled the valleys below with a black sea. Thunder and lightning began to crash and echo within hand's reach of my battlement, and the sky grew strangely, ominously dark. The Black Olympians were gathering to dictate in cannonading tones the destinies of Haiti, and the mighty Citadel was the throne room for this earth-shaking conclave.

Wave after wave of clouds, rolling in from the northern coast, were now climbing rapidly up the mountain side. They reached the lowest pediments of the walls, completely submerging the realms beneath and stretching, an ocean of black fog, far off to meet the night. Only the Citadel, for one unearthly moment, floated above this rising tide, its prow cleaving the oncoming waves so that a huge stone ship, beautiful, silent and alone, seemed to be sailing majestically forward into the supernatural darkness—on through the thunder—out across the sky—proud to bear the name of the great Black King who had launched it, the most defiant challenge in the annals of his race.

CHAPTER VI

ONCE, several years before the date of this story, I hired a seaplane in the city of Miami, Florida, and flew out over the Bahamas, hoping to settle in my own mind which one of them was the landfall of Columbus.

Historians know that the island is one of these. Columbus called it San Salvador. But which island on modern charts is the original San Salvador? There have been almost as many claims as there have been historians, or indeed, as there are islands.

Unfortunately, Columbus' original log-book disappeared soon after his death, but fortunately not before Fray Las Casas, a contemporary, had made faithful copies of parts of it, one part being dated October 12, 1492. The cleric, no man of science, failed to preserve the mathematical reckonings which would have located the island exactly. He did, however, extract word-for-word Columbus' report of the discovery and his picturesque description of the landfall.

And that is how we know a stiff wind was blowing toward the west on the night of October eleventh-twelfth; and that Rodrigo, a seaman, was the first to see the tongue of land gleaming in the moonlight.

The same Spanish copy of the original record describes "San Salvador":

"This island is quite large and very level. It has a large lake in the center. The shape of the island is that of a bean, and the vegetation so luxuriant that it is a pleasure to behold it." On October fourteenth, after two days ashore, Columbus also wrote: "At daybreak I had the boats of the caravels made ready and went along the island in a northeasterly direction in order to see the villages. The inhabitants, coming to the shore, beseeched us to land there, but I was afraid of a reef of rocks which entirely surrounds the island. But within this belt is a harbor of such size, that there would be ample room for all the vessels of Christendom."

This is not a great deal of information. But it is nearly all that exists, and with it my pilot and I laid our course for the Bahamas.

In this archipelago there are thirty large islands and over six hundred islets. Fortunately I didn't need to explore them all, for Columbus, coming from the east, must have encountered, first, one of the string of islands—ten in number—which face the open ocean. Each of these has had its strong advocates among geographers, and since I came with an open mind I meant to visit all ten.

From the coast of Florida the two of us flew for five hundred miles down the outer chain, circling over each in turn, looking for one that offered the special features Columbus described. Great Abaco had the size—"a large island"—but no lake. We flew on to Eleuthera. From the air it resembled a snake, but not by any stretch of the imagination "a bean." Conception, the next island, was only half surrounded by a reef, not "entirely surrounded"; and Yuma Fernandina had no reef at all. Samana looked like a bean, but that was its only claim.

Cat Island (where the *Maria Teresa* went on the rocks) occupied me for an entire day. This has always been a strong contestant for the honor, since Washington Irving, following the conclusions of a U. S. naval officer, chose in his great biography of Columbus to name Cat Island as the landfall. Consequently most of the maps of the ninetenth century call it San Salvador. But search though I might, I could not find even the weakest argument in its favor. There is no lake, and a ridge four hundred feet high running down the center prevents it from being "very flat." I had to conclude that Irving had accepted a careless identification.

Next morning I flew on to Crooked Island, Mariguana, Rum Cay and Grand Turk. Not one of these had a harbor fit to shelter a single sailing boat, much less "all the vessels in Christendom."

Four days I had spent exploring from the sea and the air, and so far not one of the islands had remotely fitted the description given in the log-book. There still remained, however, one island to be explored—Watling's Island, the seawardmost and the likeliest of all.

Watling's Island was in the news in 1892, when the directors of the Columbian Exposition accepted it as San Salvador. That year Walter Wellman, the journalist, raised a small monument on the east shore to mark the place where Columbus presumably landed. An excellent and authoritative book by Dr. Rudolf Cronau,* more carefully reasoned and more persuasive than the

---

* *The Discovery of America and the Landfall of Columbus;* privately printed, 1921

others I had read, also lent almost conclusive proof that Watling's was the right island. Dr. Cronau had explored all the islands long before my own visit, and by a process of elimination decided that Watling's was undoubtedly the landfall.

But when I flew over the Exposition's monument and down the east coast, I saw, as Dr. Cronau had noted before me, not one coral reef paralleling the coast as Columbus described, but three. The caravels would not have dared come within a league of this shore, day or night, and certainly not while a high wind was blowing, as the log-book recorded.

But the flight disclosed something else—"a large lake in the center of the island"—very large, and precisely in the center. Suddenly alert, we climbed higher in the seaplane, to eight thousand feet. Watling's Island was visible below in its entirety, and it was shaped like a bean. I looked for the encircling belt of coral reef. It was there, surrounding the island with scarcely a break. But what about the harbor? The coast was without any indentation whatsoever. And then I saw the harbor too. It was made by the reef swinging far out from shore at the northern end and back again, leaving a perfectly calm basin a mile wide inside the barrier, which acted as a natural breakwater. The basin was indeed big enough to hold all the ships of fifteenth-century Christendom.

This, unmistakably, was San Salvador.

But since it was apparent, even from the air, that the landing-monument was wrongly placed, I decided to search further, with Dr. Cronau's book still as my guide, and find the actual spot where Columbus stepped ashore in the New World.

The east coast, facing Spain, was obviously out of the question, for its unbroken phalanx of reefs makes it unapproachable from the sea. Columbus would not have ventured such a hazard in a rowboat, much less a sailing ship. However, on the *west* coast—the coast facing Florida—right beside the hamlet of Cockburn, there is a beautiful beach, which boats can reach through a wide break in the coral wall.

Columbus, as he reports in his log-book, having seen the moonlit tongue of land, lay to until daylight, and with the prevailing east wind must have drifted past the northern tip of the reef. Then, during the morning, he sailed south, and finding the breach in the barrier, steered through and dropped anchor before the unobstructed beach. And it was here, on the leeward, the safe side of the island, that he went ashore.

My seaplane, descending to within thirty feet of the sea, easily spotted the low coral cay that Rodrigo had first seen at the northern tip. We followed Columbus' course down the west coast, into the opening in the reef, landed on the lagoon inside and came to a stop on the very same spot, I suspect, where the *Santa Maria* dropped her sails.

What schoolboy has not seen the painting of Columbus disembarking on the beach with his sword aloft, his flag unfurled, and the Indians staring at him in wonder? I should have liked as dramatic an arrival. But instead of a Spanish admiral and his captains all dressed in purple velvet, two grimy aviators came ashore dressed in cotton coveralls, and unfurling nothing more royal than a couple of pongee mufflers, with which we were removing the spattered oil from our eyes. The "Indians" however (the inhabitants are entirely Negro, and number no more than seventy-five) were sufficiently astonished, for ours was the first flying ship ever to visit the island, and the first most of them had ever seen.

Next day, in a small boat, still following Columbus, we rowed back up the west coast reef, and found the "very narrow entrance" to the harbor which had so impressed him. "True, there are some rocks in it," he wrote (the rocks are still conspicuous), "but the water is as calm and motionless as that of a well"; as indeed it was while I was there. He continued: "I also wanted to find out the best location for a fort. And I discovered a piece of land resembling an island although it is not one, with six huts on it. This piece of land could easily be cut through within two days, thereby converting it into an island." And jutting boldly out into the reef-harbor is just such a piece of land. *It has been cut through* (no doubt by old pirate Watling himself) and made into an island—and into a fort as well, for I found a very ancient cannon guarding the excavated canal.

Dr. Cronau, I felt sure, was right. In only a single respect did the island fail to meet Columbus' description: it is as barren of "luxuriant vegetation" as its neighbors, for whatever forests there once were have long since been cut down by the English buccaneers.

Returning to Cockburn, I resolved to cross the island to the misplaced 1892 monument, dismantle it, and re-erect it on the western beach where, by all the proofs of Columbus' log-book, it belongs. But Bessie, the island's horse, was lame that week, so my noble plan to move the stones came to naught. Not three weeks later, however, Count von Luckner, aboard his schooner with Lowell Thomas, came to Watling's Island and, likewise convinced that it was San Salvador, succeeded in doing most skilfully what I had failed to do.

And I am certain that the monument now tells the truth, and that it marks as nearly as we shall ever know the very spot upon which the great Admiral first stepped ashore in the Americas.

This little expedition of mine naturally added fresh fuel to my interest in Columbus. I soon found out that the identification of his landfall was not the only controversial point. Historians were likewise disagreed upon his burial place. Over this question prime ministers have fallen, bishops have been libeled, and nations have all but gone to war. Even today two continents dispute the possession of the bones of the man who was probably the most important world figure since Christ.

Columbus died in 1506, in the Spanish city of Valladolid. His repeated request, when he felt death approaching, was that his body be buried in Hispaniola, the rich and beautiful island he had discovered on his first voyage. On this island had risen a thriving port, Santo Domingo, toward which the eyes of all Spain were turned, for as Columbus' first permanent colony it had become the goal of a vast migration of fortune-seekers.

To this New World cross-roads, therefore, Columbus' remains were transferred in 1540. The leaden casket, when it arrived from Spain, was reinterred with proper ceremony in the newly built Cathedral on the gospel side of the altar. At the same time the body of Diego Columbus, the son, was taken to Santo Domingo and placed beside that of his father. Both graves were marked with marble slabs, which remained there to identify them for a hundred and fifteen years.

Then in 1655 the English attacked Santo Domingo, and the church authorities, to protect the grave from desecration, destroyed the marble slabs and obliterated everything which might reveal the location of the bodies. Nor were new slabs ever put in place. For another hundred and forty years no inscription marked where Columbus' bones lay.

Perhaps that might be the situation even today had not Spain, in 1795, been forced to cede Hispaniola to France. Unwilling to surrender the body of their great national hero, the Spaniards decided to remove the Columbus casket to Cuba. They dug into the Cathedral floor, below the altar, just where tradition said the grave lay. Coming to a lead casket they reverently removed it to the Cathedral in Havana, and sealed it in a vault in the presbytery wall. Across the vault was placed a relief-image of Columbus, and an inscription: "O remains and image of the great Columbus, for a thousand ages rest secure in this urn, and in the remembrance of our nation."

After that the Santo Domingo Cathedral, bereft of its glory, was allowed to fall into such decay that by 1877 it had to be completely rebuilt. Delving below the stone floor before the altar, the workmen came upon an ancient lead casket just like the one removed to Havana in 1795. On the lid was inscribed the abbreviation,

D. de la A. per. Ate., which Dr. Cronau,* continuing his researches on Columbus, has translated as *"Descubridor de la America. Primer Almirante"*—that is, Discoverer of America, First Admiral. On three sides of the box were engraved, one to each side, the letters *C C A*—which could stand for Cristoval Colon, Almirante.

Realizing that this find was probably of extraordinary importance, the Bishop of the diocese invited all the Dominican dignitaries of state and church, as well as the foreign consuls, to witness the opening of the casket. When the lid was raised it revealed on its under side a third inscription, *Illtre y Esdo Varon Dn. Criztoval Colon,* which could only be interpreted as *"Illustre y Esclarecido Varon Don Cristobal Colon"*—Illustrious and Famous Baron Christopher Columbus.

There could be no doubt whose bones were these, crumbling in the bottom of the box.

The Cathedral at Havana was honoring the wrong Columbus. During the period when the graves were unmarked, it had been forgotten that the son was sepultured beside his father. It was Diego's casket, not Christopher's, which had been moved with such pomp to Cuba.

The discovery of the true grave of Columbus caused a sensation at that time throughout the world. Spain indignantly denied its authenticity, insisting the discovery was a hoax, despite the array of unimpeachable witnesses. She recalled her minister from Santo Domingo in disgrace when he reported the find was genuine, and has steadfastly refused to credit any claims except her own in the long controversy which arose.

---

* See *The Last Resting Place of Columbus;* privately printed, 1921.

In 1898 Cuba gained independence; and Spain, still declaring that Christopher Columbus must rest only in Spanish territory, moved the uninscribed casket a third time, back to Seville from which it had departed more than three hundred and fifty years earlier. There it was entombed magnificently, in an onyx sarcophagus marked CRISTOBAL COLON, and enthroned in the transept of the great Seville Cathedral, for all the world to see.

But all the world can now be certain that Cristobal Colon is not there.

Naturally the Dominican citizens are fully aware of the importance of their trust. They too have built, in their Cathedral, a shrine to guard the remains of their Columbus. In the center of the shrine is a heavy bronze chest, the sides of which fold down and reveal the precious casket within. Once a year, on October twelfth, the sides of the chest are removed, exposing the lead box to full view of the patriots who file past.

All this, I say, I had learned some years before from Cronau's books. The hope of seeing that box for myself was one of the two reasons I had come now to Hispaniola. Having visited Christophe's Citadel, I said good-by to Cap Haitien, traveled south again to Port-au-Prince, and again took to the air. Our seaplane followed the rugged southern coastline and crossed the frontier from Haiti, a black republic where the speech and culture are entirely French, into Santo Domingo, a white republic where the speech and culture are entirely Spanish. Looking down at Hispaniola, at the intensely blue water along the beach and the smoky mountains climbing inland tier on tier, I could understand why Columbus loved this great island more than any other place on earth, and why he wanted to be buried in the city he had founded on its shore.

It was not October twelfth when I reached the city of Santo Domingo—only the middle of September. Nevertheless a friendly church official granted me an extraordinary favor by opening the bronze chest and permitting me to examine the casket privately and at length.

I had a profound feeling of awe when these actual bones of Columbus were revealed. Every detail of the relic was indelibly fixed on my memory.

The lead box is seventeen inches long by nine inches square, and on the sides the initials *C C A*—Cristobal Colon Almirante—stand out boldly. The lid was lifted back, so I could read the inscription on the inside also. Of Columbus' remains, only a few bones are still intact; the rest have crumbled to dust which half fills the receptacle. The skull has disintegrated entirely, or else it was never there. Beside the leaden box is a rusty iron musket-ball, a third of an inch in diameter. This bullet had lodged itself in Columbus, no one knows how or when, but probably long before he became an admiral. It was never extracted, and went with him to his grave.

The lead box itself has corroded sadly, and the sides have warped away from the bottom. Time and inadequate protection have combined to threaten the casket and its sacred contents with complete dissolution.

But this alarming condition is not to continue, we may hope, much longer. The Pan-American Union has been striving for the last twenty years to bring to reality the Columbus Memorial, a monumental sepulcher which will guard the casket and the bones throughout the ages.

As the result of two international competitions, a design of noble beauty has been selected. Formed as a recumbent cross sloping upward, eight hundred feet long and two hundred feet high at the head, it will lift aloft, where its arms intersect, an eternal beacon. All the nations of both Americas, moved by admiration and gratitude, have agreed to subscribe to this heroic project.

At Santo Domingo, the cradle of civilization in the West, it is planned to build this monument to the great Discoverer: a monument from whose summit a flag of fire will shine in the heavens to guide the ships of the sea and the ships of the air in their courses across the hemisphere Columbus gave to the world.

CHAPTER VII

HOW TO BUY AN ELEPHANT

Seven League Boots . . . California to Key West to Fort Jefferson to Santiago to Cap Haitien to Santo Domingo . . . "go any place in the world you choose, and write about whatever pleases you.". . .

Where did I choose to go now? I sat in the park in Santo Domingo before the Cathedral, feeling almost embarrassed by my surfeit of freedom. Other islands in the West Indies attracted me, Martinique, Tobago, Trinidad. They were all beautiful and historic, but I was already familiar with them. I wanted new scenes, new quests for mountain tops unvisited. Why go to the old ones when there was so much of the world I'd not yet explored?

I reached for my pocket atlas and opened it to the map of Europe, to find some inspiration. And I found not one inspiration but two . . . my eye fell upon the Alps dividing Switzerland from Italy, over which my special hero, Hannibal, had led his elephant-borne army of Carthaginians. I'd always wanted to follow in his tracks and ride over the Alps on an elephant of my own. "I think," I said to myself, "I'll do it now. Hannibal crossed in October. Today is September twentieth. If I hop along I can make the crossing not only by the same route as Hannibal but at the same season. And then when I've reached Turin on my elephant, or Rome, or wherever else I decide to halt, I'm going to make a long jump to Ekaterinburg in western Siberia. There, perhaps, I can learn first-hand the story of the massacre of Czar Nicholas and his family. After that I think I'll go to Abyssinia—and maybe Mecca. But first I'd better get to Paris and see about that elephant."

There was a boat sailing in six hours for France. I took passage aboard her.

And ten days later, October first, I reached Paris and began to ask the price of every elephant in town.

The season, I realized, was already dangerously late. True, Hannibal's expedition had taken place when the snow lay deep in the Alpine passes. But as a consequence, of the thirty-seven elephants with which he started his mountain climb, not half of them reached Italy.

The thought of such fearful casualties made me press forward with my plans, for unless cold weather was delayed longer than it had been for twenty seasons past, all roads across the Alps would be closed for the winter in another fourteen days. I had not a moment to lose.

The logical place to look for an elephant properly trained to march down the highway and up the mountains, was a circus. Circus elephants would be accustomed to carrying howdah and baggage and passengers, and accustomed likewise to automobiles, motorbuses, bicycles, with which they must share the road.

Straightway I went to the Cirque d'Hiver, and bought a ticket with the intention of closely watching the elephant act, in order to pick out the beast whose beauty, grace and intelligence most appealed to me.

Of the sixteen elephants performing, one—a lady—completely took my heart. She could stand on her two front legs, sit upright on a red stool, and lift her trainer on her trunk into the air. Her deportment, so demure and genteel, contrasted sharply with the manners of her companions, who pushed, raised their voices and made rude gestures at the audience, putting their noses to their toes.

After the show I called upon my new inamorata, fed her three bags of peanuts and scratched her back with a steel-pronged rake. She rocked with pleasure and seemed to return my romantic glances. Hannibal, I felt sure, never had such a beautiful and affectionate mount as this. I had visions of myself, seated in my howdah, riding Lulu proudly down to Rome.

The circus manager seemed a bit surprised at my request to buy or rent Lulu for an Alpine expedition. Such a project had never been heard of in elephant history since the time of Hannibal himself. Fortunately the manager had a sense of humor and responded properly to my plans. But alas, I could not have Lulu for a rather personal and intimate reason. Lulu was in trouble. Her excessively affectionate nature had led her from one *affaire du cœur* to another; had caused, in fact, no end of scandal among the other circus performers. And just as all the malicious gossips had predicted, Lulu was about to have a baby. It was expected any time now within the next twelve months. Such a strenuous mountain journey at this critical period would be most unwise.

I was heartbroken. However, the manager had other elephants. There were Marie, Josephine Baker, Yvonne. Whatever elephant I took must be a female—males might become too obstreperous. For a thousand francs a day I could rent Yvonne. *Her* morals were beyond reproach. I didn't wonder that they were. She didn't have half the sex-appeal my Lulu had. Her skin looked dry and old. When she stood on her hind legs she groaned from rheumatic pains. I could foresee that the Alps were going to bore her terribly. But it was Yvonne or nothing; so after considerable bargaining to lower the price I paid down my deposit and found myself the owner, for a month, of several tons of elephantess.

The howdah that went with Yvonne fulfilled all my dreams of glory—gilt wood frame covered with scarlet bunting, and carrying a gilt armchair inside for me to sit on. The native East Indian mahout who was to go along as chauffeur had a costume of red embroidered coat and red leather boots. For me there was a white satin coat, with turban to match studded with huge imitation diamonds. The manager thought it would look nice if I hired a slave to sit in the rumble seat and hold a big palm sun fan over my head. So hire one I did.

Everything was ready now except the insurance. Nobody in Paris would insure Yvonne against death or damage on such a crazy journey. The Alps—at this season! Only Lloyd's in London would deal with me. And they pondered long and solemnly before naming a rate. They had written policies for almost every known risk, but never had they insured an elephant against the dangers of the St. Bernard Pass.

Even *that* was settled. "Lloyd's will insure any-thing."

But Yvonne and I never even started. At the very last minute her owner thought of something desperately important which he had overlooked: his enormous cir-cus posters with which he had plastered Paris, announc-ing his elephant act with *sixteen* elephants—"The great-est troupe of elephants in the world—*sixteen*—come and count them!"

And now, if I took Yvonne, there wouldn't be six-teen. There would be only *fifteen*. What would his audiences say who came to count the elephants? They would be outraged. They would feel swindled. They would ask for their money back. No, not for any price could he take this terrible risk.

So all my negotiations came to nothing. I still had no elephant, and four precious days had passed.

I next went to one of the Paris zoos, located in the Bois de Boulogne. Perhaps the manager there could make some suggestions.

He was delighted with my idea, and insisted that he had an elephant made to order—Elysabethe Dalrymple. She was the pet of the zoo, tame and gentle as a puppy, and conveniently small. The size of the elephant was a serious consideration since I would have to quarter her at night in stables and garages. A full-size beast would never get through the average stable door. The zoo-keeper said he frequently took six children at a time for a ride on Dally's back along the quieter paths about the park. The children's saddle I could use for myself and baggage. He regretted the fact that he could not provide me with a gilt howdah and white satin coat and turban, but reminded me that Hannibal didn't have them either.

Once more the price was agreed upon, the insurance settled. We were to leave the next noon on a freight car especially reinforced to keep Dally's weight from breaking through the floor.

That morning I brought my suitcase, typewriter and cameras to the zoo and loaded everything aboard Dally's uncomplaining back. A French mahout sat on her head with his sharp iron hook, and I climbed up beside the baggage.

Several hundred people had gathered to watch our trial trip to the freight yard which lay three miles away, across half of Paris. Just for the sport of it I had charted our course along the Avenue de la Grande Armée leading straight to the Arc de Triomphe and then right down the Champs Élysées to the Place de la Concorde.

We left the Bois in perfect order, Dally stepping along gaily at four miles an hour. But outside the zoo we entered the Porte Maillot—a typical Paris square seething with motor traffic, and Dally, brought up in the quietness of the Bois, had never seen such a bewildering sight. She began to tremble and shy like a timid horse. One experimentative taxi-driver, approaching from behind, sounded his electric horn, full blast, within two feet of Dally's tail. The poor beast leaped panicstricken into the air, and then with trunk turned skyward, and trumpeting in terror, she bolted wildly and blindly down the Avenue de la Grande Armée at what seemed like forty miles an hour.

I was the first of her burdens to be flung off—then

the typewriter, then the suitcase and camera. One final toss of her head got rid of the yelling mahout . . . and some six thousand pounds of elephant went hurtling along the street, scattering pedestrians and bicyclists, banging into taxicabs, oblivious of every obstacle. Frenchmen shouted and Frenchwomen screamed. Gendarmes and urchins and dogs ran after her as she plunged on, leaving consternation and destruction in her wake. A solid mass of motors halted by the traffic light finally blocked her course, but not till she had bolted nearly half a kilometer. Jammed in the middle of this tangle of motorcars, Dally, still squealing frantically, found herself trapped. The chauffeurs in the surrounding cars, once they got over their surprise, had the good sense to hold their places and keep Dally imprisoned till the pursuers overtook her.

When the mahout and I arrived she was still shaking from fright and breathlessness. Another block and she would have gone head-on into the Arc de Triomphe.

By now a huge crowd had gathered, and no wonder— the neighborhood hadn't known such excitement since the French Revolution.

It took us an hour to get Dally back to the Bois de Boulogne.

The zoo-keeper apologized no end. He had never suspected the poor beast would be so frightened by motor horns. But we both agreed that since she had this fear, it would never do, without long and careful training, to take her on a mountain motor-road where another runaway might mean death to us all.

He gave me back my francs—and I stood in the Place

Maillot, elephantless. And in six days more the St. Bernard would be closed till spring.

There was just time for one more effort—in Germany. I knew that both in Hanover and Hamburg trained elephants were for sale. Perhaps I could secure one of these.

A long-distance telephone-call turned the trick. Hanover offered a magnificent giantess, nearly eight feet high at the shoulders, named Big Bertha. Her specialty was marching about the streets carrying cinema placards on her mountainous sides. Consequently, automobiles were no bad news to her. But I would have to buy her outright and sell her back, at considerable loss, to the owner when my journey was over. Also I must agree to feed her not less than three bales of hay and twenty pounds of bread each day.

Bertha was obviously too big and too expensive, but I had no choice. Racing against the Alpine snowstorms, I scraped together the purchase price in marks, and crossed the frontier into Germany.

In Hanover my beast, saddled and insured, awaited me. Telegrams began to fly back and forth to Switzerland. The Great St. Bernard leading directly into Italy was still open, though flurries of snow had already fallen and all the lakes and streams in the neighborhood were frozen.

This pass climbs to eighty-one hundred feet and is the most difficult and dangerous of all, but it is the most direct. Also it gave me the opportunity of calling upon the famous St. Bernard monastery. The monks there, being fond of dogs, would surely be pleased to greet an elephant. The Swiss police agreed to let me use the highroad up their side of the Alps, and the Italian foreign office instructed their frontier guards to facilitate in every way my descent down the Italian slopes.

November first had now arrived. But I still had hope of getting over, for the weather, at least in Germany, was unusually mild and sunny. It encouraged me to take the chance.

But just in time to prevent my going on to Switzerland, the weather suddenly changed—and won the race. A telephone call came through: "Since last night blinding snowstorms raging in the passes. Snow in Great St. Bernard already two feet deep. Little St. Bernard likewise blocked. No traffic of any sort possible."

I realized there was now nothing left to do but give up all hope of success, for the time being, and try again next spring.

This postponement of my elephant expedition by no means left me at loose ends. My interest in the elephant march over the Alps was only one of two interests that had brought me to Europe from the West Indies. The other, equally strong, was a desire to learn more of the facts about the Romanoff massacre at Ekaterinburg. With the first of these interests folded up and put away for at least eight months, I was free to pursue the second.

So, after a brief visit in Berlin arranging for a Soviet visa, I boarded an airplane and sped on to Moscow. And a few days later, at the end of an eighteen-hundred-mile journey across the Urals into Siberia, I descended at old Ekaterinburg, destined to experience one of the most extraordinary encounters that ever befell a journalist.

CHAPTER VIII

THE MASSACRE OF THE ROMANOFFS

1. *The Assassin*

LYING prostrate in his bed, desperately ill, Peter Zacharovitch Ermakov, one of the three Bolshevik officers who, on the night of July 16, 1918, murdered Czar Nicholas II of Russia and all six members of his family, poured out with semi-delirious violence the whole dreadful story of the slaughter of the Romanoffs.

Until that moment he had kept mute on the subject of this massacre—one of the three men who knew everything. He himself helped organize it and carry it out. And then, for seventeen years, he listened, half-amused, neither denying nor confirming, to the wild rumors that spread around the world concerning the "facts" of the assassination.

Ermakov's confession was a matter of historic interest, for though half a generation has passed since that tragic and bloody night in Ekaterinburg, the story of the execution of the Romanoffs remains, like the beheading of Marie Antoinette, or like the assassination of Lincoln, one of the most dramatic and most vivid chapters in history. For years to come it will continue to be a familiar subject of discussion not only in Russia but in the entire world, such a towering symbol of oppression had the Czar and Czarina become—deservedly or not—and so appalling was the fate which overtook them.

The facts about the Czar's death known to the general public, heretofore, have been meager and controversial. They can be summed up as follows:

In August, 1917, the Czar, his wife and five children, having been arrested by the Revolutionists and held prisoner five months in Petrograd, were transferred to Tobolsk, in western Siberia. Later, in April, 1918, they were moved again, to Ekaterinburg—now Sverdlovsk, the metropolis of the Ural Mountains, a city also in western Siberia, but three hundred miles nearer Moscow.

Immediately the royalist army of Whites in Siberia, reinforced by many liberated Czech war prisoners, learned of the Czar's new prison-site, and began to press toward Ekaterinburg with all the force they could muster, in the hope of liberating the Imperial Family.

By July, 1918, Ekaterinburg, almost surrounded by Whites, was preparing to surrender.

But the Reds guarding the Czar felt that his rescue would be a staggering blow to the Bolshevik cause, and that the only way to prevent it was to kill not only Nicholas, but his wife and son and four daughters as well, lest one of them, free once more, become the inspiration and rallying point for counter-revolutionary activities.

Orders came from Moscow to the Ekaterinburg Committee of Workers and Peasants to shoot all the Romanoffs.

The Czar and the members of his family, with their several attendants, were told on the night of July sixteenth that disturbances had broken out in town and that fighting might spread any minute to the streets before their house. Consequently, for safety's sake, they must gather in a specified semi-basement guard room, where they were to await the arrival of an automobile that would take them to new and less exposed quarters in a different part of the city.

When they had collected in the room, and found chairs, their death sentence was read to them, and—to quote the long and illuminating report of the official Bolshevik investigator—"they were shot."

Exactly by whom they were shot, by how many, and the events immediately preceding and following the massacre, have always been subject to argument, since not one of the actual executioners had ever revealed the facts. Reports about the number and identification of the attendants who also died have likewise varied. Some stories said there were only two attendants, others said six.

The nine—or eleven—or thirteen bodies, all told, were taken eighteen kilometers out of town and:

> buried—
> burned—
> flung into a mine shaft—
> spirited away to an unknown destination—
> recovered by the Whites.

Historians have written that:

> the bodies have never been found—
> the bodies have been found, and numerous jewels. ikons, etc., with them.

It has been reported that these relics were sent:

> to Moscow—
> to London—
> to Pekin.

Czar Nicholas II and Czarina Alexandria on their wedding day in 1894. The Czar was twenty-six, his bride twenty-two.

The Czar and the Czarevitch (twelve years old), taken in 1917 just before the arrest and imprisonment of the Romanoff family.

The four Grand Duchesses, photographed about 1914. From left to right: Maria, Tatiana, Anastasia, Olga. In 1918, at the time of their assassination, Olga was twenty-two years old, Tatiana just past

The very meagerness and elusiveness of the facts have given rise to endless rumors, impostures and speculations.

A very persuasive book has been written to prove that Anastasia, the Czar's youngest daughter, escaped and is still alive.

But another book—just as persuasive—has been written to prove that she isn't alive and didn't escape.

The most authoritative account we have is in the report made by Sokoloff, the Whites' Chief Magistrate, who was commissioned by them, on their capture of Ekaterinburg, to conduct a relentless and exhaustive inquiry into the assassination.

The inquiry was a masterpiece of its kind. It left no stone unturned, no *available* witness unexamined, in the effort to learn the whole truth. All the testimony, however, had to come from circumstantial evidence and from witnesses whose participation in the crime was of such an innocent nature that they dared to remain in Ekaterinburg and face the Whites' wrath. For we may be sure that the chief murderers had discreetly fled, knowing they would be crucified if caught.

Despite these handicaps the inquisitors pieced together from second-hand evidence a generally correct outline of what happened. The report revealed the hideous brutality of the massacre, and the revolting cruelty with which this cold-blooded and deliberate slaughter of a defenseless family had been carried out.

But we have had to wait all these years to get the full and final truth. The occasion was the delirious, reckless and complete confession of one of the assassins himself.

His father-confessor, by a strange twist of circumstances—was myself.

On reaching Moscow by air from Berlin, I had one thought foremost. I was eager, of course, to explore Moscow and to inquire into the condition of the Russian people under Communism. But those things could wait. My first interest was in getting to Sverdlovsk to see with my own eyes the Romanoffs' execution house (now a public museum) and if possible to interview some member of the firing squad, if any one of them still lived in the district—and dared to talk. I felt that I would be able to understand the new régime better if I knew more about the last tragic chapter of the dynasty that it had destroyed and supplanted.

I soon found an excellent interpreter, willing to travel with me in Russia wherever I wished to go. Together we boarded a Trans-Siberian train and made the forty-eight-hour journey to Sverdlovsk.

This same journey, for the same purpose, had been taken numerous times before by various diplomats, historians and foreign correspondents, beginning as early as 1920. Always they were able to explore the prison house from top to bottom; it's open to the public from nine to five. But none of them had been able to meet, much less to question, a single one of the men who carried out the execution and were its only witnesses.

In Moscow I had found it difficult to believe the report that no trace remained of the ten or twelve soldiers who presumably took part in the shooting. And after considerable inquiry, I discovered that one of them had been traced, although his identity and whereabouts were known to only a few.

I had Stoneman, the Moscow correspondent for the *Chicago Daily News,* to thank for this clue. In 1933 he made the first progress toward solving the mystery when he learned that Peter Ermakov, whom Sokoloff in his report had accused of being one of the chief murderers and personally in charge of the cremation of the bodies, was not only still alive and still in Ekaterinburg, but was actually warden of the local prison, a post he had received from the grateful Soviet nation for his glorious contribution to the cause of Communism. But when Stoneman tried to arrange an interview for the *News,* Ermakov asked to be excused. No amount of persuasion could budge him. And thus the situation stood when I arrived in Sverdlovsk.

Acting on the tip from the Chicago correspondent, I went with my interpreter straight from the railroad station to the prison. The museum could wait. Yes, Ermakov was warden there. But he was not in, nor had he come to his office for the past three weeks. Reports said he was extremely ill.

That was bad news indeed, after I had traveled so far. Nevertheless, I called his house by telephone, and talked, through my interpreter, with his wife. The report of his sickness was all too true—cancer of the throat. Doctors were calling day and night . . . blood-transfusion just that afternoon. He had not been out of bed for three weeks, was not allowed to raise his hand. His voice was almost gone. The doctors would not allow him to try to speak to anyone. Madame Ermakov regretted that I had come at such an unhappy time, because any interview now was obviously out of the question . . . perhaps later when her husband was well again . . . thanks for calling . . . good-by.

I hung up the receiver feeling defeated and discouraged. Suppose he should die, without revealing the full facts! The story would die with him and history would probably never come any closer to the truth about the execution and burial of the Romanoffs than the second-hand accounts already current.

Not knowing quite what to do next, my interpreter and I wandered on down the street—when I had an inspiration. Madame Ermakov! She had been so agreeable on the telephone, though obviously troubled. Why couldn't I ask *her* for an interview? Only five minutes. She might know all her husband knew, and be willing to answer a few questions . . . if I could find her at a time when the desperately ill patient didn't need her whole attention.

So I called back a second time, stated my case quite frankly, and pleaded for the privilege of interviewing her, at any hour or place she would name. To my delight—and astonishment—she invited me to come to the Ermakov apartment at eleven next morning. But I must appreciate the tension and anxiety in the household, and make my questions short.

Only another reporter who has been on the trail of such a dramatic story as this one knows with what hopes and fears I looked forward to seeing Madame Ermakov.

A handsome and pleasant woman of about forty, she received me and my interpreter as she had agreed. The tiny apartment contained a hall and two small rooms, furnished so simply as to be almost bare.

The moment I entered the hall, I could hear Ermakov, through the half-open door, coughing and gasping in the next room. His bed was not six feet away from where I stood. Realizing his wife had not overstated the degree of his illness, and that every moment I remained added to the imposition of my call, I prepared to be brief.

"I understand that your husband is one of the men who executed the Romanoffs," I began.

"How did you know?" she asked, thereby answering my question.

"The correspondents in Moscow told me," I said.

"Well then, it's true."

"I'd like to hear about the firing squad," I continued, trying to be as direct as possible. "It is generally believed that it contained from ten to twelve soldiers. Have you ever heard your husband state the exact number?"

And then there came a hoarse and half-choking whisper from the sickroom, through the crack in the door:

"Tell him there were only three of us!"

Madame Ermakov looked startled. She had not intended for her semi-delirious husband even to be aware of my visit.

"There were only three," she repeated nervously.

I was trying to think fast. . . . Ermakov was listening to every word, and evidently in a rashly talkative mood. . . . But perhaps I would be allowed only one more question—only one more minute—before his wife cut short this conversation, and closed this first, and no doubt last, authentic revelation about the assassination.

I turned to my interpreter. "Ask about Anastasia," I said, "and speak *louder*. Say that in America we understand that all the Czar's family were killed except Anastasia—who escaped and was smuggled out of Russia and taken to New York."

The interpreter repeated in Russian, with raised voice. Before Madame Ermakov could reply, the door was pushed wide open by a heavy, hairy arm extending from the bed. . . . "What's this? What's this—about Anastasia?" came that same straining whisper. "You come inside here—*I'll* tell you what happened to Anastasia!"—I crossed the threshold with fast-beating pulse—"I spread her ashes with a shovel across five versts of Siberia . . . if you want to know where she is . . . tell *that* to New York!"

Ermakov lay on a low, crude Russian bed. Red cotton quilts were piled around him, but in his thrashing about he had pushed them off his body. I saw a huge and rather fat man of fifty-three turning restlessly in his feverish efforts to breathe. His heavy fat chest rose and fell painfully with every gasp. He had not been able to shave for a month, so a thick black beard covered his face. His hair, too, fell about his ears. His mouth hung open, and from one corner there was a trickle of blood. Blood stained his beard, his pillow, his sheets. Two bloodshot and delirious black eyes gleamed at me.

"Sit down—sit down," he ordered the three of us in that rasping whisper. "Don't stand there staring."

We sat down in unconscious, unresisting obedience to that tyrannical voice and those wild eyes—I on the edge of the bed. "You ask *me* about the execution," he continued, apparently in some anger. "Don't ask my wife—what does *she* know about it?"

I looked at Madame Ermakov. Should I leave? Should I stay? She was frightened at his violence, but realized he was determined to talk and might become more violent if we did not hear him out.

I would ask just one more question, and then—for decency's sake—depart.

"Tell me, Comrade Ermakov, how did you kill the Romanoffs?"

It was shortly after eleven when, straining and gasping for each word, he began to answer me. When I finally said good-by to him it was half-past two.

CHAPTER IX

THE MASSACRE OF THE ROMANOFFS

2. The Victims

To APPRECIATE fully the revelations Ermakov made to me about the last act of the Romanoff tragedy, it is necessary to review briefly the events in the earlier scenes that led up to it.

Few rulers in history have been so hounded by misfortune—and so impervious to it—as Nicholas II of Russia. While he was still a small boy, his grandfather, Alexander II, was blown to pieces by a Nihilist bomb—an event that left the boy Crown Prince. His father, Alexander III, though a powerful and successful ruler, was singularly disinterested in his oldest son, and failed completely to give the child an education befitting a future Czar.

Nicholas ascended the throne at twenty-six, in 1894, a mild and inconsequential little man, unaware of the realities of life. At his coronation in Moscow *three thousand people* were crushed to death when a great mob tried to press, all at once, through the gate of an amusement park where gifts were being distributed. And later, during the coronation ceremony, his badge of sovereignty fell from his shoulder to the ground. Being of a fatalistic and resigned nature, Nicholas was convinced that as a ruler he was doomed, and ever afterward he accepted, rather than contested, his unhappy fate.

Only one virtue in Nicholas' character can historians find to praise—the trait which more than anything else was to bring him to his fearful end—his passionate and lifelong devotion to his wife, who had been in her earlier years extremely beautiful; a German Princess from the little Duchy of Hesse. They were married just before the coronation, Nicholas being twenty-six, his bride twenty-two.

As Czarina, Alexandria soon proved to be as positive and wilful a figure as her husband was apathetic and ineffectual. The moment she became Empress she began, with her whole heart, to champion the autocratic system of government when already the political trend was definitely in the opposite direction. To this unfortunate trait in her personality were added chronic neurosis, religious mysticism, profound melancholia, and a tendency to hysteria whenever she was thwarted.

However, it must not be forgotten that the Empress had many exceptionally fine, even heroic qualities. The example of courage, industry and self-sacrifice she set her countrymen during the first years of the war endeared her, despite the general mistrust of her motives, to millions of Russians. Day and night she worked, organizing her war hospitals. No Cossack in the Czar's army was a better or braver soldier than the Empress—especially noteworthy as she had been born and bred a German, and had her family fighting on the other side.

But her well-intended interference in Romanoff rule was fatal. Under pressure from her, the Czar, with his lack of character and determination, was led from one folly to another and into defiance of every progressive political move. Inevitably the Russians turned against him. He came to be hated for his stupid blunders, and to be despised for his helplessness in the hands of his misguided but resolute wife. The spirit of revolt, long suppressed, grew stronger under her despotism and his incompetence. To suppress this rebellious movement, thousands upon thousands of political offenders were sent to prisons in Siberia.

Among these were Nikolai Lenin and Peter Ermakov.

Not content with the other misfortunes heaped upon the Czar, Fate now sent him four daughters in succession, when all Russia was praying for a son and heir to the throne. But at last, in 1904, their prayers were answered. A boy, Alexis, was born to the Czarina. The parental joy, however, was short-lived, for almost immediately the baby was found to be a victim of hæmophilia (inability of the blood to clot and staunch its own flow), inherited from his mother's family. Anna Viroubova, the Empress' confidante and closest friend, writes in her vivid and fascinating book, *Memories of the Russian Court,** that "the whole short life of the Czarevitch, the loveliest and most amiable child imaginable, was a succession of agonizing illnesses due to this congenital affliction. The sufferings of the child were more than equalled by those of the parents, especially

---

* Published by The Macmillan Company, 1923.

his mother, who hardly knew a day of real happiness after she realized her son's fate."

This disease, for which no treatment was then known, doomed the little Czarevitch to be a pain-racked invalid all his life. Who can blame the despairing Czarina, therefore, for inviting into the palace the illiterate but designing peasant-priest Rasputin, when she heard, after all the doctors of medicine failed to help the Czarevitch, that he had remarkable healing powers in his hands and gaze? And who can blame her for keeping him there when, through some hypnotic power, he was able instantly to relieve the tortured child whose screams of pain had driven her almost insane with despair?

The rest of the story of Rasputin is too well known to need repeating . . . his subtle absorption of power through his grip on the Czarina, gained by means of his ministrations to Alexis, until for the last two years before his murder by Prince Yusupov he was the real ruler of Russia.

The scandals of Rasputin and his reign—scandals based partly on fact and partly on malicious fabrication—permeated to the furthermost frontiers of Russia. These evil stories, coming to a climax in 1916 when Russia's armies were being steadily defeated in the war with Germany, deprived the Czar of the last vestiges of support from the people. To recapture his authority, he allowed his wife to persuade him to take over the supreme command of the army—his final and greatest folly, for he revealed himself to the few loyal soldiers who remained as a rather foolish and pathetic child walking around in a general's uniform and wear-

ing a beard. The army also noticed that he spent most
of his time admiring the flowers, keeping notes on the
weather, and writing love letters to his despotic wife,
totally unconcerned with the fact that the living soldiers
had only sticks to fight with, and that the dead were
piled up in countless thousands all about him.

The wonder is that the Russian people did not turn
upon the Czar and remove him sooner than they did.

On March 15, 1917, the Revolutionists under Kerensky being in control everywhere, Nicholas was forced
to abdicate. Four days later, he and his entire family
were placed under protective arrest by the Provisional
Goverment which feared, even then, that otherwise the
Romanoffs would be executed by the Bolsheviks. The
family's first prison was merely their own palace at
Tsarskoe Selo, some twenty miles outside Petrograd.
Here the Czar, the Czarina, Alexis and the four daughters, Olga, Tatiana, Maria and Anastasia, lived much
as they had lived in the old days. The Czar turned the
lawn into a vegetable garden, rowed on the lake, sawed
wood, kept the weather reports up to date in his
incredibly artless diary, and received visits from
Kerensky.

This ill-fated family, living this placid life when the
whole world around them was a roaring bonfire—what
were they really like? Did the titles of Emperor and
Empress and Prince and Princess make them less
human than other people? Were they handsomer, or
kinder, or wiser, for being so exalted? The characters
of the Czar and Czarina have already been sketched.
But the Czarevitch and the four Grand Duchesses—
what about them?

I'm again indebted to Anna Viroubova's book for a
brief description of the Czar's children:*

"Alexis, due to the care and seclusion under
which he lived, remained throughout his short life
an almost mythical being. A more tragic child
than the last Dauphin of France—indeed one of the
most tragic figures in history—he was, apart from
his terrible affliction, the most beautiful and most
attractive member of his whole family. Because of
his delicate health Alexis began life as a rather
spoiled baby, indulged by everybody. It is easy
to understand why, because nothing more heart-
rending could be imagined than the little boy's
moans and cries during his frequent illnesses. If
he bumped his head or struck his hand or foot
against a chair or table the usual result was a
hideous blue swelling and a subcutaneous hemorrhage frightfully painful and often enduring for
days.

"At five Alexis was placed in charge of the sailor
Derevanko, who for a long term of years remained
his constant body-servant and companion. I can
still in memory hear the plaintive, suffering voice
of Alexis begging the sailor to 'lift my arm,' 'put
up my leg,' 'warm my hands.' I ask the reader to
remember that the Imperial Family firmly believed
that they owed much to the prayers of Rasputin for
the fact that Alexis' health, once the priest began
his ministrations, steadily improved. Alexis himself believed it.

"The boy, like his father, dearly loved the army
and all the pageants of military display. He made
everybody salute him—particularly the Marshals in
his father's army, and the Admirals of the fleet.
The Czarina scolded him for such discourtesy, but
the officers themselves were delighted, and never
failed to salute their military little Czarevitch with

---

* Quoted with the permission of The Macmillan Company.

exaggerated formality—though it was not more exaggerated than the salute which he returned.

"As for the Czar's daughters, all four, because of the simple life they led, had manners that were unassuming and natural without a trace of *hauteur*. They all had happy, loyal natures, and were absolutely normal, mentally and physically.

"Of the four, Olga was the cleverest as well as the oldest. Her chief characteristics were a strong will and a singularly straightforward habit of thought and action. Had she been allowed to live out her natural life, she would have become, I believe, a woman of influence and distinction. Extremely pretty with brilliant blue eyes and a lovely complexion, Olga resembled her father.

"Up to the time of their imprisonment, Olga was the only daughter for whom marriage had been considered. In 1914, when she was eighteen, Crown Prince Carol of Roumania (now King Carol), prompted by his mother, Queen Marie, negotiated with the Czar for Olga's hand. But the Princess herself, in her usual direct manner, declined the match. In 1916, during the war, Prince Carol again visited the Russian Court, and now the young man's fancy rested upon Maria—age seventeen— and he proposed again. But the Emperor declared that Maria was only a school girl and laughed the Prince's proposal aside.

"Maria and Anastasia, the third and fourth daughters, were also blond types, and both unusually attractive. Maria had splendid eyes and rose-red cheeks. Anastasia, a sharp and clever child, was the gayest and most mischievous of the four.

"But it was in Tatiana, the second daughter, that her friends saw a reincarnation of her mother. Taller and slenderer than her sisters, she had the soft, refined features and the gentle, reserved manner of her English ancestry. Kindly and sympathetic of disposition, she displayed toward her younger sisters and her brother such a protecting spirit that they, in fun, nicknamed her 'the governess.' Of all the Grand Duchesses, Tatiana was the most popular with the people, and I suspect in their hearts she was the most dearly beloved by her parents. Certainly she was a different type from the others even in appearance, her hair being a rich brown and her eyes so darkly gray that in the evening they seemed quite black. More than the others Tatiana suffered from the social isolation in which they lived. She liked society and longed pathetically for friends."

Such were the royal children as they were known by a most intimate friend. And now—back to the palace-prison at Tsarskoe Selo.

After holding the Imperial Family there for five months, Kerensky, seeing and fearing the growing strength of Lenin and his ruthless Bolsheviks, bundled the prisoners onto a train, and shipped them off to a new and far less pleasant prison in the Siberian city of Tobolsk.

Three months later, in November, 1917, Lenin overthrew the Provisional Government. Civil war seethed throughout the country. Laborers, soldiers and peasants ran amok and slaughtered every member of the cultured and educated classes they could get their hands on. And their loudest yells were for the head of the Czar.

Meanwhile the royalists continued to plot to rescue Nicholas and smuggle him and his family to England. Such a large number of their agents were caught in Tobolsk that the Red commissars there decided to send the Romanoffs to the better garrisoned and more loyally Bolshevik city of Ekaterinburg, three hundred miles nearer Moscow.

At that time the Czarevitch was suffering from another one of his painful attacks . . . and no Rasputin came to relieve him. He could not possibly be moved. Nevertheless, the Czar was ordered to go on ahead, under escort.

For the Empress this was a heartbreaking order. She had to choose between her husband and her son. Alexis, with an internal hemorrhage, she knew to be in deadly peril. But she also felt that the Czar, without her guiding presence to protect him, would surely be murdered. Alexis had the family physician. The Czar had no one. Consequently, after several hours of inner torture, the Czarina, with death in her soul, decided to abandon her sick child in order to follow her husband because she feared his life was the more seriously menaced. If he was to die, then they would die together.

When she and the Czar departed they took Maria along, leaving the other three girls with Alexis. The four children remained behind for three weeks. Then, the Czarevitch having recovered sufficiently to travel, they joined their parents.

The best house in Ekaterinburg belonged to a rich merchant by the name of Ipatiev. He was dispossessed on twenty-four hours' notice, and the Czar and his wife and daughter installed, to be joined three weeks later by the other four children. A wooden stockade ten feet high was built around the house to prevent the townspeople from spying on the prisoners, or the prisoners from communicating with confederates outside. An officer and eight soldiers guarded the entrances.

Defending Ekaterinburg from the Whites was a ramshackle army of several thousand Bolshevik irregulars. But dominating the town was the usual Cheka, a council of Red extremists created to exterminate counter-revolution and "speculation" (any form of personal commercial enterprise). The Cheka ruled by the simple expedient of assassinating everybody who they suspected did not harbor a passionate devotion to the Red Revolution. At their service in Ekaterinburg, as everywhere else, was a formidable company of professional torturers and executioners. For the most part, these were footloose Hungarian war prisoners, or Chinese. In Ekaterinburg the ringmaster of this murder committee was one of the most savage and fanatical characters in Russian history, a man named Yourovsky; his chief ally, a thirty-six-year-old ex-convict named Peter Ermakov.

Two and one-half months after the delivery of the Romanoffs into the hands of this Cheka, shortly after one o'clock in the morning, a muffled fusillade of what sounded like rifle-firing was heard issuing from the basement of the Ipatiev house.

This much of the story about the Czar's life and death I had known when I walked into the sickroom where Peter Ermakov lay prostrate.

CHAPTER X

3. The Death House

PETER ZACHAROVITCH ERMAKOV, one of the three men who murdered Czar Nicholas, the Czarina, their five children, and four attendants, began his training for the terrible rôle he was to play in history long before the assassination took place.

According to his own statement made to me on that memorable morning, Ermakov from his youth had been a domineering and violent character, and a fanatical anti-Czarist. From his twentieth to his twenty-fifth year (1902-1907), living in or near Ekaterinburg, he had been arrested and imprisoned three times by the secret police for revolutionary agitation and terrorist activities. Each time his rage against the Romanoff Government only increased. Each imprisonment only goaded him to further and more desperate plots. On the fourth arrest he was shipped off to a prison camp in his native Siberia, with a life sentence.

There he continued to be as rebellious as in Russia. As punishment for his furious and destructive outbursts, he was beaten, starved, chained. For a solid year he wore handcuffs, and as a result had two broad purple scars around his wrists. Several times he barely escaped execution. But his spirit never cooled. Thirst for, and plans for, revenge burned in his soul—revenge against the tyrants who kept him in this torment and this exile.

Nineteen hundred and sixteen. Already Imperial Russia was disintegrating. More and more revolutionists were emerging from cover—and being rushed to Siberia to join Ermakov. But discipline in the prison camps had ceased to exist. The guards were mostly at the battle-front. Prisoners were escaping as fast as they arrived.

In March, 1917, the exiles heard that the Russian Army fighting Germany had mutinied, that the Czar was a prisoner, that the whole autocratic system they hated and fought against had crumbled.

En masse they had swept aside their prison bars, and marched off to join the Revolution. For many of them, their destination was Ekaterinburg, the nearest big city, Ermakov's home town. And at their head marched Peter Ermakov himself, with his glowing eyes and murderous intention, annihilating every royalist in his path.

But meanwhile the royalists, reinforced by several regiments of Czechs and by all others west of the Urals who opposed Red rule, formed an army of their own and called themselves the Whites. Enrolled in this army were the property owners, the nobles, the Czar's military officers. They had much to fight for. They were not going to be just sheep for the Bolshevists to slaughter. They resisted heroically and desperately, and slaughtered as many Reds as the Reds slaughtered Whites—back and forth across Siberia.

It was Ermakov telling me all this as I sat, during

that incredible interview, on the edge of his sick-bed. I should have made my departure long before. But I had ceased to remember that I ought to go. And his wife forgot to remind me. These chapters of his life she, herself, evidently had not heard before. She and my interpreter and I kept silent and listened, as Er-makov, recklessly and deliriously, relived those harrow-ing days.

Expansive and unguarded though he was, he still managed to conceal one feature of his past. Official records found in Ekaterinburg by the Whites, upon their capture of the city immediately after the Czar's execution, revealed that Ermakov had been sent into exile not so much because of his revolutionary activities as for being a highway bandit and incorrigible thief.

Ermakov's story about his own early history—even the part he told—you may be sure did not flow smoothly. He dragged out each word, one at a time, from his can-cerous and bleeding throat. At times his voice faded completely, and he would force himself to a half-sitting position once more, and try through sheer will-power to speak again.

"I killed, killed, killed," he gasped in that strained, strangled voice, "—during the civil war. Nobody in Siberia killed as many Whites as I did. No time for bullets—they were too few. I used my sword, and split their —— —— heads in two. We never took prison-ers. Every White and every Czech I caught, I killed."

It is easy to understand how so fanatical a partisan of the Revolution soon plowed his way to a position of im-portance in Ekaterinburg. And it is not to be thought strange that to him it seemed as if heaven had answered his prayers, made daily during nine years of imprisonment, when in the spring of 1918 *all seven* Romanoffs were delivered over to the tender mercies of the Ekaterinburg Cheka, of which Ermakov was a leading member.

"I was at the station when the Czar's train came in," Ermakov continued, still forcing his voice. "The Czar got off, along with the Czarina and their daughter Maria. The other four children were in Tobolsk. The Czarevitch was suffering from his sickness and too weak to travel."

Ermakov rested, struggled for breath, continued:

"I'd never seen the Czar before—only his pictures. But I recognized him right away from his beard. There wasn't a thing royal about him—just pale, undersized, and weak-looking. I remember noticing his colorless, watery eyes. But he was the one who had kept me in prison all those nine years—the prison where I'd seen over half my fellow exiles die. . . . Undersized or not, I could have strangled the little —— —— right there on the station platform.

"There was nothing weak-looking about the Czarina. She looked like a sharp-tongued German housewife, but terribly nervous and haughty. I remember she was wearing a long black coat, had two big pearls in her ears, and a stupid little lap dog under her arm. I'd heard about the high-handed way she ran the Czar—and the government too—and I believed it now. She looked as if she'd insist on running everything. I knew we were going to have trouble with *that* dame. She'd probably have another Rasputin in the house before night. She wasn't so awfully old—only about forty-five—but she had gray hair. Maria was about eighteen or nineteen."

Every time Ermakov paused to gather strength, I held my breath, fearing he would become completely exhausted and speechless before he came to the execution . . . and I knew there would never again be a chance like this to hear the truth. I could only hope and pray. He struggled on again.

"Two of our commissars took charge of the prisoners, and detailed an officer with eight men to act as guards. We had Ipatiev's house on the Cathedral Square ready for the Czar; and he and his wife and daughter drove there in a carriage. Next day we ordered a solid stockade, ten feet high, built around the house. We didn't want them communicating with White spies outside.

"You should have seen the linen, and curtains, and tablecloths, the Czarina brought along. You'd have thought they were moving back into the palace instead of into prison. Right off, she began writing out her menus on gold-crested menu cards, and ordering this, and ordering that. But we soon fixed *her*. We gave her and all her family exactly the same food the workers and my soldiers had. It all came from the same kitchen . . . soup and a plate of vegetables for lunch, and the same for supper.

"We'd had the Czar for our prisoner about three weeks when Dr. Botkin and the other three daughters came on from Tobolsk, bringing the Czarevitch. I was at the train to meet them too. Some sailor got off carrying Alexis in his arms. I'd seen so many pictures of the Czarevitch I recognized him as easily as his father. He looked white as wax, and very sick. We had to lift him into a carriage."

Painfully and haltingly, Ermakov continued his story:

"When the second batch of Romanoffs settled in the house, we had about twelve in all to watch—the Czar and the six members of his family, Dr. Botkin, a valet, and a maid named Anna Demidova. There were two imperial cooks—one a boy named Leonide about the same age as the Czarevitch." Ermakov laughed mockingly at the superfluity of cooks under the Cheka's régime—and choked on blood.

"We gave them twenty minutes each morning to walk in the garden. But we never allowed them to see anybody from the outside. The Whites and Czechs were getting closer to town every day—too close—and we knew they meant to capture Ekaterinburg and release the family if they could. We didn't want any little escape plans made under our noses. We nipped one plot when we found a diagram of the house drawn by the Czar and put in a letter he was trying to smuggle out to his friends. After that we increased the guards: kept one soldier outside the Czar's room, and one outside the girls' room. We had to imprison Alexis' sailor—we shot him later—for being so rebellious to authority. After that, we had to detail a special guard to carry the Czarevitch about in his arms. Alexis was still sick, and couldn't walk a step. We kept a soldier outside the lavatory too—didn't want any funny business going on there.

"Nobody seemed to mind much except the Czarina.

The Czar kept very quiet . . . smoked cigarettes all day. Nothing disturbed the Czar. He didn't seem to realize he wasn't Emperor any more, but just an ordinary Russian, and a prisoner. He was always sure he'd be back in Petrograd in a couple of weeks. He used to read the Bible every night, as I remember—the old hypocrite. And there was a big fancy book on the table called *The House of the Romanoffs*. He often looked at that too.

"The Czarina, though, she was always angry and quarreling about something. She asked me one day please to have the soldiers stop making so much noise outside her room. I told her the soldiers could make all the noise they liked. They weren't the prisoners, *she* was.

"I wasn't in command of the house myself, but I was in and out all the time. I saw whatever went on. The first house-commander we had was named Avdief. He drank too much, but we thought he was tough enough to keep Alexandra in her place. The guards were all workers from the same factory—a factory here in Ekaterinburg. They asked to be given this special post—promised they'd never let the crowned murderer escape.

"There was only one dining-room for everybody— and we had to keep the family reminded that they were our prisoners, so we made them eat with Avdief and the guards. I sometimes ate there, but Avdief was such a drunkard and the guards were such animals, I didn't like it.

"Avdief turned out to be not so tough after all. He went soft and sentimental toward the Romanoffs. The guards too. I caught them myself several times talking to the girls, and laughing. And they began to accept cigarettes from the Czar."

(Pierre Gilliard,* the Czarevitch's tutor, reaching Ekaterinburg just after the Bolsheviks had fled, was able to question people familiar with the situation in the prison house, and from them learned that "the guards, little by little, had become humanized by this contact with their prisoners. They were astonished by their simplicity, won over by their sweetness, subjugated by their serene dignity, and soon felt themselves dominated by those whom they believed they held in their power.")

"We couldn't have that going on. They'd be helping the prisoners escape the next thing we knew. I told Yourovsky about it. Right away next day he threw out the whole bunch—Avdief and everybody. And *he* took charge. I thought I was hard—I must have seen a thousand people killed—killed a lot of them myself—but I was a softie compared to Yourovsky. There wasn't going to be any talking to princesses under *his* régime. In place of the factory workers, Yourovsky called in a squad of our executioners from the Cheka—Hungarian war prisoners mostly. There were a few Russians in the Cheka too, but Yourovsky didn't want any of them. He felt he could trust the foreigners better."

Ermakov fell back on his pillow, seized with a paroxysm of coughing. I felt sure I'd hear no more. But no—he roused himself again, wiped the trickle of blood

---

* *Thirteen Years at the Russian Court*, by Pierre Gilliard. Used by permission of Doubleday, Doran & Company, Inc., publishers.

from his beard with the back of his fist, and seemed to be determined to tell every detail he could drag from his memory.

"Princesses," I whispered to my interpreter. "Ask him about the Princesses."

The interpreter asked how the four girls passed the day. Ermakov understood.

"Oh, they had a lot of games. They played dominoes with the Czar. And they read a lot and talked a lot— I don't know about what—wasn't important. They all seemed to love Alexis. Some one of the girls was with him all the time—handsome little fellow . . . but a hopeless invalid . . . no sort of Czar for Russia.

"Olga was the oldest daughter—nothing special. About twenty-two; maybe twenty-three. I remember Maria had her nineteenth birthday party in the prison house—one of the guards took her some cakes. She seemed to be the Czar's favorite. They always walked in the garden together. Anastasia still had her hair down her back. She wasn't more than seventeen, maybe younger. Tatiana came between Olga and Maria. I thought she was the prettiest of the four. She had lots of dignity too, and was always looking after the others. We all liked her the best." *

Tatiana! Waiting for Ermakov to recover sufficient breath to speak again, I remembered the beautiful and moving chapter about this particular Princess in *From*

---

* At the time of their death, Olga was twenty-two and six months, Tatiana just past twenty-one. Maria's nineteenth birthday came five weeks before. Anastasia also celebrated a birthday in the prison house—her seventeenth. Alexis was fourteen years old less fourteen days. The Czar was fifty, the Czarina forty-six.

*Double Eagle to Red Flag.** The story places her in
the Czarina's war hospital in Petrograd. There, working unceasingly, never sparing herself because she was a
princess, Tatiana won the unqualified respect and worshipful devotion of every wounded soldier in the place.
She seemed to them more like an angel than a human
being, with her clear eyes and fresh young face and
generous heart. Each day she made the rounds of the
wards, seeking out those who were suffering most, and
touching their hands and foreheads with her finger-
tips.

And they forgot their agony, so healing was the presence of this sweet divinity. She walked beside them
as they were wheeled into the operating room, and they
never felt afraid. She stood beside them when they
died. Or if they lived and left the hospital, she escorted
them to the door, and gave them as a parting gift some
small memento which she herself had loved.

One wounded lad, just seventeen, worshiped her as
he did the Holy Virgin. He spent his hours just waiting for her return . . . his glorious, beautiful Princess.
When his time came for an operation, she escorted him
to the table and began to help the surgeon remove the
boy's bed-dress. Shamed, horrified, at the thought that
she—this immaculate and heavenly being—would see
his nakedness, the poor lad fainted dead away.

He left the hospital, some time after, hearing only the
music of Tatiana's good-by, clutching in his hand her
own prayer-book that she had given him. Inspired, he

---

* *From Double Eagle to Red Flag,* by P. N. Krassnoff. Used by permission of Dodd, Mead and Company, publishers.

rushed back to the front, flung himself recklessly at Russia's enemies, and in the first charge perished, for Tatiana—the same Tatiana who within little more than a year was to be held in an Ekaterinburg prison by these savage and vindictive assassins.

Ermakov was struggling to speak again—to answer my question about the source of the Czar's death sentence.

"Yourovsky," he said in that painful whisper, "—he wrote it."

Moscow, dreading the approach of the Whites, had already decided on the death of the Imperial Family. An Ekaterinburg commissar had gone to the capital to get his instructions from the Central Committee. Ruling this committee was Jacob Sverdlof. (In his honor the name of Ekaterinburg was changed to Sverdlovsk—a reward for the part he played in the Romanoff tragedy.)

The instructions were—execute!

Yourovsky was then commissioned, about July twelfth, to carry out the sentence. He chose Ermakov as his first assistant, and instructed him (who had been born and bred just outside Ekaterinburg, and knew every inch of the surrounding country) to find a proper place for the cremation of the corpses. The place was all-important, since the cremation must be done in secret and not a trace of the bodies be left for the Whites to deify.

"How did the death sentence read? Do you remember?" my interpreter asked.

"I don't remember all of it," Ermakov whispered. "It was only about five lines. It said:

" 'You think the Whites are going to rescue you—but they aren't.

" 'You think you're going away to England, and be a Czar again—well, you're not.

" 'The Soviet of the Urals sentences you and your family to death for your crimes against the Russian people.'—That was something like it."

Ermakov, to my unspeakable relief, was breathing easier and speaking more clearly. The approach to the execution itself had given him new strength, new spirit. Apparently no more than half conscious of the presence and identity of the two strangers in his room, he raised himself up from his pillow with straightened arms, looked fiercely at the ceiling, and released a fresh flood of memories. It is possible he had never allowed himself so to overflow in speech before, possible that once liberated by his own delirium he found a certain ecstasy in unburdening his soul. Coughing, strangling and suffering, but never stopping, he talked straight on for another half hour. His revelations, however, cannot possibly be recorded verbatim from this point, for they came out in disconnected phrases. But the facts of his story, rearranged in proper sequence, are correctly reported.

I still sat on the edge of his bed, not daring to move lest I break the spell.

"It was on July twelfth we had our final meeting and got our orders," Ermakov continued. "We set the night of July sixteenth for the shooting—four days later. I had to make all the plans myself for the destruction of the bodies. We wanted to do the thing as quietly as possible, to be sure the Romanoffs didn't suspect in advance. And I wanted to make doubly sure that the bodies would be thoroughly destroyed. I didn't want the Whites to find a single bone.

"On the fourteenth, my aid and I, a sailor named Vaganof, went eighteen kilometers out of town to a place where I knew the miners had been prospecting for ore. They had dug cave-like holes in the ground, and abandoned them when they didn't find anything, to try some other place a few meters away. There were ten or twelve of these old mines, with the piles of excavated earth all around—and not too far from the road. I couldn't think of a better place to burn the bodies. Vaganof and I then came back to town and got Yourovsky, and we three returned to the mines on horseback.

"Yourovsky said I couldn't have chosen a better place.*

"Next morning we took an army truck and carried several big tins of gasoline out to one of the deepest mines. I also sent along two big buckets of sulphuric acid, and a truckload of firewood. One of my soldiers stood guard over these supplies to frighten off any curious peasants who might be wandering around.

"On the sixteenth—the day we'd set for the execution—Yourovsky ordered the same truck and same crew to bring a dozen blankets at midnight to the Cathedral Square before the prison house.

"When they got the signal, later, they were to move on with the truck to the basement entrance of the Czar's house. Yourovsky told the chauffeur he was to stop his

---

* One of the Russian house-guards, testifying at the Sokolov inquiry, reported that Yourovsky, having decided upon the spot for the cremation and destruction of the bodies, rode back to the prison house, called upon the Czarevitch, and sat on the child's sick-bed for a "friendly chat."

truck as close as possible to the door and *not* to kill his engine—leave it wide open so as to make as much noise as possible.

"If there was a lot of back-firing—so much the better.

"This would be the moment, with the engine roaring and the truck ready, for the shooting. People outside might not even hear the shots.

"Yourovsky took charge of all arrangements for the execution itself. We had decided to kill—beside the Czar and the Czarina and the five children—the doctor, the Czarina's maid, the cook and the valet. That made eleven.

"The Bolshevik maid working in the house we decided to take along to allay suspicion until we got everybody into the execution room, but we didn't mean to kill her.

"Yourovsky and I agreed that it would be best if only he and I and Vaganof did the shooting. Vaganof was always with me. He was a good Bolshevik who hated the Czar as much as I did. We could count on him to shoot straight!

"Yourovsky had a Nagan repeater. Vaganof and I had Mausers. We each carried twenty extra rounds of ammunition.

"Yourovsky also gave revolvers to three or four members of the Executive Committee, and rifles to seven of our Hungarian house-guards. But we didn't intend them to use these—just stand by in case of trouble." (Trouble! From the Czarevitch? From the four Princesses?)

"There were to be just we three executioners.

"That afternoon we had looked all over the house for

a good place to do the shooting, and decided on the basement guard-room. Being below ground the shots wouldn't sound so loud. It was the right size too—about eighteen feet long and twelve wide. And it was the room nearest the basement entrance—where the truck would be waiting for the bodies.

"There was a double door leading from the end of the room into the basement corridor. We executioners would have to stand in the doorway and fire at the family all crowded together in the small room. If there were more than three of us we'd be in one another's way.

"About midnight Vaganof and I drove in the truck to the far side of the Cathedral Square, and left it there with some soldiers. I told the driver to come to the basement entrance at the side of the house when I sent for him.

"Yourovsky and the three commissars and seven guards were waiting for us at the main entrance. We all inspected our pistols. Everything was ready.

"Yourovsky then knocked on the Czar's door. The Czarina and Alexis were sleeping in the same room. Yourovsky woke them up and went in. I stood just outside.

"He told them that a lot of fighting had broken out in the town, and was spreading this way. For their own security they must dress and collect in the guard-room by the basement entrance. An automobile would come there to pick them up, and take them to other quarters—at least for the night.

"It took the family a long time to get ready—nearly an hour. I heard them walking around in the bedrooms putting on their clothes and talking.

The Czar's office desk at Tsarskoe Selo reveals his passion for family photographs. The calendar shows August 31, 1917. The Czar had been removed to Tobolsk a few days before. Souvenir-hunters later tore off a few pages.

Rasputin greets the Czar and Czarina as they enter the church in Leningrad. An attendant carries the Czarevitch. Notice the expressions of awe on the faces of the two women on the extreme left.

Bedroom of the Czar and Czarina in their palace at Tsarskoe Selo, near Leningrad, containing the Czarina's collection of six hundred ikons and the Czar's collection of one hundred and fifty family photographs.

A drawing room at Tsarskoe Selo. On the wooden slide the Romanoff children played on rainy days. Alexis' toy automobile, latest 1917 model, stands beside it. Before the windows are seen the Czarina's court dresses.

"Yourovsky got impatient. He was about to go in and hurry them. It was after one o'clock.

"But just then the door opened and the Czar came out carrying Alexis. They both had on military caps and jackets. The family followed behind. The Czarina and the girls were all dressed in white and carrying handbags. Two of the girls were also carrying sofa pillows. . . . Yourovsky must have told them to carry pillows to sit on in the automobile. Anna, the Czarina's maid, came out with *two* pillows.

"Behind her came Dr. Botkin, the cook, the valet and our Bolshevik maid—I don't remember her name. Nobody seemed excited. I'm sure they didn't suspect. The Czar was saying something in English I couldn't understand. But he turned around and spoke to the servants in Russian. I heard him say, 'Well, we're going to get out of this place.' He felt sure the Whites had broken into town, and that we were moving the family in order to delay the rescue as long as possible.

"It was dark in the hall upstairs, and the Czar, right behind Yourovsky, was groping his way forward with his heavy burden. I offered to take Alexis myself and carry him down to the guard-room, but the Czar refused. Yourovsky led them on down the steps. He told the rest of us to wait for him right where we were."

When Ermakov mentioned this gesture toward the Czarevitch, I could not help thinking to myself: You would have taken that helpless child carefully in your arms into the execution chamber—and sat him on a chair—and calmly blown out his brains . . . when you had a seven-year-old son of your own waiting for you at home. (Ermakov had already mentioned his son to me—born in Siberia during the father's exile.)

But I didn't speak my thoughts. I knew Ermakov would only hold up his two wrists as he had held them up once before—wrists scarred by the handcuffs he had worn for a year—and ask me to see *that,* and ask if I thought he could forget how the Romanoffs had done this to him, and would do it again if they had the chance. He would say Alexis was just another tyrant in the making—to be exterminated before he grew old enough to indulge his tyranny. I didn't give Ermakov a chance to say all this; I didn't want to break this flow of information right at the brink of the climax of the story.

Ermakov, panting and gasping, was whispering on:

"In a minute or two Yourovsky came back, and told Vaganof and me that the time had come to kill. I said we mustn't forget the truck. I sent a guard across the square to tell the driver to come on at once to the side entrance—and not to forget about the motor noise.

"We waited till we heard the truck begin to grind in low gear across the square. Then we went down in the guard-room, followed by the commissars and the seven guards. They all had their bayonets fixed.

"The Czar and the other ten prisoners were there, being watched by two Letts.

"There were only three chairs in the room—no other furniture.

"Alexis was seated on one chair in the middle of the room—he was still so sick he couldn't stand.

"The Czar had another chair and was sitting beside Alexis.

"The Czarina sat just under the window, by the right-

hand wall, with Anastasia standing beside her. . . . I'd
nailed the window down to help muffle the shots.

"Dr. Botkin stood right behind the Czarevitch. Anna,
the maid, was standing in the far right-hand corner,
clutching her two pillows; the cook and valet together
in the left-hand corner.

"Leaning against the back wall were Olga, Tatiana
and Maria. None of the girls had on hats or coats.

"In the left corner by the door was the Bolshevik
maid.

"Each one of us had rehearsed exactly what he was
to do, so there'd be no mistake:

"We would wait in the corridor—with the guards—
for the truck to reach the side entrance. Then, when
the engine was racing, we three would move to the door
of the room. I was to beckon to the Bolshevik maid to
come outside. We had no intention of harming her.

"Then Yourovsky would read the death sentence, and
we would all three start shooting at once. Yourovsky
told Vaganof and me not to shoot at the Czar or the
Czarevitch—*he* wanted them.

"I was to get the Czarina, Dr. Botkin, the cook and
the valet.

"Vaganof would kill the four girls and the Czarina's
personal maid.

"Each of us would be ready to reload the moment
his six bullets were used up.

"We got to the corridor before the truck reached the
side entrance, but we heard it coming.

"The family heard it too. The Czar stood up. Alexis
put on his cap. The valet reached for the pillow on
the Czar's chair to take it along.

"The truck stopped outside—not fifteen feet away from us—right in front of the basement door. The driver began to race his old war-torn engine, faster—faster—faster—till it fairly roared.

"Yourovsky and Vaganof and I moved to the guard-room door.

"I beckoned to the Bolshevik maid. As she walked out I said something about putting her first in the automobile.

"The others scarcely noticed it.

"Then Yourovsky took a step forward into the room, and faced the Romanoffs—the death sentence in his hand."

CHAPTER XI

4. Slaughter

PETER ERMAKOV, still gasping and choking, pushed himself up from the pillows of his sick-bed, thoroughly aroused now by his own recital. Staring straight ahead of him, he whispered on in that half-strangled voice:

"Yourovsky and Vaganof and I stood in the doorway. The commissars and guards stood just outside in the corridor. Yourovsky began to read the death sentence. He had to shout to be heard above the pounding of the truck motor just outside. . . .

" 'You think the Whites are going to rescue you— but they aren't.

" 'You think you're going away to England, and be a Czar again—well, you're not.

" 'The Soviet of the Urals sentences you and your family to death for your crimes against the Russian people.'

"The Czarina understood—instantly. She jumped up and stood rigid. The others understood likewise. But they were all too stunned to speak. Only the Czar seemed not to comprehend. 'What?—what?' he shouted back at Yourovsky over the roar of the engine, '—aren't we going to get out of here after all?'

"Yourovsky's answer was to fire his pistol straight into the Czar's face.

"The bullet went right through his brain.

"The Czar spun to the floor and never moved."

Ermakov's eyes had become so wild and bloodshot he looked almost maniacal. . . .

"I fired my Mauser at the Czarina—only six feet away—couldn't miss. Got her in the mouth. In two seconds she was dead.

"I fired next at Dr. Botkin. He'd thrown up his hands, and turned his face half away. The bullet went through his neck. He fell over backwards.

"Yourovsky had shot the Czarevitch out of his chair, and he lay on the floor, groaning.

"The cook was crouching in the corner. I got him in the body and then in the head. The valet went down. I don't know who shot him.

"Vaganof made a clean sweep of the girls. They were in a heap on the floor, moaning and dying. He kept pouring bullets into Olga and Tatiana.

"The two younger girls—Maria and Anastasia—had fallen beside Dr. Botkin.

"The light was bad and smoke filled the room, so our aim wasn't always sure. Somebody must have crawled all the way forward to the corner beside the doorway—perhaps the valet. We later found bullet holes in the baseboard there.

"I don't think any of us hit Anna, the maid. She had slid down in her corner and hidden behind her two pillows. We found afterward that the pillows were crammed with jewels—maybe the jewel cases turned the bullets away. But one of the guards got her through the throat with his bayonet . . . we had called in our Cheka executioners from the corridor to help finish off the job, and they were clubbing and bayoneting everybody.

"The Czarevitch wasn't dead . . . still groaning and twisting on the floor. Yourovsky shot him twice more in the head. That finished him.

"Anastasia was still alive too. A guard pushed her over on her back. She shrieked—he beat her to death with his rifle butt. . . ."

My interpreter, looking sick and pale, was repeating rapidly in low, flat whispers every word of Ermakov's labored phrases. I myself was wondering how much more of these cold-blooded horrors I could stand. There was no promise of a respite. Ermakov, driven on by his own story, had more to say:

"The guards in the other parts of the compound heard the shots—they knew what had happened. Several of them came running in to see the corpses. In a few minutes the corridor and guard-room were full of soldiers. Some of them got sick at the sight of so much blood and had to go out again.

"Yourovsky ordered the guards to take the hats and coats off the bodies, and gather up the necklaces, watches and rings, and put all the valuables in one place. Then we wrapped the bodies in blankets and piled them on the truck. We left a dozen men or so to clean up the guard-room—there was blood everywhere, and slippers and pillows and handbags and odds and ends swimming around in a red lake.

"Vaganof and I went along with the truck—out to the abandoned mines. Yourovsky stayed behind to set the house in order. We didn't get started till after two in the morning. And then it somehow took us two hours to cover the eighteen kilometers—the road was terrible. By the time we arrived at the mines there was a streak of dawn breaking in the sky.

"I decided we didn't have enough time to dispose of the bodies before daybreak. We'd do it the following night. I was determined to have strict secrecy—we didn't want any of the peasants to know where I was burying the bodies—if only to confuse the Whites.

"We piled the corpses up beside the tins of gasoline and sulphuric acid and the firewood I'd sent out the day before. Then as I wanted to go back to town and see Yourovsky, I left Vaganof and a squad of soldiers behind to guard the corpses and form a cordon around the field. I planned to come back as soon as it was dark again.

"That day, July seventeenth, I spent helping collect the personal property of the Imperial Family—jewels, ikons, diaries, correspondence. All this was turned over to one of our Bolshevik commissars to take to Moscow. But everything had to be finished off hurriedly—the Whites were one day closer . . . nice little surprise *they* were going to have.

"About ten that night, when it was dark enough, I went back to the mines—and found everything in order. By the light of the lamps we stripped the corpses of their clothes. Found a lot of diamonds sewn in the Czarina's bodice—and more necklaces, gold crosses, and a lot of other such things on the girls. These were sent to Moscow along with everything else.

"Then I made a big pile of all the clothes—just

clothes—on top a layer of pine boughs, poured gasoline over everything, and flung in a lighted match.

"By the light of that fire I lifted the corpses into the army wagon, and took aboard the tins of gasoline and the acid and the firewood, and drove two kilometers farther off the highroad to another abandoned mine I knew about.

"Here in the mouth of this mine we built a funeral pyre of cut logs big enough to hold the bodies, two layers deep. We poured five tins of gasoline over the corpses, and two buckets of sulphuric acid, and set the logs afire. The gasoline made everything burn rapidly. But I stood by to see that not one fingernail or fragment of bone remained unconsumed. Anything of that sort the Whites found I knew they would use as a holy relic. I kept pushing back into the flames whatever pieces were left, and building more fire, and pouring on more gasoline. We had to keep the fire burning a long time to burn up the skulls. But I wasn't satisfied till our pyre and everything upon it was reduced to powder.

"Then I took a shovel and filled the gasoline tins and acid buckets with the ashes—corpse-ashes and wood-ashes all together. We didn't leave the smallest pinch of ash on the ground. There was a big pool of rain-water close by. We even poured that over the place where the pyre had been. I put the tins of ashes in the wagon again, and ordered the driver to take me back toward the highroad. I wanted to scatter the ashes with the shovel. There was a strong breeze blowing that night, so I pitched the ashes into the air—and the wind caught them like dust and carried them out across the woods and fields . . . and it rained next day . . . so if anybody says he has seen a Romanoff, or a piece of a dead one—tell him about the ashes—and the wind—and the rain."

CHAPTER XII

5. Postscript

ERMAKOV collapsed back on his pillows, fighting foɪ breath and voice. His pajama coat fell open, and revealed his fat chest. He put his hand on his body. "I'm fat and tired now," he said. "Oh, but I wasn't like this when I fought the Whites. I was a devil, thin and strong. I could kill fifty Whites a day and never stop for food or sleep. After the Romanoff execution I fought day and night for a week."

The Whites and Ekaterinburg! That was a chapter I had to know, to finish off the fearful story. I had stayed much, much too long, though it eased my conscience to see that Ermakov seemed to be suffering less now and choking less than when I had come two hours before. Perhaps this confession had done him good. I'd ask just one more question. If the bodies were disposed of so thoroughly, what were the relics which the Whites were supposed to have found in the mines and taken away in a casket?

So I tried to get Ermakov talking again:

"How soon after the execution did the Whites reach the prison house?"

Ermakov rose up once more. "I'll tell you," he whispered. "Six days after the cremation we got orders to evacuate the town. We didn't have a chance to stop the

Whites. They were three times as strong as we were—and fighting like wild men. On the eighteenth the Whites learned that the Czar had been put to death. They went almost crazy with rage. . . ." Ermakov laughed, but his laughter was so blood-choked it made me shiver. "They pushed forward twice as fast—I knew they would. They were swearing they were going to capture and torture every man of us who took part in the execution. They especially wanted Yourovsky and me. They swore they'd nail us to a tree . . . and they would have too.

"On July twenty-third we were surrounded on three sides. Only the railroad to the west was still open. Next day the Whites closed the gap and seized the railroad.

"I was still in Ekaterinburg. I had kept only twenty men with me—but I knew I could fight my way out when I had to. That night my guards and I got on our horses and dashed right through a whole mob of Whites blocking the road. They shot at us, but we came at them so fast they didn't know what was happening until we had gone.

"And weren't they happy when they learned it was *I* who got away!

"Next morning they had the town. They rushed to the prison house. The heavy furniture was still there, but that was about all. Of course the bullet holes and bloodstains in the guard-room showed them where we had done the shooting. The White commander took a hatchet and dug out those sections of the wall and pieces of the floor. I heard he wanted to analyze the blood and see if it was the Czar's—or some such stupid business.

"The commander moved into the Czar's room upstairs. He made this his headquarters. Somebody brought him the Bolshevik maid we had employed to serve the Czarina and watch the family—the same one I had pushed out of the guard-room just before the execution. The Whites stood her up against the wall in the same place where the Czar was shot, and shot her.

"They found my own seven-year-old boy next. I wanted to send him on to Moscow when we were retreating, but he was sick with measles, so I decided to let him stay behind . . . he was in good hands, friends of mine. I didn't believe the Whites would learn about him.

"But somebody gave him away. The Whites forced a confession from his guardian. And then they got a message to me saying that unless I surrendered myself, and stood trial for shooting the Romanoffs, they would do to my son what I had done to the Czar's son.

"But I refused to answer—didn't believe going back and getting shot myself would help the child any.

"When the Whites saw I didn't mean to surrender, they took my boy onto a freight train, and when the train was going full speed downhill, two soldiers grabbed him by his hands and feet and pitched him out the open door of a boxcar. Nobody knows why he wasn't killed. Maybe he landed in soft earth. Anyway he was found still alive by some Bolshevik peasants and smuggled safely back to town. The Whites were sure he was dead and I suppose never thought of him again.*

---

* Ermakov's son is now a full-grown man, and a shock brigader in a Sverdlovsk shoe factory.

"It didn't take the Whites long to learn about the abandoned mines, where we'd burned the corpses. But they thought we'd just buried the bodies, and they dug and dug for six months looking for them. They finally found the charred remains of the clothes. We hadn't burned them very well. They announced they had found the ashes of the Romanoffs—and believed it too. I've heard that these charred bits of clothing were taken to Pekin, and kept in some church there."

Ermakov in mentioning "bits of clothing" was guilty of an understatement. There were actually sixty-five objects, burned and broken, found by Sokolov and his investigators. The list included images of saints from the Czar's pockets, military insignias, belt-buckles, Dr. Botkin's eye-glasses, corset-stays, buttons, half-burned shoes, keys, and a handful of unset pearls and diamonds.

The story about these relics being taken to Pekin is one of a dozen such stories in circulation. London, Moscow, New York, have all been named along with Pekin as the resting place of the tragic box. But there are no grounds whatsoever for their claims. This is what happened:

The Whites, in 1919, on being in turn expelled by the Reds from Ekaterinburg, were driven eastward. Sokolov took the box to Harbin, and there, seeing danger pursuing him and wishing the greatest possible security for his casket, he requested the French General, Janin, to accept the relics and take them to Paris for safe-keeping. This Janin agreed to do. In Paris the box was first sealed up in a government vault, but later turned over to a Russian ex-diplomat named de Giers, who had served under the Czar as ambassador to Italy.

The box is now in de Giers' keeping. He refuses to state whether or not it is still in Paris, but gives assurance that it is in a safe place. (A recent rumor has the box buried in the Luxembourg Gardens.) He insists that the relics belong to the Russian nation—not to the present Soviet Government—and that they will not be delivered to the nation until the time comes when they will be received with proper honors and proper respect.

I do not know how much more Ermakov would have talked, how much more he might have revealed, if there had not been a ring at the doorbell. It was the doctor, who had come to give his patient another blood transfusion.

I still had one more question to ask:—What ever became of Yourovsky? But my time was up. It was not till much later that I heard (and then only a rumor) that Yourovsky had been executed by the Bolsheviks themselves on the fantastic charge that he had been personally responsible for the dastardly murder of the Imperial Family!

I said good-by quickly, and thanked Madame Ermakov for having received me. Her husband was still gasping and looking about with those wild eyes. I think my departure was as vague to him as my arrival.

Outside, in the cold November air again, my knees felt weak. I entered the nearest grog shop for a drink of brandy.

Whatever opinions I may have had, before seeing Ermakov, about the world-wide controversy over the escape of Anastasia, I came away completely convinced

that his emphatic statements in regard to this matter
definitely settled it. Anastasia could not possibly have
escaped. I felt sure that he had burned her body along
with the rest, and that the case of the woman who, with
evident sincerity, claims to be Anastasia—and who has
been accepted as Anastasia by many Russian royalists—is one of the most astounding and baffling imper-
sonations in history, but no more than that. Pierre Gilliard, the Czarevitch's tutor, and an intimate member of
the Romanoff household from the time Anastasia was
four years old until three months before the assassination, interviewed the woman in question. He denies
that she is the Czar's daughter, and has written a book,
The False Anastasia, to prove that she cannot be. Ermakov's detailed and positive avowal that he had burned
Anastasia with the rest was sufficient proof to me that
Gilliard is right.*

Shortly after leaving Ermakov's apartment—once I
had my composure again—my interpreter and I went
to the Ekaterinburg prison house museum where the
Imperial Family had died. The house has been largely
repaired since the ghastly massacre in 1918, and shows
no signs of its tragic past.

A guide took us through. The house is filled with
relics of the Revolution—pictures of the Bolshevik
leaders in the district, their hats, their coats, their

---

* The story accepted by "Anastasia's" champions is that the youngest
Grand Duchess, at the moment of the assassination, was not "beaten to
death" by the Hungarian Cheka guards, but only beaten unconscious; and
that two Russian house-guards, detecting this fact on removing the corpses,
instead of placing her body in the truck, smuggled her to their own house,
and later escaped with her to Rumania. I do not doubt their belief in the
truth of this story. I am convinced they are mistaken.

medals. There are posters and diagrams on the wall, announcing the glories of Communism, and showing how many more tractors and ingots of steel were made under Bolshevism than under Czarism, and how many more airplanes and suits of underwear . . . as if, in this house, anybody cared. I had to manhandle the guide to get him away from his glories-of-Communism rigmarole long enough to ask him which room was occupied by the Princesses, which by the Czar and Czarina—the room where Yourovsky brought the fatal message to "assemble below" on that fearful July night. I soon found that the guide didn't know exactly, and wasn't interested. . . . This was a temple of the Red Revolutionists—not a memorial to their victims.

But fortunately I had seen Ermakov first and was able to work out the identification of the rooms for myself.

First of all I followed the route of the doomed family through the building, from the Czar's bedroom to the basement guard-room . . . down the steps, along the corridor. The guard-room remains today as in 1918. The bullet holes are not all there, since, as Ermakov stated, the Whites removed small sections of the wall containing some of the holes, and parts of the flooring where the blood had flowed. The pock-marks in the woodwork are still to be seen. At this time the room was used to store old packing boxes which I found piled up to the ceiling. Because of these boxes and the lack of light, I was unable to take any kind of picture.

Standing in the double doorway, where Ermakov and Yourovsky and Vaganof had stood at the reading of the death sentence, I could imagine the picture as they saw it: the Czar and Czarevitch, both in their military

blouses, seated in chairs in the middle of the room—
the Czarina, likewise seated, beneath the window by
the right wall—Anastasia standing beside her—Dr.
Botkin standing behind the Czarevitch's chair—Olga,
Tatiana and Maria leaning against the back wall—Anna,
the maid, standing in the far right-hand corner—the valet
and cook in the left-hand corner—and then those savage, slaughterous ten seconds . . . killing, and reload-
ing, and killing anew . . . with Vaganof "pouring
bullets into the bodies of Olga and Tatiana"—Tatiana,
the sweet divinity of the war hospital, who had worked
so heroically to bring relief to the living and peace to
the dying—with no one to raise a hand, now, to defend
her . . . and the little Czarevitch, shot out of his chair
and groaning on the floor—"Yourovsky fired two more
bullets into his head—that finished him." . . . "Only
thirty-eight pistol shots to kill eleven people," Ermakov
had boasted. Not bad.

The basement door is just the same as when the eleven
corpses, wrapped in blankets, were carried through it
and heaped upon the truck waiting close by.

Upstairs only two walls in the room that had been
occupied by Anna Demidova, the maid, were devoted
to the Romanoffs. On one of these I found a mural
painting, ten feet long and seven high, depicting the
arrival of the Czar and Czarina and Maria at Ekaterinburg. The train which has just brought them from
Tobolsk is in the background. Three Bolshevik commissars are taking them in custody.

On the opposite wall were glass cases containing
photographs, letters, documents. The first letter to take
my eye was one from Rasputin to the Czar, written at

the end of July, 1914, just before the Great War, in which the priest begs the Czar to avoid war at any cost, since Russia was unprepared, and a disastrous war would surely bring about the fall of the dynasty. Prophetic words!

Displayed also in the case were sections of the Czar's and Czarevitch's diaries. Pages from the Czar's diary showed that he had continued, right up to the day of his death, to keep a close watch on the weather.

A front page from the Ekaterinburg newspaper of July 19, 1918, spread these headlines: EXECUTION OF NICHOLAS, THE BLOODY CROWNED MURDERER—SHOT WITHOUT BOUR-GEOIS FORMALITIES BUT IN ACCORD-ANCE WITH OUR NEW DEMOCRATIC PRINCIPLES. . . . New democratic principles . . . the butchery of six helpless women and a crippled boy. . . . "I got the Czarina in the mouth." . . . "Anastasia shrieked—the guard beat her to death with his rifle butt." . . . Sentenced without trial, murdered in secret, bat-tered shapeless after they had fallen by seven hired Hungarian assassins—Hungarians, because the Rus-sian soldiers themselves could not be trusted to take a proper part in so foul a deed. . . . New democratic principles as practised among the Bolsheviks!

Three days later I was in Leningrad.

My encounters in Sverdlovsk, and my visit to the death house, had given me a keen desire to see the Czar's palace at Tsarskoe Selo, where, so I learned, every room remains exactly as the Romanoffs left it on the day they departed for their Siberian exile.

On reaching Leningrad I took a motorcar at once to
this country place, and spent an afternoon wandering
through the great empty house that once had been home
to a man and his wife and their five children.

Empty—but only of people. Every book and picture and bed and chair is there, untouched since the
family walked away one morning and never came back.
The Czarina's gowns of silk and satin still hang in the
wardrobe. From every appearance of the Czar's desk,
he might have left it five minutes ago. Arranged around
the top are eighteen photographs of his family: Olga
and her first court dress; the Czarina and little Tatiana;
Alexis as a baby, playing with his dog; the Czar and
Czarina on their wedding day. . . .

In one of the formal reception rooms is preserved a
wooden slide which Alexis and Anastasia kept polished
on rainy afternoons. And there is Alexis' miniature
automobile, the latest 1917 model—rubber tires, cut-
glass lamps—in which he could pedal himself about the
palace corridors, honking his horn furiously as he pursued his shouting sisters. If one has ever had a child
who owned and loved a similar tin automobile, or if one
has ever been a child and pedaled one's own play wagon,
the sight of this toy, so lonesome and neglected looking, will make the memory of its imperial little chauffeur's cold-blooded assassination, in the guard-room at
Ekaterinburg, doubly poignant and doubly cruel.

The Czar's and Czarina's bedroom gives us some in-
sight into their minds. The Czar's passion for family
photographs runs riot here. One hundred and fifty
clutter every space. The tables, the walls, the cabinets,
are hidden under photographs. The Czarina has ex-

pressed herself too. In the alcove, above the two brass beds, are six hundred ikons. At the side of the room is a cheap wash-stand supporting a china wash-bowl and pitcher.

But the Czar and his wife were happy here. This was their sanctuary, to be adorned as capriciously as they liked—a refuge where they could be at peace, surrounded by the love of their children and their saints.

The billiard room reveals the key to the final chapter of the family's history. Here, during the war, the Czar and his generals spread the war maps on the billiard table, and worked out each new campaign, each new attack, retreat and strategic move. Just above is a half-hidden balcony. In this balcony the Czarina, remaining unobserved, and not trusting her husband's ability to direct the course of the war, listened to the discussions below. And then, after counseling with Rasputin she secretly aided—or blocked—the military plans as she, a patriotic and well-meaning but irresponsible woman, thought best.

It is interesting to speculate what might have happened had a less neurotic, more comprehending Empress been hiding in that balcony. It is possible that the Czar, with his susceptibility to guidance, good as well as bad, might still be on the throne today. Undoubtedly there would never have been the national disgrace of Ekaterinburg—an atrocity which future generations of Russians, when the political prejudices of the present day have passed and a dispassionate viewpoint has been attained, will acknowledge to have been one of the blackest and most shameful pages in history.

CHAPTER XIII

THE WHEAT AND THE EMERALDS

THAT night, my first in Leningrad, there was a soft rain falling. About twelve o'clock, unable to sleep, I put on my raincoat and splashed out into the streets. Because of the weather and the hour scarcely another person was in sight. I passed St. Isaac's Cathedral, its glorious granite columns shining faintly in the rain, strolled beside the beautiful yellow-hued Admiralty Building, around the enormous square before the Winter Palace and, via the bridge, on across the broad Neva River to walk past the house where Prince Yusapov murdered Rasputin.

Tomorrow morning these streets, these squares, these bridges and buildings, would make up a roaring new city called Leningrad. Tomorrow morning the sidewalks would be thronged with the proletarian pedestrians, clad in threadbare clothes, hurrying to work. Before each dispensary of bread, meat and butter, there would be a long and weary-looking line, clinging to the cards that ration food. But right beside these lines would be other lines of concrete mixers, turning furiously, preparing concrete for rows of houses; and steam rollers smoothing the new pavements, and riveters welding together the new ten-story apartments for the new society.

But tonight in the dripping darkness Leningrad slept, and St. Petersburg, regal and proud, surrounded me, the haughty capital of the old empire, scornful of the swarms of peasants and factory hands that had come to take possession of its grandeur.

St. Petersburg in the days of its glory was one of the noblest, most beautiful cities on earth. It had spaciousness, dignity, leisure, wealth, power. Peter the Great, who built it on marsh islands at the head of the Gulf of Finland, set an all-high mark in vigor and imagination, a mark still far beyond that of the Workers' Councilmen of today. With a wave of his sceptre, he swept aside all obstacles to create public squares of vast area and surround them with public buildings that are among the largest and most lavish in Europe. The richest class of people in the world during the eighteenth and nineteenth centuries—the Russian nobility—flocked to St. Petersburg. Each noble tried to outdo his neighbor in the construction of palaces and in his show of splendor. In this competition the Czars kept well in front, spending money and gathering treasure to an extent incomprehensible to us today.

The resulting magnificence, built on the anguish and enslavement of the masses, shone with a blinding light. The Russian aristocracy became distinguished throughout all Europe for its extravagance, its ostentation, its incomparably beautiful women and lordly men. The biggest emeralds in the world glittered from the crowns of Russian queens. The greatest collection of pictures outside the Louvre found its way to the Hermitage Gallery. The music of the Russian masters flowed from every orchestra. The art of ballet-dancing became a Russian monopoly. St. Isaac's Cathedral, an architectural wonder of the first magnitude, rose from the marshlands. Summer palaces were built to rival Versailles in splendor. In the art and the grace of living, St. Petersburg, right up to 1914, led the great capitals of the earth.

But all this atmosphere of elegance and all the people who created it are gone, utterly, irretrievably vanished. Leningrad hates, defames and jeers at all that she used to be.

My second night in Leningrad I went to the Marinsky Theater to see a ballet, *The Hunchbacked Horse*. I felt a real surge of excitement. Here the most exalted of the old nobility gathered. To attend the Marinsky, they donned their richest jewels, their whitest gloves, their most lavish gowns and uniforms. Here the Czar and Czarina with their son and daughters came frequently, to sit in the Imperial Box and applaud the lavish spectacles. Such a glittering, royal gathering has probably never been seen elsewhere.

A charming and intelligent English-speaking Russian girl, a leader in the Communist Party, accompanied me. On the way I remarked that the Marinsky Theater must feel proud to have had the privilege of first seeing Pavlowa dance, and of presenting Nijinsky in his early days of triumph. My companion looked puzzled. "Who?" she asked vaguely. Here was one of the keenest young people I met in Russia, a "shock brigader" of the Soviets, a fountain of Communist faith and zeal. But she had never heard of two of the three most widely celebrated Russian artists of the twentieth century (Chaliapin, the third, she had heard of) because they had happened to live before the Workers' Party seized the government.

This experience proved typical of a hundred similar cases I later encountered, all revealing the distorted sense of values from which the Bolsheviks are still suffering. Nothing is good, nothing is right, nothing is worth remembering, except their own theories, their own faith and the works thereof.

No theater have I ever seen as beautiful as the Marinsky. The walls are covered with yellow damask, and each seat in the orchestra is an individual armchair upholstered with the same rich silk. At the back is the Imperial Box, and on the sides the smaller boxes of the grand dukes. The decoration has faded very little since they sat there.

Into this regal auditorium the new masses were pouring. Some had no coats, few had neckties, only half the men had shaved that day. Not one woman wore anything but the plainest, cheapest, sack-like dress. Not a jewel, not a flower, not a graceful attitude, not a beautiful person. A sailor and his girl sat on one side of me. Two students in red wool blouses sat behind. Next to them were two women who must have been standing at their jobs all day—they took off their shoes. From the Imperial Box leaned six comrades, probably from the police force, eating pastry. The musicians in the orchestra wore wool shirts, without coats.

The ballet which this audience had gathered to see was superlatively good. Here is one Czarist art the proletarians have not let die. I would have enjoyed it more, however, had the audience not eaten apples all during the performance.

The violent transformation of Leningrad from imperial to proletarian is evident on every side. The ducal palaces, run-down and woebegone, are now workers' apartments. The palace where Rasputin was murdered is a House of Culture and Rest for teachers. The great suburban estates have been turned into pleasure grounds where the workers go to escape the desperately crowded quarters in which they live.

The old Nevsky Prospekt, now called the Prospect of October Twenty-fifth, once one of the smartest and richest streets in the world, has become one of the dingiest. True, three times as many people parade it as before, but they are dressed in shabby, shapeless clothes instead of furs, and have kopecks to spend instead of gold roubles. The shops that once offered only the best and the most beautiful are now poverty-stricken, half empty, and display only the cheapest and shoddiest goods. No individual shop-keeping is allowed. Every place is state-owned and state-supplied. Taste and quality are incredibly poor. Beside any store in Leningrad, any ten-cent-store branch in an American cow-town would seem like a treasure house. There are book stores—but the books have only one theme. There are cinema houses—but only political, sermonizing, Soviet-glorifying films can be shown.

It seems to me that the Soviets discourage their people from having anything more than the barest necessities. Clothes, flowers, motorcars, books are considered dangerously counter-revolutionary. There is very little money among the workers to buy these things, since any accumulation of money is a crime. And if the Russians *did* have the money there is almost nothing worth while on which to spend it. In one fur shop I bought a sheepskin Cossack hat. Poor as it was, it cost one hundred Soviet roubles. The average monthly pay for a worker is a hundred and fifty roubles.

My good American camera was stolen right off the desk of the manager of the Intourist Bureau. Had I permitted, the Bureau would have docked the clerk who was responsible, for the value of the camera—*six months' wages*. But even if I'd taken the money there was not a single camera to be bought in all Leningrad, other than those offered for sale, second-hand, by private citizens in the commission shops. Apparently the only way to get a new camera in Leningrad was to steal it.

This famine of goods that would be considered essential in any other country, does not shake the people's conviction that theirs is the best of all possible lands, for most of them either never knew better times, or have forgotten that they once did. When any progressive-minded comrade becomes discontented and yearns for an extra pair of socks or a good watch, he is reminded that such things are anti-social as long as the state needs every kopeck and every cogwheel for heavy industry. But while this endless self-sacrifice is going on, the people as individuals are being made drab, dull and poverty-minded. More than once, while in Russia, I asked myself this question: When the heavy industries, which the Bolsheviks are paying for so dearly, at last begin to turn out articles of personal comfort in useful quantities—will there be schools to teach people how to use these things and live like human beings?

On an island in the Neva River stands the Fortress of

Peter and Paul, built by Peter the Great to protect his newly founded capital. This place is held in particular disfavor by the Soviets, for to its prison were sentenced the political enemies (now heroes) of the former government. Some of them were shot to death here, too, for such public services as bombing a carriage-full of Romanoffs to little bits—which, as we know now, was a pious and glorious act of rebellion against the capitalistic system.

As a prison, the place is unspeakable, and the agonies endured there in the name of political faith helped bring on the bloodthirsty Bolshevik revolt.

But a greater reason for the Bolsheviks' abhorrence of the fortress is that its church shelters the tombs of all the Czars from the time of Peter the Great to Alexander, the father of the last Romanoff. Large groups of workers are led through this church—now ugly and unkempt, and stripped of all the splendor it once knew—and shown the tombs of their vanquished enemies, the Czars. The explanatory lecture, in brief, is this: "Here lie the tyrants who fought against the demands of the workers. Let us be thankful that the Romanoffs are all dead and that every vestige of the old system by which they ruled is overthrown."

With the dungeons fresh in one's memory, it is difficult to deny that the Revolution was indeed an emancipation, in many ways. But among the Bolsheviks one does not hear a single note of pride in what Russia accomplished under the Czars—her enormous expansion to the present boundaries that are the boast of the country, her advance from semi-barbarism to equality among the nations in two hundred years, her fruitful concern with the arts. There is no attempt to instill in the minds of the young people who come to stare at the tombs any respect for their country's past glories, but only contempt and hatred for its blemishes and scorn for everything not sprung from the Bolshevik Revolution.

I saved St. Isaac's Cathedral until I could spend half a day there. The Cathedral, reminiscent of St. Peter's in Rome, and once the Imperial Church, is now an antireligious museum, filled with artless posters revealing the iniquities of the old orthodox religion, its ignorance and greed, its indifference to the workers' struggle against the capitalists There are crude pictures of priests hidden in belfries, turning machine guns on workers' demonstrations; and pictures of drunken orgies in the monasteries. The priceless marbles and mosaics (which at least they could salvage from the past to benefit the present) are hidden by strident placards which boast about the Five Year Plan and tell how many more tractors and nails and sausages were made under Stalin than under the tyrant Nicholas.

I remarked to the English-speaking lecturer, who escorted me, that it was shocking to find the superb mosaics covered over by these hideous posters.

"Religious art is only a tool of the capitalists to lull the workers into submission," he replied, from his replybook.

"But aside from the religion, aren't you proud of those enormous columns across the façade outside?" I asked him. "I understand they weigh sixty tons apiece. They must be the handsomest granite columns in the world."

"We are *not* proud of them," he said. "Think of the

suffering the workers had to endure to bring them from Finland. We have drawings made at the time showing how badly they were housed and fed. The workers were not even allowed to have a union."

"But do you know why this sacrifice was made, why this marvelous church was built?" I asked him, seeing he had no real enlightenment about the place.

"To enslave the workers with the opium of religion," was again his mechanical answer.

"It was built to commemorate your Czar Alexander's victory over Napoleon and the expulsion of the invading French army from Moscow, from Russian soil," I corrected him—and waited to see what the reply-book had for *that*.

"We workers do not believe in war."

I gave up, not troubling to remind him that "the workers" at that moment had the biggest army in the world.

On another day I visited two of the most celebrated summer palaces: Peterhof, and the palace of Catherine II at Tsarskoe Selo, where I had previously gone to see the royal residence of Czar Nicholas. Peterhof is famous for its fountains, which when they play create a scene of extravagant loveliness and luxury. There the courtiers and their ladies danced, and the Czarinas wore their emerald crowns. In Tsarskoe Selo, Catherine lived in glittering splendor, amid her forty drawing rooms, her rooms walled with amber, with silver, with priceless murals, and dined with a hundred dukes in her banquet hall of jade and lapis-lazuli.

Now these two monumental relics of Czarist autocracy are public museums.

On the occasion of my visit to them, it was a "rest day." (Sunday is abolished—every date of the month divisible by six is a rest day.) The sun shone brightly, and attracted thousands of workers to the grounds. They came in overalls and undershirts, carrying their lunch in paper parcels, eating everywhere, bestrewing with refuse the marble statues, the fountains, and making themselves thoroughly at home. In Versailles the great palace is still haughty, still royal, and greatly respected by all Frenchmen as a symbol of a glorious period of their past. But the Russian counterpart is dilapidated, muddy and ill-kept. Serves it right—it gave shelter to the enemies of the laboring classes.

Back home that afternoon I sat, decidedly depressed, at my hotel window, and looked out over Leningrad, and saw the ancient domes and golden spires of St. Petersburg, still rising high and proud, fade in the November twilight. It made me sad to·realize that so much which was fine and distinguished in this beautiful city had to perish to give birth to the new society. It is not St. Petersburg alone that is gone, but all the style, refinement, grace and charm that went with it.

Leningrad is now only a drab, hard-driven workshop in which everybody has just enough food to keep from starving, and a place to sleep, but nothing more. Everybody is desperately poor. No one has time to make love, no one is allowed to write a song about a lark, or travel to Venice for a holiday, or read a book of adventure or romance. There is no glamour, no poetry, left to life, no freedom for one's soul, as the rest of the world understands these things. Instead, the workers have committee meetings and the joy of seeing new factories arise.

This all seems to me to be as lopsided a system as was the previous one. Formerly a few people had too much caviar and too many emeralds, while the masses were hungry for wheat. Now the masses all have wheat (when the government lets them keep it) and no emeralds. But man cannot live by bread alone. The supply of emeralds is just as vital as the supply of wheat, if life is to be worth living—the purely decorative and esthetic is just as necessary as the useful and practical. In Leningrad, alas, the emeralds have all been trampled under foot.

Only the wheat remains.

CHAPTER XIV

ACROSS the table from me, in her small but very busy Moscow office, sat the First Lady of the Land of Russia. She was Citizen Krupskaya, widow of the great Lenin—Mrs. George Washington of the Soviet Union. And seventy-five years old.

Partly because of her age, with a life behind her filled with honor and unparalleled achievement; partly because of her steadfast devotion to the Revolution and its great leader, her husband; but chiefly because of her own personal courage, vision and generalship, Mme. Lenin has become the best known, the most admired and the most beloved woman in her country.

Her husband was the father of the Russian Revolution. She was its mother.

Hers is the one name always mentioned by every Russian in the Soviet Union, no matter how much the Communist conquest may have uprooted him and despoiled him, with reverence and deep affection.

The first thing I did on reaching Moscow again, from Leningrad, was to call upon this celebrated woman. And to my delight she granted me an interview.

When I entered her office (she is a commissar of education), I saw a strange figure waiting to greet me. I

say strange because the figure offered such a sharp contrast to the very young and very alert girl-secretaries
outside.   She sat, leaning on her desk, as if extremely
tired, a black shawl held close about her shoulders
and snow white hair falling in careless wisps about her
strong but kindly face.   Her weary lids were half
closed.   Here was a woman who had endured appalling
suffering, who had fought, fought, fought, all her long
life for what seemed to be, for most of it, a hopeless
dream.   She followed her husband in exile to Siberia.
With him she returned in 1917 to help overturn a world.
She saw him shot down by enemies, but live.   She saw
perhaps a quarter of the population of Russia perish
from the Great War, the Civil War, banditry, famine,
pestilence, before her party triumphed.   And her eyes
reveal the anguish they have beheld.

But when those eyes gave me a smiling welcome,
that weary face seemed to spring to life.   And when she
spoke, forty years vanished from her age.   She talked
rapidly, vigorously, although her English was difficult.
The clarity of her mind and the force of her character
arrested me immediately, as they arrest everyone who
comes in contact with this veteran Communist.   I understood why, as an orator and a leader, she had been one of
the greatest forces of the Revolution.   Even now, at
seventy-five, she speaks often at public gatherings and
on the radio, and when she does, all Russia listens.

I was allowed to talk to Mme. Lenin for more than an
hour.   Her great interest—now that she and her husband have dethroned dynasties, suppressed rebellions,
expelled foreign enemies, and clamped Communism on

one-sixth of the land area of the world—is the education and emancipation of women. In this respect Citizen Krupskaya and her department have accomplished stupendous things.

From a condition of almost oriental enslavement and ignorance before the World War, the masses of Russian women under Communism have leaped overnight to the other extreme. Now they have absolute equality with men in every respect—economically, legally, politically. In no way are women set apart, protected, or favored. There is no longer a "Mrs." or a "Miss"—only "Comrade" and "Citizen." They are given the same work and the same wages as men. They must struggle for life on exactly the same footing as men, fighting with their own fists.

Half the work in the vast new industrial plants is done by women, in the machine shops, the automobile and tractor factories, the mines. Women build the military tanks, the airplanes, the artillery, the locomotives.

In one electric-motor factory I visited, the manager apologized for having so few women workers—*only thirty-five per cent*. In this plant, as elsewhere, they were wearing men's clothes, boots, caps. They were as grimy, as greasy, as the men—and as hard.

Moscow is building a new skyscraper hotel and a new subway. And the "sand-hogs," the rock-miners, the steel-fitters, are as likely to be women as men. Squat and red, they shovel gravel eight hours on a stretch into the concrete mixers, run the steam derricks, excavate foundations with picks and dynamite.

A new street is being paved. There is hardly a man

in sight. The rock crushing and the asphalt spreading are done by gangs of women. And the final steam roller is run by a girl wearing overalls.

Women have seized not only the heavy industries as their province. The professions have fallen too. *Seventy-five per cent* of all students in medical schools in Russia today are women. That means that soon three-fourths of Russia's doctors will be women; likewise three-fourths of the dentists. In the state bank ninety per cent of the clerks, tellers, vice-presidents, directors, are women. So are half the lawyers in the country.

In Mme. Lenin's Department of Education I didn't even see a man. Out her window I caught sight of a new building going up. The brick masons were women. Down in the street women were running the street cars; and out on the river they captained boats and manned barges. A major in the military aviation corps, a general in the Red Army, the Ambassador to Sweden, the Secretary of the Treasury, are women.

In Soviet Russia every man could be exterminated, and the women, in so far as their economic independence goes, would never know it.

Only in the fields of art, music, poetry, and similar esthetic professions, have men held their own. The symphony orchestras do not attract the women. To the exhibitions of painting and sculpture, only men contribute. The new operas and ballets are man-made. Women are too busy mixing concrete and riveting girders, too greasy and tired, to think about the creation of art.

But what about homes, I asked Mme. Lenin.

There aren't any, such as we know them. The babies are in government day-nurseries, the children in government schools. The mother works all day in the new subway shoveling government gravel, the father all night making government shoes. Most likely they'll all be fed in government kitchens. They live in one room allotted by the government.

Among Soviet women the marriage ceremony has become so casual a gesture that it's often dispensed with altogether. There is no distinction between married mothers and unmarried mothers. For there is no such thing as illegitimacy.

A Soviet woman may mate with whoever will accept her; and then she need keep her mate only so long as he pleases her. Divorce is easy. Alimony is rarely granted, as the wife is working just as hard, and earning just as much, as the husband.

If there is disagreement about the future of the child, the courts award it to the parent most able and likely to raise it according to proletarian standards, or else place the child in a Soviet institution where its proper political training can be assured.

Perhaps Russian women are happier, now that they have all the privileges of men, and none of the privileges of women.

At Mme. Lenin's suggestion I later visited a marriage and divorce bureau. It was, of course, staffed entirely with women. The bureau consisted of three small rooms, plainly furnished with chairs and desks. In the first room were also benches where the couples sat waiting their turn. On the wall facing them are huge lurid posters asking: "Are you diseased?"

The couples, already embarrassed and self-conscious, are not greatly cheered by the greeting on the wall.

The first couple is called "to the altar." The altar consists of a table supporting a registration book, and controlled by a very businesslike woman official. She asks the bride and groom if they are in good health. From their identity-cards, ages and names are recorded. The bride states whether she takes her husband's name or keeps her own. The groom pays one rouble—three cents—if he is a factory worker, five roubles if he is a factory director. They sign the register and are pushed along to make space for the next couple. The ceremony takes about sixty seconds.

In the adjoining room is the divorce court. The dissatisfied woman, or man, likewise waits in line to report to the officer behind the book. The applicant merely says: "I want a divorce from my husband, Ivan Ivanoff."

"Are there children?" is the only question asked. If not, the bureau sends Ivan Ivanoff a penny postcard, saying:

"Dear Ivan: You and your wife are divorced. Regards.
                              The Government."

If there are children, the bureau must know what arrangement has been made for their welfare, before the postcard is mailed.

The day I went to visit the marriage and divorce bureau, I was so taken with the casualness of the Soviet system that I decided to get married and divorced myself, just to experiment with a new sensation. There were several girls lined up in the entrance hall, but not one of them seemed inclined to exchange her escort for me. The only bride available at the moment was my lady interpreter who had come with me from the hotel.

I'd never seen her until ten minutes before, and still didn't know her name. She wasn't at all my type, weighing about two hundred, but I found no one else about, so I proposed. She accepted me, admitting that she frequently married visitors like myself whom she brought to the bureau. The other betrothed couples snickered at my overly-buxom bride. But I tried to appear absorbed in the posters and not notice them.

Our turn came. We showed our passports. For the first time I learned that my new wife's name was Leda. Of course I made the inevitable remark and apologized for not being a swan. Leda said she'd keep her own name, and not take mine, as she didn't expect our marriage to last very long.

It lasted just one minute and ten seconds.

Leda and I walked into the next room. Leda said, "I want a divorce from my husband."

"Have you any children?"

"No!"

"Sign here."

We signed.

"Now you're divorced," said the official.

"What!" I exclaimed. "Don't I even get a post-card?"

"If you insist."

I gave the bureau my address and next day got a postcard saying my marriage was *kapoot*.

But back to Mme. Lenin.

I asked her about women who, unlike Leda, *stay* married. One point that she made impressed me: Soviet wives, just because they are married to husbands holding important positions, in no way benefit from it. They are accorded honor only when they themselves have served the Workers' Party and achieved prominence as active Communists. There is no such thing as social rank in the government. There are no such affairs as official entertainments where social rank might intrude. And if there were, only worker-wives would be invited.

Mme. Lenin is a heroic figure in Russia not because she was married to Nikolai Lenin, the patron saint of Bolshevism, but because she herself, as Citizen Krupskaya, has achieved heroic things. Otherwise she would live in complete obscurity.

Stalin's first wife died at the outset of the Revolution. His second wife, a nineteen-year-old office secretary, not being conspicuous in the Communist Party, never once appeared in public. In fact, the public was hardly more than conscious of her existence until the time of her state funeral in 1932. There are rumors that Stalin has married a third time. But not even members of the government are sure. The prominence given a Mrs. Roosevelt, a Mrs. Hoover, a Mrs. Coolidge, because of their being wives of Presidents, is in direct opposition to Communist practise.

Citizen Krupskaya talked on. It was natural that our conversation should have turned presently from women to children, and from children to the new Bolshevik schools.

"We have here in Moscow," she said to me, "a school that I am sure is unique in the world—a state school for boys and girls who want to run away and join the circus!"

That struck me as an inspired idea. I asked for the address. She gave it to me gladly, and suggested that since I was interested in such institutions, I might visit the state ballet school too.

And a few moments later, when a secretary came in to announce other visitors, I took leave of the most winning old lady I had met in many a day. I walked down the steps of the dilapidated building and out into the streets. Once more I was surrounded by shabby clothes and cheerless faces. Nevertheless I realized that my opinion of Bolshevism, an opinion sunk very low in Leningrad, had taken a bound in the last hour. For surely, I reflected, any political system that has such a warmly human, truly noble woman for a champion, must have, somewhere, a human and noble quality at its heart.

CHAPTER XV

THE HUNDRED HAPPIEST CHILDREN IN THE WORLD

THE ballet academy happened to be the nearer of the two schools Mme. Lenin had told me about. I went at once to see it, eager to discover how the superb dancers in the Soviet theaters had learned their art. They were so splendidly proficient, it was difficult to believe that they had not been born dancing. Except for the now almost legendary stars of the former Imperial Ballet, the world has never seen such grace and skill in human movement. But the Imperial school had taken absolute possession of its dancers from their earliest childhood, had removed them from their parents and their playmates, in order to school them in the art. Now, under the liberating Revolution, how did the new order manage such perfection?

Exactly as the Czars had managed it.

The state ballet students start their instruction at the age of four. Almost as soon as they can toddle, physically perfect children begin training at the exercise bar, and are cut off from the ordinary pursuits of ordinary childhood in order that their whole energy can be turned toward dancing. Not only muscular proficiency, but expression, gestures, rhythm are taught the boys as well as the girls. The average American boy would die of shame if he were caught taking lessons in looking ethereal and imitating a swan. But in Russia, ballet instruction is a deadly serious business, and one must be hard as nails to keep pace.

The results are marvelous. By the time they are twelve years old, the children have conquered the most intricate and difficult steps. At the one-hundred-and-twenty-fifth anniversary performance of the Moscow ballet school, with Stalin and all his ministers on hand, a fifteen-year-old boy, inspired by the presence of these divinities and by the crash of the hundred-piece orchestra, leaped and whirled about the stage with such winged toes and such incredible skill that he brought the dance-wise audience to its feet, and completely stopped the show. One of the greatest favorites among the ballerinas—one who is sure to pack the house whenever she performs—is sixteen.

Out of every ten babies who enter the ballet school, perhaps only two finally graduate. No one can tell, when the child is four, what it will look like at fourteen. Often the boys grow up to be six-feet-three, and too tall to imitate a swan. Or a girl, because of her ruthless exercising, may develop into such a husky half-back that it would take *two* dance partners instead of one to stagger with her on their shoulders across the stage. The discharges, therefore, are frequent. But the child meanwhile has had the finest education possible in Russia, and is always provided with a livelihood elsewhere.

From the ballet academy I went to the school for the children who want to run away and join the circus.

In America the circus-impulse in young people is merely tolerated by parents who look upon it as a form of juvenile restlessness that will pass. But in Russia the circus-urge is considered highly commendable and is encouraged by financial support in order that the child may realize his dreams of becoming a clown, or an acrobat, or the man on the flying trapeze. His circus education, lasting three years, is paid for by the state, and when he at last has his degree in clowning, or tumbling, or juggling, he is assured a job with the Soviet troupes, where the demand for new "artists" is always greater than the supply.

I had supposed that only in heaven could such a lovely and romantic institution ever become a reality . . . and I found it in the middle of the capital of despotism.

The circus school is advertised far and wide, from Vladivostok to Samarkand. The advertisement reads: Soviet Boys! Soviet Girls! Do you want to join the circus as an *artist?* Are you over fourteen and under eighteen? Come to us and learn clowning, juggling, tight-rope walking, acrobatics, horsemanship. We send you a ticket and pay for everything. The Soviet State Circus needs you!

What boy, or for that matter, what girl, could resist such a truly wonderful, magical invitation?

Thousands of applications pour in. At present the school directors can choose only a small fraction of those who plead to be admitted, accepting, preferably, the orphans and the homeless.

A strict entrance examination is given. If a girl applicant can already stand on her hands, or a boy juggle three lemons, their chances of being accepted are greatly increased. But they must be physically flawless.

The freshman class numbers forty—the forty children as fortunate as it is possible to be, if we are to accept the conviction of the others who must just look on from the outside, and yearn.

All freshmen take the same courses—acrobatic dancing, tumbling, bareback and bicycle riding, gymnastics, tight-rope walking, flying trapeze. They also have three hours each day of academic study. Of course no geography is taught lest the children become too inquisitive about the existence of a foreign world; and no history, for nothing that happened before the 1917 Revolution is of any importance. The children don't care, since at best they study their books grudgingly. It is the circus lessons that they love. And when *these* classes are being held, the school's sawdust ring is filled with a swarm of tumbling, swinging, juggling, jumping, shouting children, the girls in bathing suits, the boys almost naked.

The classes of freshmen, gawkish and clumsy, are followed by the second-year students who are already excellent performers. When the seniors appear one sees marvels of muscle and agility, with barrel chests and bulging legs.

But no matter what the class, everybody goes through his tricks with the utmost joyousness and enthusiasm. The acrobats have to be pulled out of the ring to make way for the next performers. They retreat into the street and carry on with their hand-springs there. The clowns, having gone through their daily half hour of routine clowning, continue to fall down and paddle each other all over the school. The bareback riders, both boys and girls, drive the poor old practise horse almost to death, pleading to be allowed just one more time around the ring, just one more dive through the paper hoops. The jugglers hide behind the scenery to steal another period of rehearsal. The entire student body has to be driven home to the dormitories at night by means of angry threats of punishment from the director.

The day I visited the school the young aerial acrobats, flying and swinging high over the head of the instructor, positively refused to come down, and only shouted defiance back at him as they continued to sail through the air with the greatest of ease. The instructor finally had to turn the lights off in order to get his overzealous flying-trapezists home to supper.

In no other school on earth, I'm sure, are the students so profoundly in love with their "studies." Here, for once, a sport-loving child gets all the sport his heart desires, accompanied by spangled costumes, and colored lights, and music, and white horses, and applause—all the glory of the circus.

Sometimes the young student, probably from a primitive village on the Siberian steppes, feels a joy in this new life that is almost more than he can bear. I saw one wildly tumbling sixteen-year-old girl become so exhilarated by her own prowess that she made her final leap onto the shoulders of her teacher, and sat there pounding on his head, out of sheer exuberance of spirit. The teacher dragged her down, gave her an affectionate embrace, and tossed her back into the ring to do more somersaults.

As the practise horse gallumped around the ring carrying one of the girl bareback riders, three boys, yelling like wild Indians, leaped aboard behind her—then another, and another, and another. When the seventh tried to climb on, there was no room, and as he slid off he pulled down with him the other six. They all lay in the sawdust, a jumble of arms and legs, and shouted with laughter.

Exuberance of spirit! I left the circus school, feeling I'd had a glimpse of a race of youths who had been touched and blessed by some loving god whose hobby was to select imaginative boys and girls, and give them, without stint, the complete and glorious realization of all their young dreams.

In Russia the Soviets may be exiling thousands, tears may be flowing in oceans, and no man may be able to call his soul his own. But right in the midst of it all are the hundred happiest children in the world.

CHAPTER XVI

From the moment I left America I had been looking forward to visiting Russia. Russia seemed to me the most important and most interesting story on earth, a story with which I could fill pages, and settle the Russian question in my own mind once for all.

When I sat down in Moscow to write my story, I found it strangely unmanageable. To write forcefully and well about this infuriating but astounding country, one must have definite convictions and opinions. But in keeping with the experience of most other foreigners, my convictions suffered such violent and such frequent changes that I hardly knew myself from day to day what I believed.

Each morning, having to face the bayonet-regimented existence in Moscow, I swore anew that the rule of the Soviets was the cruelest, most brutal and most colossal racket ever rammed at pistol point down the throats of a helpless people. And yet before night I would have seen some isolated feature of Bolshevism that was so enlightened, so advanced and so inspiring, that for the moment I forgave and forgot the tyranny that had produced it.

The Soviet system of persecuting and imprisoning the family of any Russian citizen who tries to escape from

this gangland's grip seemed to me as inhuman and barbarous a custom as ever existed in the most savage ages
of history.   But just when I was exploding with indignation because of it, I would visit one of the model prisons, and—though I realized these show-places were far
from typical—still I would feel that it is we Americans,
with our dismal and degrading prison system, who are
the savages.

The ruthlessness and mercilessness with which the
Bolsheviks go about exterminating all classes of society
except the third class—themselves—outraged my sense
of justice, and sent me off on the warpath in defense
of human liberties.   But again, my hostility against this
crucifixion of the civilized minority cooled when I entered such an institution as the circus school, and saw
the protection and sympathy being poured out to young
people who, before the Revolution, would have had no
prospect except to become beggars, thieves, or illiterate
and bestial peasants.

For two months, with headquarters in Moscow, I explored the U.S.S.R., accompanied by a clever and
companionable young German photographer who spoke
Russian, and who bore the inevitable name of Fritz.
Together we filed respectfully through Lenin's tomb on
the Red Square and looked at his startlingly life-like
mummy.   We visited the Kremlin several times, only to
be impressed anew each visit by the marvelous beauty
of the gold-domed churches and the oriental red-
brick towers joined by the long white medieval walls.
We saw the imperial treasures in the Kremlin Museum,
the jewels, the extravagant riches, of the Czars; saw the
biggest cannon in the world—which has never fired a

shot, and the biggest bell—which has never rung. As often as possible we passed St. Basil's Cathedral, the most glorious building in Russia. Sometimes in the sunset light I looked at this intoxicated Tartar dream come true in stone, and felt sure that it was the most imaginative structure in the world. The architect who designed St. Basil's must have been a madman, but a madman with a passion and a genius for exciting and fantastic beauty, who was given complete freedom to build this, his wildest fancy.

There was little in Moscow, or Kiev, or Kharkov, and all the points in between, that Fritz and I didn't see. But we kept as far away as possible from the shining false façades which Communism-ballyhooing Intourist guides show foreign visitors.

With the approach of winter we left Moscow for the Caucasus, traveling third class by a night train. For three days we had stood in line, trying to buy better class tickets, but all first and second class seats had been taken by Party members. Our coach, fitted with the hardest and crudest benches, was packed to suffocation, and smelled like a slaughterhouse. We all sat in complete darkness. It was a Soviet train, and consequently the electric current, like the water and the food, had completely disappeared, and no one knew why. However, no one except Fritz and myself seemed to care, as the other passengers, accustomed to life in Communist Russia, had long since ceased to expect such bourgeois conveniences as light and water on trains. There was no hope of sleep, no chance to read. I could only sit on my suitcase, look out at the frozen darkness—and think. . . .

For eight weeks my eyes, ears and nose had been

filled with new Russia, its woes and its achievements.
What, after all this intimate contact, were my reactions
to Communism, Russian style?

Certainly one reaction—strongest of all—had been a
conviction that Russia is a land of miracles. There is
no word to describe the picture of the Soviet States,
other than miraculous. And I definitely do not mean
that the picture is miraculously beautiful. In many
ways it is unbelievably and tragically ugly.

Never in modern times, perhaps never in ancient
times, has there existed a country ruled by a government as super-despotic as the Russian Communist régime. The old Czarist Government gained the detesta
tion of its subjects because of its notorious tyranny.
But compared to life under the present dictatorship of
peasants and laborers, life under the Czar was free as a
spring breeze. And the wonder of wonders is the ease
and power with which this super-despotism works. Today a handful of labor-leaders consumed with Communist theory and fanatical zeal sit on high within the
Kremlin walls, their eyes fixed on a book of political and
social notions, and proceed, unopposed, to experiment
on the lives and souls of 160,000,000 human beings, with
as much impersonal detachment as a bacteriologist experimenting with germs.

In the beginning—1917—these labor-leaders who had
seized control of Russia, said:

"The Czar has proved himself the greatest obstacle in
the way of our lifting the masses of workers out of their
slough of ignorance and misery. First of all, then, if we
are to improve our lot, we must exterminate the Czar,
his wife, his four daughters and his young son. Per-

haps a bit brutal, but you've got to be tough to get anywhere."

And so the Czar and his family were slaughtered.

"And the aristocrats and intelligentsia must go next.
They'll never take to our ideas about exalting the factory workers and the *moujiks* to the throne. That means
murder and imprisonment for about a million of our nobility and gentle people, of our educators, religious
leaders, scientists, military and naval officers, merchants,
architects, diplomats—in fact of all civilized and educated Russian citizens."

So this million was murdered or imprisoned.

"Now," said the leaders, "we can accomplish something for the masses. Rid of the bourgeoisie, we will
give the masses the great privilege of being made over
to conform to our sacred theories.

"Of course some of the stubborn ones may not like
their new medicine. But *we* know what's good for
them—they don't. We must lock them in. From now
on no Russian may leave Russia."

So the frontier was closed by a steel ring of bullets
and bayonets. It became extremely difficult and dangerous for any Russian to escape from the social experiment.

"There will probably be a few fools," the leaders continued, "who will fail to appreciate the blessings we are
going to give them, and will try to run away. And perhaps some of them will succeed. But we'll take care of
that. If any Russian does escape we'll persecute his
mother and sisters and children, and send *them* off to
starve and freeze in Siberia. That will teach the other
rebels a lesson!"

What man, however miserable, would attempt to break free if he knew that this freedom for himself would inevitably bring anguish and death to those he loved?

"Now we've got 'em," said the leaders. "What is our first vivisection experiment going to be? Let's amputate the church."

A labor-leader waved his hand and exterminated the church.

"The family must go next. Family unity is a capitalistic and bourgeois custom dangerous to Communism. Our children must be taught to spy upon their parents and testify against them. Our men and women must be able to love whom they please, when they please; to marry and divorce on impulse. Our state will care for the unwanted offspring, and do it better than the parents."

So the family was abolished too.

"Money," they said, "is the source of all evil. Money was the support of the gentry and intelligentsia. We must destroy all private wealth, all private property, and all means of accumulating it, lest these old classes come back."

Money went next. Everybody was, and still is, allowed to share the same poverty together.

"But we must have industry and commerce to keep our people employed. We must sell our wheat and buy machinery. We haven't enough wheat for our own needs, but we've nothing else to export, so we must seize the peasants' private food supplies."

The supplies were seized. *Five million people starved to death* within two years. There was no mourning for them—mourning would be only sentimentality, a cardinal sin among Bolsheviks. The sacrifice had to be made for political expediency. The wheat was sold and machinery obtained to make guns and tanks with which to defend the dictatorship.

"There is one last and very important gap to be closed to complete our benevolent system," said the leaders. "We must use every means in our power to protect our new theories and our new liberated masses from foreign capitalistic influences. No information, no counter-revolutionary enlightenment must come in from the world outside. Russia must be a sealed box. Only then can we be complete masters. No books not supporting Communism will be published, or brought in from abroad. No newspapers or magazines that might reveal the false happiness and prosperity of other people living under the enemy's system will be tolerated. The movies, the theater, the radio, must be rigorously censored and adjusted. Nothing must emerge that does not glorify the working man and damn the other classes."

And nothing *has* emerged. Not in all Moscow can one find a single book not in step with Communist teachings, or a single movie that is not political propaganda.

The newspapers, too, are only echoes of the dictatorship, mechanically repeating proletarian slogans interlarded with sermonizing, flag-waving and boasting. Most of the non-Russian news (what little there is) concerns the fearful atrocities being inflicted on the sacred persons of the working men in England and America by the capitalists—stories which would insult the intelligence of a six-year-old anywhere outside Russia. Strikes, race-wars, unemployment, are given strident headlines. Any news showing the comparative security and prosperity of the majority of working men in America is immediately and methodically killed.

Red rule, one must admit, has made a vigorous attack on illiteracy. But once people have been taught to read, what reading have they been given? Communist propaganda. There is no other literature.

The great Soviet Library, the pride of the nation, housing six million volumes, is another glaring case of this intellectual enslavement. It shelters, supposedly, the accumulated wisdom of the world. It should be the chief fountain of enlightenment and learning without respect to creed, political party, or nationality. But when I sought there a history of the life and times of Nicholas II—of Russia from 1900 to 1917—the librarian was horrified. What! Czar Nicholas! That personification of despotism, that enemy of the workers! I most certainly could *not* have such a book. Why didn't I choose one of the hundreds of histories of the glorious Bolshevik Revolution instead?

Even the great National Library, the last bulwark of intellectual liberty, is gagged.

The same warping of education, the same blinding to all else but proletarian prejudices, goes straight down to the kindergarten. Even Mother Goose, rewritten according to Karl Marx, lives on a soap-box instead of in a shoe.

I asked a fifteen-year-old schoolboy what they were taught in school about America and western Europe.

"We are taught the history of the Communist revolutionary movement in America and England," he said.

"No other history?" I asked.

"History is just the lives of kings and capitalists. There is nothing in it about the working classes."

This distortion of "education" practised in Russia, this direction of education by fanatics, struck me as forcefully and unpleasantly as anything I saw. Not a day passed in my travelings about, that I did not talk through my interpreter with children and students. And the moment the fact came out that I was an American citizen, the children looked at me with pitying reproach.

"Why," they ask, "did you torture and execute those two innocent men, Sacco and Vanzetti? Why do you keep Mooney in prison when he is innocent? Why do you wish to lynch those innocent negro boys at Scottsboro? Why do you wish to kill innocent strikers, and gas innocent veterans who wish to petition your President?"

These questions, and these only, are asked any American who meets and talks with young Russians. They have learned no other information about America, for they are not allowed to learn. No wonder they look upon America as a savage and sadistic land that spends its time thinking up new torments for its enslaved working classes.

To these charges I always replied that we are not savages, but a civilized and, in most ways, progressive people; that their teachers have picked out detached controversial cases over which we ourselves are most unhappy, and beaten up clouds of dust in regard to them. When I told the children about the freedom and material well-being in America, they only scoffed at me for inventing such lies.

As for Sacco and Vanzetti, the Bolsheviks still scream

from the housetops about these "murders," but no hands in history have ever so dripped with blood as their own. While we were executing two Communists for murder, the Bolsheviks were executing, starving, imprisoning, a million mere nonconformists. Sacco and Vanzetti were given trials and, rightly or wrongly, found guilty by juries. The million victims of the Bolshevik régime were innocent of any crime, except the crime of having property and education, and of desiring to rescue their country from the fanatical agitators and the debased elements which in 1917 and 1918 had seized it.

The Bolsheviks wail, and spread headlines, about America's methods of handling strikes, about Scottsboro, and the veterans' demands, but they keep quiet about their own despotism which instantly slays any protest against the existing order. In Russia strikers are not allowed to strike. Bullets or Siberia would be the fate of anyone who even thought of it. The demands of our veterans, during Hoover's administration, were no doubt badly handled. But we may be sure that had they picketed the Kremlin instead of the White House not one of them would have been left alive.

"Counter-revolutionary" is the word used to describe any resistance offered by a Russian to being treated like an experimental guinea-pig. Opposition to the Soviets is looked upon with more horror than child murder, and as ruthlessly punished. Thousands upon thousands, *hundreds* of thousands, have been shot in order that Communist ideals may prevail. Estimates of the number of people held today in concentration camps, many within the Arctic Circle, reach as high as three million. The prisoners are the former property owners whose property the Bolsheviks wanted, the politically unconverted, the old intelligentsia, all of whom are being "liquidated" and subjected to the most savage and inhuman treatment.

The very day I left Moscow *one hundred and eight men,* accused of counter-revolution, were stood up against a wall and massacred in a revengeful fury over the assassination of a Soviet commissar by a fellow Communist. For the Bolsheviks human life is the least important and the cheapest commodity they possess.

The Bolshevik leaders—exiling, imprisoning, terrorizing, killing, to maintain their dictatorship over the peasants and laborers—have one battle cry which they shout interminably: "The working classes! Forward, the working classes!" To exalt the workers, to exterminate all others, is the one aim of the government.

The working class is the new Russian aristocracy. If you toil with your hands making boilers, or stoking furnaces, or digging ditches, you inherit the earth—the Soviet earth. You are housed in new apartments, fed enough to sustain you, hospitalized, schooled, amused, adored by the government.

But if you work as a clerk in a state bank or a state bureau or if you teach school or write for the newspapers, you get the short end of everything. Your children will be allowed in the schools only when the quota for the children of the factory workers and peasants has been filled. As for the children of the former nobility and aristocracy—the few who remain—these heathens are not allowed within a mile of a school house.

All these restrictions and suppressions have made Soviet Russia into a vast escape-proof prison filled with helpless inmates who are forced to do what the Soviet theorists think is good for them. There is no pretense at pity, no soft talk about "humanity." Every new move is made with a broadside blow, without the slightest consideration for the human agony and disruption it will cause.

The Bolsheviks know how difficult it is to force the older generation to swallow this particular brand of salvation—the generation that once was accustomed to the vices of personal liberty and unhampered access to knowledge. But the Soviets have successfully seized the children and brought them up to be perfect, hand-made Communists, inoculated from infancy with a driving desire to keep the working classes in the saddle, and with a profound fear of capitalism and of any country where this iniquitous system is allowed to flourish.

In order to rule, the Bolsheviks have not hesitated to enthrone ignorance and persecute knowledge. They smash with sweeping decrees one lighthouse after another of intellectual and personal liberty. History, religion, journalism, they have already executed. Even the theater and the ballet, two civilizing influences in which the Bolsheviks excel, would be promptly strangled if they tended to become counter-revolutionary. Such a gesture would seem utterly senseless and savage, but no more so than the strangling already accomplished in other sources of culture and knowledge.

Still more discouraging is the fact that the Communists see nothing wrong about these appalling amputations from their cultural body. They not only do not seem to miss freedom and refinement, but actually hold them in contempt. Decent clothes, an attractive personal appearance, tasteful apartments, comfort and distinction of any sort, are considered bourgeois, and inimical to the Revolution. A Russian man appearing in evening clothes at a gathering of his fellow countrymen would be stoned!

The Bolsheviks boast that they have outlawed religion. It is true that the churches have been closed or torn down, or turned into anti-religious museums where, as in St. Isaac's, the walls are covered with shrieking, hideous posters depicting the ignorance and vices of the clergy and the enslavement inflicted by them upon their superstitious congregations. It is also true that the very possession of a Bible is considered counter-revolutionary, and that any study of Biblical subjects is forbidden.

But religion is not dead. It has merely shifted its focus from the old Christian saints to the new Bolshevik saints. Bolshevism has substituted Karl Marx for God, and Lenin for Christ. The new converts have become as dogmatic, as intolerant, as militant, as the fiercest Christian zealots of pre-Revolutionary days. I have seen violent cases get up in public and tell how Communism has redeemed them from political sin—with trembling voices and shining eyes, just like those who hit Billy Sunday's sawdust trail. These types will suffer gladly, even die, for their Communist convictions.

It is this very fanaticism, combined with a convenient primitive ignorance, that has enabled the Bolsheviks to achieve so astonishingly much. It is this religious mania that has brought miracles to pass.

You need only look about to see the evidence of these achievements.

One miracle has been the revolutionizing of peasant

life. With one great gesture, as sweeping as that which abolished the church, the Bolsheviks have forced millions of little farmers to gather with their families on big farms and to work collectively. This uprooting caused broken hearts without number, and violent resistance. But the state, crushing all opposition, soon controlled the imagination and enthusiasm of the children, who had not yet developed any special attachment to their old homes, and through these young converts the government managed to raise the efficiency, comfort and cultural level of the farming classes, as well as the quality of the farm products, almost to the standard of capitalistic countries.

Under this same violent new spirit Russian industry has leaped from last place almost to the forefront. Her factories, her mines, her steel mills, roar and hum and belch smoke twenty-four hours a day. The demand is constantly ahead of the supply. New office buildings, new apartments, are rising with incredible speed. The builders, spurred on by their state religion, work with a selfless frenzy. Volunteers beg to be allowed to help, as in the old days volunteers once begged to help build a new cathedral.

Before I left Moscow I saw a thousand university students fling themselves, with a storm of cheers, into the job of paving a public square, and without any material compensation whatsoever drive through with an enthusiasm that allowed them no rest till the work was done.

Half the population of Moscow has helped, manually, as volunteers, one way or another, to build the new subway.

These workers, paid or unpaid, skilled or unskilled,

go marching and cheering and singing along the streets, day and night, bands playing, banners waving.

On the occasion of the great national holiday, November seventh, the date in 1917 when the Bolsheviks seized control of the government, I witnessed a gigantic demonstration of this party support, on Moscow's magnificent Red Square. I stood within a hundred feet of Stalin and his ministers, and for hours watched the pageant pass by Lenin's tomb, on one corner of which was Stalin's reviewing stand.

One hundred thousand soldiers took part in the parade, and saluted the Master as they passed, wave on wave. With the great square packed with these armed men all standing at attention, Comrade Voroshilov, Minister of National Defense, stepped up to the radio loudspeaker at Stalin's elbow. His voice roared out: "I salute you, comrade soldiers. I salute you, comrade visitors. And I shout to the whole world that Russia does not want war. Russia hates war with her whole soul. But let our enemies beware. We have—we are— the finest army in the world. We will defend our policies to the last man. Not an inch of land, not one ounce of pride, will we surrender."

As he spoke his last dramatic word a military band of one thousand pieces burst forth with the *Internationale*. The volume of tone made one's ear drums ache. Waves of cheering broke over the ranks and were tossed back by the people waiting around the Kremlin walls— cheering, cheering, cheering—down the packed streets, across the river, along the quays, on beyond the city. Five million people joined in the loudest, longest cheer in history.

Once more the columns moved. Ten thousand cav-
alrymen galloped by. And tanks! The Bolsheviks
boast that more tanks passed that day than are owned
by all the other armies in the world. I counted four
hundred, then gave up. Some were monsters weighing
forty tons. Some of the smaller ones dashed across the
square at sixty miles an hour. Overhead the sky was
black with fighting planes. The Russian Army is supposed to possess five thousand. I believe they were all
flying at once that afternoon.

Then, when this bewildering array of fighting men
had marched, ridden, rolled and flown before Stalin,
the workers' parade began.

*Two and one half million workers marched through
Red Square,* a river, a tidal wave, of humanity. Every
factory, every trade, every school, every bureau, turned
out with all its members, with floats, placards, music,
of a thousand sorts, to prove their loyalty to the sacred
cause.

I left Red Square after the first million had passed.
I was too dizzy to endure more—dizzy from the numbers of moving legs and heads, dizzy from standing
seven hours, dizzy from the waves of enthusiasm and
energy that had engulfed me.

I tottered home, asking myself how any political system as ruthless and tyrannical as Bolshevism could
achieve so much. But I knew the answer: Education
for the peasants—ninety per cent of Russia, economic
liberation of women, an industrial boom that for the moment gives every good Bolshevik a job—and the complete control of their uninquisitive minds. Surely, I
said, despite all the slaughter and destruction upon

which Bolshevism has been built, there must be great good and great power in their ideals.

The intolerance, the bigotry and brutality, the intellectual gagging, which at present cut Russia off from the good will of the world, some day are going to weaken and pass. They are already weakening at a rate that shocks the Bolshevik fundamentalists. Russia, I believe, will evolve, say in twenty-five years, out of its bath of blood and despotism into a really civilized and liberated nation, with a number of social institutions so far ahead of ours that, compared to her, we will seem in some ways as backward as she now seems to us.

Many of these new ideas, born with such cruelty and travail, *we must accept,* and the sooner the better. Thus is America going to develop, perforce, in the direction of new Russia's enlightened attitude toward the working masses, while Russia at the same time gropes toward America's ideals of personal and intellectual liberty. Then perhaps the two potentially greatest nations in the world will some day meet on the common ground of friendship and understanding, for each will have contributed to the other something vital and enduring.

Zapara Kiut, a native of Abkhazia in Caucasia, and the oldest man in the world. According to the Soviet scientists who investigated this extraordinary case of longevity, Zapara was born in 1782.

Members of the tribe of Negroes living on the Black Sea shores of Abkhazia, descendants of a shipload of slaves blown eastward from the Bosphorus over two hundred years ago. The old Caucasian soldier was included in the photograph to indicate that the picture was not taken on a Mississippi cotton plantation.

Richard Halliburton dressed in Khevsoorian chain armor. Tradition tells that this armor was brought to Caucasia by the Crusaders in the twelfth century. In any case all the Khevsoorian mountaineers own, and, until recently, wore these coats of mail to battle. On each shield is a crude Crusader cross, and sometimes the letters *A. M. D.—Ave Mater Dei*, the Crusaders' motto.

CHAPTER XVII

"He's been drunk for the last hundred and thirty years," sighed the great-granddaughter of the old Caucasian soldier who was seated before me clutching a vodka bottle. "I've given up all hope of reforming him."

"When did he first take to drink?" I asked.

"About 1803," she said, motioning her own grandson out of a chair so that I might be seated.

Zapara Kiut, either because of or in spite of his alcoholism, has lived to be a hundred and fifty-three years old. He is the oldest person in the world, if we accept the verdict of the Soviet scientists who came all the way from Moscow to the Caucasus to make a special study of this extraordinary case of longevity. Zapara had no birth certificate, but from things he remembered and historical events he took part in, the birth date of 1782 was agreed upon as being most probable.

As might be expected, the most long-lived race of people on earth—whose oldest member is Zapara—are mountaineers. They live in Abkhazia, a province of Georgia, in primitive villages perched on the Black Sea slopes of the Caucasus Mountains. From his shack Zapara can look directly down upon the sea, a thousand feet below, or up at the snow-covered peaks rising ten thousand feet above. For a century and a half he has been contemplating the sea and the snow. This contemplation, plus his mountain heritage, plus the everlasting sunshine, plus his vodka, seem to have combined ideally to prolong Zapara's life to more than twice the length allowed the rest of us.

When I heard about this notable relic, I felt that an interview would be worth the long hard journey to Abkhazia. His country is too rugged to permit railroads. But there is a motor road of a sort along the coast, and donkey trails give access to the settlements. If a committee of scientists could reach his house, Fritz and I (having continued in our third-class coach on across Russia to Caucasia) could reach it too—and did.

We found Zapara living in a crude plank shack, the very same shack in which he was born in 1782. When we presented ourselves at his front door Zapara refused to see us. For the first time in his life, so his great-granddaughter reported, he was sick—bronchitis—and felt ashamed and unclean.

I sent a bottle of vodka in to him as a present. He drank half a tumbler of the potent liquor and decided his bronchitis wasn't so bad after all. Another half tumbler and he decided to come on out and play. In fact, he would put on his best clothes in our honor.

And so this modern Methuselah appeared, wearing a goat's hair turban and a long Cossack coat adorned with cartridges.

Zapara Kiut proved to be a rather small and slender man, no more than five and a half feet tall. (Among the many centenarians living in Abkhazia not one is more than five-feet-eight. The taller they grow the sooner they die.) He had a lean gnarled face with the usual Abkhazian hooked nose, and a short gray beard. In America he could have easily passed for no more than a mere hundred.

His eyesight was very dim, but he could still see well enough to get around. We had to raise our voices only slightly to make him hear. He was particularly proud of his teeth, some half of which remained.

Seating him in a chair in the sunshine, and pouring more vodka into his glass, Fritz managed to start him talking. His earliest recollections were of his father's goat flocks which as a boy he shepherded on the higher slopes of the Black Sea coast. In those days he lived summer and winter in the open, and was blissfully unaware that *George Washington was serving his first term as President.*

Young Zapara at an early age came into possession of a rifle, and with it he scoured the peaks and forests in search of deer and bear. Schools were unheard of in this mountain country, so he never learned to read or write. For a hundred and fifty-three years he has never signed his name. This fact started me wondering if illiteracy were the first requirement for longevity.*

The end of the eighteenth century found Zapara's native Georgia resisting conquest by the Russians. He joined the armed bands of mountaineers and for several years kept up a guerrilla warfare against the invaders. But by 1805, when Zapara was twenty-three, these

---

* A recent census taken in Bulgaria revealed the fact that there were eighteen people in that country over one hundred years old. All eighteen were peasants living close to the soil; all were illiterate; all drank alcohol and smoked tobacco; all were women—and widows several times over!

bands had all been defeated and dispersed, and the Russian Army was in complete control.

A few years later, the conquerors, in need of new regiments to fight Napoleon, offered Zapara money and glory and travel if he would join the Czar's Cossack troops. He accepted, for the money.

When he came to this chapter in his early life, and mentioned Napoleon, I'll admit my pulse jumped a beat or two. For I believed I was about to hear the immortal story of Napoleon's march to Moscow, and his retreat, from an eye-witness, the only eye-witness left alive in the world.

While I was practically holding my breath in anticipation, Zapara slowly helped himself to another hopper of vodka.

"And did you see Moscow burning?" Fritz asked impatiently. "Did you fight the French? Did you pursue Napoleon back to Paris?"

My hopes were too high. He *had* been actively engaged in 1812, but on the Turkish front in what is now Rumania.

Zapara's memory of those dramatic days was growing very misty. He did not remember much about the war. Likewise the fact that regiments from his army had executed one of the most devastating military maneuvers in history—cutting Napoleon's retreat four hundred miles west of Moscow and practically annihilating what was left of the French Army—was all news to Zapara.

"They used to give us vodka on cold nights!" was his contribution to history.

So I asked him questions more easily answered.

When did he marry? About 1815, soon after his return from the Turkish war. His wife had borne him eighteen children, the last in 1850 when he was sixty-eight. For the last forty years now he had been a widower, watching his seventy-five grandchildren dying of old age, one after another. He didn't expect to remarry; modern women didn't suit him.

What did he think of the younger generation?

Well—*which* younger generation? His own grandchildren had been pretty good, when one made allowances for the natural irresponsibility of youth; but *their* grandchildren had grown a little out of hand.

In 1882 Zapara had his hundredth birthday. In 1894 Czar Nicholas came to the throne, and Zapara, then a hundred and twelve, remembered a special celebration in honor of the coronation, when he got especially and scandalously drunk.

In 1904 he was already claiming to be the oldest man in Russia.

"Have you heard about Zaro Agha?" Fritz asked him for me. "The famous Turk who was invited to the World's Fair in Chicago because *he* claimed to be the oldest man in the world?"

"Oh yeah? How old?"

"Around a hundred and thirty-four, as I remember."

"Humph—a whippersnapper!"

In 1914 all Zapara's male descendants of fighting age left Abkhazia to take part in the war with Germany. Old Zapara, now a hundred and thirty-two, begged to be allowed to march beside his great-great-grandsons into Berlin.

The Revolution in 1917 more or less passed him by.

Only when the Bolsheviks came swooping down to "liquidate" all owners of property and to seize all private lands for the collective farms, did he get out his century-old rifle and prepare to fight. Fortunately, fighting wasn't necessary, for the Bolsheviks, out of respect for his years, allowed him to keep his little patch of potatoes and half dozen pigs.

I was curious about Zapara's personal habits. Perhaps from them I could learn the secret of longevity.

Did he smoke?

Of course! Constantly!

Was he a vegetarian?

He looked completely blank.

Did he eat meat?

Certainly he ate meat. He ate everything, but mutton and pork and black bread mostly.

How often did he bathe?

He used to bathe when he was young, but hadn't in the last fifty or sixty years—it was unhealthy. This bronchitis came from the scrubbing his great-granddaughter had given his neck the week before.

Since he couldn't read, what did he think about?

He didn't think about anything much—just dozed in the sun and watched the children playing.

Did he ever exercise?

Not if he could help it. For ten years he had not walked a kilometer. His mountain side was too steep for his shaky legs. And anyway, in town, what was there new to see?

"There's the hospital," his great-granddaughter cackled. "He ought to be there now. I keep telling him that he can't take a chance with a cough at *his* age.

But he won't *listen* to me—I can't do a thing with him."

I thought fast. Our own two burros were waiting at the foot of the hill. If we could get Zapara onto one of these we could lead him to the hospital. Fritz and I offered to carry him the half mile down the hillside. He objected violently, but we kept on feeding him vodka until he didn't care what happened. Then we lifted him onto my back, and fastened his hands with a handkerchief in front of my neck so he couldn't fall off. I seized the old man's knees and, feeling like Æneas escaping with his aged father from the sack of Troy, cautiously and with frequent stops descended the mountain side. During his manback ride Zapara mumbled and slept. He wasn't heavy, having far fewer pounds than years.

We sat him astride a burro, and reached the seacoast highway.

Zapara was now sleeping soundly, and we had nothing to do except to hold him in the saddle and amble along toward town.

When Fritz and I had passed this way before, we had met no one but a few Russian peasants. But now, walking toward us down the road, were a Negro man and woman as black as any that ever worked on a Mississippi plantation. They were dressed in exactly the sort of shabby Western clothes that any American country darky might wear.

What in the name of heaven were these American blacks doing over here in this hidden corner of the Caucasus? In English, as we met, I asked them just that question.

"ЧТО ЗТО, ТОВАРИМВ," replied Uncle Tom.

Except for a few Russian phrases, they spoke nothing but Georgian, nor had their ancestors, as I learned, spoken anything else for two hundred years. Local legend has it that they are the descendants of a shipload of slaves that were blown eastward from the Bosphorus by a storm about 1700, and wrecked on the eastern shore of the Black Sea.

In any case here they are, a little Russian Harlem of thirty or forty Africans, in the midst of this wild race of semi-oriental white mountaineers. When the Revolution gave absolute equality to all men without regard for race or color, the eight black bucks in the colony promptly married white Russian girls. The new generation is entirely mulatto. These, too, will marry whites, so that in another thirty years this unique colony will have disappeared.

When we got old Zapara to the crude little hospital, he had sobered up considerably, and remonstrated loudly when his clothes were removed and he was put to bed between the first sheets that had covered him in a century and a half.

At the hospital Fritz and I had a talk with one of the doctors, who suggested that if we were collecting centenarians we ought to visit a certain eagle's-nest village, forty miles deeper in the mountains, where, out of a population of ninety men and women, over one-third claimed to have passed the century mark, most of the younger people having left home during the Great War and the Revolution.

Much as I wanted to go to such a remarkable village,

we could not, for the season was too advanced and the one trail hidden under ice and snow.

The doctor, being a good Bolshevik, explained enthusiastically the progress and advantages Bolshevism was bringing to Abkhazia. He spoke of his own hospital, of schools and commerce and comforts that were penetrating the most remote valleys, and related how the mountaineers had begun to eat from plates, sleep on beds, drink less vodka, and sometimes even bathe.

But the good doctor did not mention the fact that since all these new-fangled improvements have been thrust upon them, the natives' life-span was perceptibly dwindling. Instead of living on heedlessly to five score and ten years, the new generation is lucky if the doctors can get them to the century mark.

And worse is yet to come. The Soviets have decreed that all body-lice and fleas must be driven off these tough and hardy mountaineers (who were quite content with their company), to make way for vaccinations, toothbrushes and pink soap. Cornflakes and cod-liver oil will come next. And then these champion long-lifers can be expected to die off at seventy-five just like the rest of us.

With the outlook for continued longevity among the Abkhazians so gloomy, I was lucky to have met Zapara Kiut in time—the oldest of them all. For surely, since the Army of the Light has descended upon his race, the world will never see his like again.

CHAPTER XVIII

THE LAST OF THE CRUSADERS

The city of Tiflis, capital of the state of Georgia in Caucasia, has long prided itself upon its advanced ideas, its broad boulevards, its modern architecture, and its progressive-minded citizens.

The shock was all the greater, therefore, when, in the spring of 1915, some months after Russia's declaration of war against Turkey, a band of twelfth-century Crusaders, covered from head to foot in rusty chain armor and carrying shields and broadswords, came riding on horseback down the main avenue.

People's eyes almost popped out of their heads. Obviously this was no cinema company going on location. These were Crusaders—or their ghosts.

The incredible troop clanked up to the governor's palace.

"Where's the war?" they asked. "We hear there's a war."

They had heard in April, 1915, that there was a war. It had been declared in September, 1914. The news took seven months to reach the last of the Crusaders.

And you wouldn't be surprised, if you tried, as Fritz and I did, to find the behind-the-beyond country in which these twelfth-century people live.

One of the most curious and romantic legends of the

Caucasus tells the story of the origin of this armored tribe. And as yet no historian has found any reason to believe that the legend is not based entirely on fact. The story declares that this race came, eight hundred years ago, from Lorraine, more than two thousand miles away. The argument is borne out by the fact that their chain armor is in the French style, while their otherwise incomprehensible speech still contains six or eight good German words.

When they left Lorraine, so goes the legend, the last thing they had in mind was the colonization of the frosty peaks of the Caucasus Mountains, for they were followers of Godfrey de Bouillon and planned to wrest the Holy Sepulcher from the Moslem infidels.

But during the thousand-mile march across what is now Asiatic Turkey, this particular band of Crusaders somehow got detached from the main army, and were prevented by the Saracens from rejoining it. Whether they took a northern course of their own accord, and continued on across Armenia and Georgia to the Caucasus as pioneers, or whether they were fleeing for their lives with Moslem scimitars swishing around their ears, the legend does not say. But we do know that they called a halt in one of the most rugged and unapproachable corners of the Caucasus . . . and didn't emerge again in force till 1915 when the rumors of a worth-while war brought them, wearing their ancestors' coats of mail, into Tiflis.

These strange people, called Khevsoors, have continued to occupy their hidden corner for over eight centuries. But not one inch have they advanced in general culture. In fact they have lost whatever of the arts they brought with them from Lorraine, and nearly all the crafts.

Only their Crusader chain armor, more or less indestructible, they still have, and the letters A.M.D.—Ave Mater Dei, the motto of the Crusaders—carved on their shields, and the Crusader crosses which adorn the handles of their broadswords and are embroidered in a dozen places on their home-made garments.

At the same time, the Khevsoors have developed a crude culture of their own that makes them, to me, the most interesting "foreign" race in all Russia.

Maintaining their independence unbroken for the last eight hundred years, they were walled off from the world by barriers of mountains and canyons. A highway extending ninety miles north of Tiflis approaches to within twenty miles of one of their villages. But the single cliff-cut trail that leads off to it is traversable only on foot, or with horses that can climb, slide and swim. Even this trail is closed by ice and snow in December and remains closed till May. During these five months no one can enter and no one can depart from Khevsooria.

To visit this archaic clan, this lost world, Fritz and I, having traveled inland from the Black Sea to Tiflis and motored to the starting point of the only trail into Khevsooria, made what was perhaps the last trail-passage of the season. Iron crampons on our shoes were necessary, for already ice covered everything. It was explained clearly to us before starting that one more fall of snow, after we had reached our destination, would make our return extremely difficult—we might even have to remain in the village five months, as much prisoners as our hosts—and live with only the dubious comforts and refinements they had inherited from the original Crusaders.

We took the risk, but watched the sky with anxious eyes as we advanced. Our luck held. It didn't snow, nor did we slide off the cliff-face into the frozen river below. Terrific peaks, completely sheathed in ice, rose on all sides of us. I had been used to thinking, carelessly, that Mont Blanc is the highest mountain in Europe. But the range along whose slopes we climbed includes *nine peaks higher,* and a score more that topped the Matterhorn. Elbrus, the highest of the range, overtops Mont Blanc by nearly three thousand feet.

After six hours on the steep and slippery trail we descended into a valley and saw the first Khevsoor village, a collection of rude stone huts, in which sheep, goats, pigs, cows and Khevsoors all live happily together.

The entire population of the village—some three hundred—came to look at us, the first foreign visitors in two months.

It was immediately evident that the Khevsoors have developed a communal life completely unmodified by any changes that may have occurred in the world outside. If at the end of their five months' imprisonment they found that all life at the other end of the trail had been destroyed by a passing comet, they would continue to have no more and no less than before. Their houses and all the articles in them are home made—the furniture, the cradle, the cooking pots. They weave their own cloth from wool their sheep provide. They have no wheeled transport, only crude sleds made by their own hands. Cartridges they would lack, but these have never been of any great importance anyhow in this sword-conscious community.

Everybody works, raising barley, shepherding the sheep and goats; and the produce of their common labor is shared by all. No man is richer than his neighbor. No house is better than any other. Money they do not understand and do not want.

Before I'd been in the village an hour I decided that personal beauty in Khevsooria is rare and brief. The eternal struggle to sustain life in this rugged country soon destroys their youth. The women looked old at thirty though they sometimes live to be a hundred. All women, obviously, were considered very inferior beings. They ate what the men had left, and slept together on the floor downstairs; the men in beds upstairs.

One particularly cruel custom, handed down from the darkest ages, shocks anyone who comes to Khevsooria. For ten days before an expectant mother is delivered of a child (she may have married at fifteen), she must re-tire from the community and hide, an outcast and un-clean, in an animal shed outside the village. She must never show herself. No one must be seen approaching her. Absolutely alone she must bear her baby—in the dark, beside the goats. If her cries reach the village, her husband is allowed to go and fire his rifle from the shed's roof in order to frighten away the evil spirits tor-menting his wife. But he must not, even if she's dying, go inside.

Fortunately the Khevsoor women are as tough as the goats whose apartment they are using, and give birth to their young with about the same amount of trouble.

Cruel to their women. And also cruel to their horses. While its master lives, the horse is treated like a son, loved and protected. But when the master dies the horse must die too. As the owner's corpse is being borne to the cemetery, an expert horseman mounts the animal and rides it down canyons, across rivers, up hills, at the swiftest possible speed, spurring and spurring it—to death. The corpse of the horse is left where it falls for the vultures to dispose of.

Meanwhile the greatest possible gayety is taking place at the dead man's house. His family must make any sacrifice to provide a banquet for the village. Nobody mourns. Instead, everyone drinks as much home brew as possible and eats himself sick on all the sweetmeats that have been saved up since the illness began to look fatal. It is the one event in the social life of Khevsooria to which everybody looks forward.

I asked my hosts if they had any religion . . . how much of their twelfth-century Christianity had they preserved?

Yes, they were still Christians. They even had a church. The church proved to be only a shrine in the woods, containing an altar decorated with a cross, bronze bells, and the antlers of deer—symbols both Christian and pagan. All meaning of Christianity has long since been forgotten. Christ is only a vague name to them, nor have they any idea why they wear a cross around their necks and on their swords and shields.

But they do have a code of ethics and conduct that is as rigid as iron. One clause in this code concerning honor—the honor of the clan—has caused more bloodshed than all their wars put together.

If for any reason a Khevsoor is killed by another Khevsoor, the heirs of the dead man are honor bound to kill the killer. That the killing may have been in self-defense doesn't matter. And then when this second assassination has been accomplished the latest victim's heirs must kill *his* killer. And on and on, not for generations but for centuries, these vendettas continue, spreading and spreading until families not at first remotely connected with the feud are driven into it, and the original occasion completely forgotten.

If the feud is between families of separate villages, each village spurs on its champion. The honor of the village is at stake. The appointed executioner probably has no quarrel whatsoever with the man he must kill, may scarcely even know him. That doesn't matter. Honor must be served. If the ranking relative of the latest victim does not seek vengeance he is despised and spat upon. The men will not eat or work with him. The women will not speak to him except to jeer. His own children and family are made to suffer. The poor fellow, hating to continue the bloody and useless cycle, is driven to it by the Khevsoor code, knowing full well it means, soon or later, his own death in turn.

Over one hundred Khevsoors have been sacrificed in the last thirty years to this insane custom.

On first reaching the land of the lost Crusaders, I had hoped to find every man wearing his famous coat of mail. I didn't find a single one. Instead they all wore a home-spun cross-embroidered shirt over baggy trousers. But on the wall in every house, the armor hung beside the shield and gun. The sword itself, varying from twelve to thirty inches in length, each man carries constantly. It is as much a part of his dress as his sheep-skin hat, or the ornamental row of cartridges across his chest.

Seeing how interested we were in the chain armor, the village elders took down half a dozen suits and let me examine them and try one on. The entire outfit, including shield and sword, weighs about thirty pounds.

Each mesh coat is made of some twenty thousand tiny iron rings and goes on like a nightshirt. The sleeves are short, but mesh gauntlets cover the forearms. With each suit goes a bag-like chain helmet with a hole cut out for the face. A flap folds over, so that the head can be entirely protected. For the shins there are likewise mesh greaves. Consequently when completely arrayed, the only parts of the body vulnerable are the knees and thighs. The original mesh is terribly rusty, as the owners no longer understand how to preserve it. The newer coats are made of copper wire stolen from the telegraph line along the highroad. It is both cleaner and lighter than the iron but offers by no means as good protection.

The Khevsoors have not worn their coats of mail into battle since their famous march to Tiflis in 1915. The chief reason is that those who finally did join the Czar's army soon found that modern bullets have no respect for copper wire mesh.

But for dueling, which remains the accepted way of settling all disputes, the contestants still clothe themselves in their armor. Also they enjoy fighting for fun. Like their forefathers, the Crusader knights, they have a passion for putting on their iron shirts and going at each other with broadswords. Fighting, both in good and bad humor, in this land where books are unknown and where other forms of sport or diversion simply do not exist, is the only means they have of expressing themselves.

Sunday is reserved for getting drunk and dueling.

For our benefit two of the Khevsoor braves decided to put on a show. We all went to a little plateau outside the village where the duelists faced each other. There is no referee, as everybody has known and followed the rules for centuries. Unlike the jousting in the Middle Ages when ladies were such important features of a tournament, the Khevsoorian duelists permit only men to watch. However there is an age-old custom that permits a woman to stop a duel at her pleasure by appearing on the scene and tossing her handkerchief between the two combatants.

The fighters crouch with one knee bent almost to the ground. Their small light shields, embossed with a big cross, are used to parry rather than receive the blows of the opponent's sword. The duelists jump about with astonishing agility, circling and jockeying for position like fighting cocks. Recklessly the swords thud on leather shields, crunch on chain armor, or clash as they strike together. But, unlike similar duels in German universities, wounds are rare, since the head and face, where most of the blows fall, are not exposed. There is no slit even for the eyes. A fighter must see as best he can right through the mesh screen of the helmet flap.

The duel I witnessed was, of course, friendly. Though both fighters were well oiled on home-made barley brandy and didn't hesitate to attack with full vigor, a couple of bruises were the worst that happened.

When, however, anyone actually inflicts a wound, either in friendly or in angry battle, the victim must be compensated in cows. The village elder measures the wound in barley seed, and for every seed it will contain the guilty swordsman must pay one cow.

Suppose he has no cow—or only five when the wound is ten seeds long? He can hardly steal his neighbor's. But there is no law against crossing the mountain border and stealing the cows of the Dagestan tribe as payment. In fact, it's an ancient custom, and keeps the Khevsoorian herds from dwindling. The Dagestans don't like it and yell like everything, but they are not a belligerent people and know better than to attempt to retaliate against the sword-swinging Khevsoors. This banditry has kept the two tribes bitter enemies for hundreds of years.

When night came, the mayor of the village provided Fritz and me with lodging in his own house. In the attic dormitory, where we slept beside the men of the household, it was dreadfully cold. Between the cold, and the barley brandy our host had insisted on my drinking, and the home-made rawhide beds we had to sleep on, I got no rest. But each time I stirred I saw the dim outline of the chain armor, the swords, the shields, hanging on the wall. The sight of that armor, and the presence of the men about me who wore it, gave me the feeling of being a Connecticut Yankee in King Arthur's court—the feeling that I had gone to sleep and slept eight hundred years backward, and waked up in another age, in the year 1099, to find myself part of the living Crusades.

It was easy enough to imagine that the mayor's sons, close by, were knights who had laid their armor aside only long enough to rest; tomorrow they would be marching off to Jerusalem. Perhaps in the morning I might meet Godfrey de Bouillon face to face on my way up the hill to the watch tower. Or if it were 1199 (what's a century or two after three barley brandies?) I might even see Richard Cœur de Lion riding through Khevsooria on his way to the Holy Land.

When morning arrived I looked around carefully for these two celebrated Crusaders, but couldn't find them anywhere. In the entire village I came upon only one man who still burned with the old crusading spirit—the bespectacled Jewish agent of the Bolsheviks, who had been established here to save the Khevsoorians from capitalism. He said it was a lot of nonsense looking for Godfrey de Bouillon and King Richard—they were counter-revolutionary Christians and would be liquidated if they set foot in Sovietized Caucasia . . . and anyway the Holy Sepulcher wasn't at Jerusalem any more. It was a red granite tomb beside the Kremlin wall in Red Square at Moscow.

Disillusioned and discouraged, I prepared to depart. But the agent was determined that I should not leave with a bad impression of his village. He personally would show me how much there was of interest. First, he persuaded the little Khevsoors to sing the *Internationale*—Khevsoors who had been practising thorough-going Communism centuries before the Bolsheviks ever heard of it. He showed me a text book out of which the children were learning to read. It was illustrated with pictures of American capitalists wearing diamond rings and smoking big cigars, choking the working classes to death with yards of stock market ticker-tape. He said he planned to collectivize the Crusaders on one big farm where they could learn to recite Karl Marx. And then, saving the best till last, he took me to the room used for his new school. It was crude enough, typically Khev-soorian. But over the rostrum, flanked by crimson flags, was a banner with the Russian words:

"Workers of the World—Unite! Forward to World Revolution!'

CHAPTER XIX

ON MY return to Tiflis from Khevsooria, I found bad news awaiting me.

The secret police were displeased by the unorthodox way I had been roaming about, unescorted by the usual Intourist chaperons, seeing the U.S.S.R. as it is, rather than as the Bolsheviks want foreigners to think it is. That was bad enough. But for me to have gone without permission to Sverdlovsk, and searched out Peter Ermakov, and listened to his ghastly—and politically inexpedient—confession was, as I might have anticipated, unforgivable.

I had been stupid enough (forgetting that I was in Russia) to write the details of the Ermakov interview in a personal letter to my family—and the letter had, of course, been opened at the border.

Consequently, a limitation of five days had been put upon my visa, and my point of departure must be Batum, the nearest port.

(As for my notes, they were typed single-space on both sides of thin paper and concealed in the overcoat linings of American friends when they left the country. This precaution was necessary, not because the notes were by any means all anti-Bolshevik [I had never failed to emphasize the striking accomplishments of the

Communist régime], but because I knew that even laud-
atory comment, if it contained a single criticism of some
feature of Bolshevik policy, ran the risk of being destroyed by the postal authorities—or, for all I knew,
would be filed against me in my *dossier* at Moscow.)

On receiving the notification from the police, I had
one immediate thought: If my visa is being canceled
because of the Ermakov interview—what about Ermakov himself? What punishment will be meted out to
him, if he is still alive? For it's one thing to commit
murder for the Soviets, but it's quite another thing to
talk about it afterward.

Several weeks later, at my request, the interpreter
who had accompanied me to Sverdlovsk wrote to the
prison there, and learned (or at least was told) that
Ermakov had survived the crisis he was facing when I
interviewed him, but was still extremely ill. Perhaps
his very sickness, and the knowledge that he probably
would never recover, saved him from the wrath of the
authorities. Or discipline may simply have been de-
ferred. I do not know. I've had no further news regarding his fate.

This abrupt ending of my visit to Russia did not upset my plans, for I had none. Even so, considering
what did happen as a consequence of this sudden devel-
opment, I was properly punished for whatever sins the
Bolsheviks thought I had committed.

Back in Abkhazia, on my visit to old Zapara, I had
caught a heavy cold. Instead of stopping to treat it as
I should have, I went on to Khevsooria, for I knew that
even one day's delay might give the December snows a
chance to block the trail until spring. The raw weather

and the lack of proper clothing had turned my cold into bronchitis. By the time I reached Tiflis again, the bronchitis had turned into pneumonia.

And of the five days' grace I was allowed, three had already gone.

Fritz did all he could to help me prepare for the trip to Batum. I needed handkerchiefs—badly. Fritz scoured the town in search of them. There was not one handkerchief to be bought in all Tiflis—a city that could count five hundred thousand noses. How the natives managed, I never learned. But Fritz finally bought a coarse cotton bed sheet, the best available, and ripped it into smaller squares. Nor were there any gloves for sale at any price. I had gone to Khevsooria with woolen socks, bought in Berlin, pulled over my hands. Tiflis offered no better substitute. Nor were there any overshoes. Moscow had a sufficient stock; but Tiflis, situated in a more southern latitude, was supposed to be able to get along without them. So I laid out another pair of heavy German socks, to pull over my shoes when the time came to be taken to the train. Now, I thought, I will *look* more like a good Bolshevik—but Lord help me if the government could see into my heart!

I found little consolation in the fact that my fountain pen, the innocent instrument of my downfall, had been choked to death on Russian "ink." Although I was resolved not to put another word on paper until I found myself safely back in civilization, I disliked being without a pen. Perhaps, if I were well enough, I might be able to write on the boat. So again Fritz made the rounds of the shops; but there were no fountain pens to be had, not even for good capitalist money.

No handkerchiefs, no gloves, no overshoes, no fountain pens—or for that matter, none of a dozen other perfectly ordinary necessities—were on sale in Tiflis.
Goods that are staples in the most remote country stores
in other lands, simply did not exist in the fifth largest
city in the Soviet Union. The lack of any one of these
articles might be of no consequence—but the lack of
them all, after nearly two decades of the Soviet system,
seems profoundly significant.

I didn't bother to inquire into the reason for this situation—I knew the answer already. The famous Five
Year Plans! Russian industry was too busy turning out
pamphlets and tanks and locomotives and things for export, to supply fancy bourgeois luxuries like handkerchiefs for home consumption.

With socks on my hands and my shoes, with
squares of bed sheet in my pockets, and burning up with
fever, I got to Batum (thanks only to Fritz's assistance)
right on the deadline. There I expected to catch an
Italian boat scheduled to sail for Istanbul that same
afternoon. But I was met by officials, who notified me
that the boat had been delayed, though it was expected
any hour. In the meanwhile, I would have to remain in
custody. As a special favor, since the time was too
short to enter the hospital, they would allow me to live
at a hotel, which they gave me to understand was one of
the best in the Black Sea region.

Afflicted with a first-class case of pneumonia, I welcomed the promise of reasonably comfortable quarters.
But instead, I found that this show-place among Bolshevik hostels was like all others in Russia, except the
three or four "foreign" ones in Moscow and Leningrad.

The management had installed central heating the previous winter; but no one had ever succeeded in mastering its mysteries. Not since the Revolution had there been any current in the electric fixtures. Each room had one candle. Vermin had apparently been collectivized in my bed; and as for the toilets (two for a hotel of forty rooms)—no pigsty was ever so foul.

This utter indifference to filth in Russia was no new discovery. As every foreign traveler has found, toilets are the same from the Finnish border to the Pacific Ocean. In the hotels, trains, restaurants, government bureaus, wherever Russia's new liberated masses foregather, the toilets are so revolting that no one would care to describe them in print. Not until I traveled through the U.S.S.R. did I realize the practical meaning of that ringing Communist war-cry, "We have only our chains to lose!" But even *they* have been lost—in Russia. If these quagmires are ever cleaned at all, it's only according to a Five Year Plan. And if you complain to the manager or janitor, he looks at you in surprise. It's a toilet—what else should one expect? Yet these dirt-enduring comrades, indifferent to the first principles of animal decency, are offering us a glorious new system for the salvation of humanity, a sunrise of social truth and beauty!

I suspect the Hammer & Sickle would make more converts if they did not have such scorn for the mop and the broom.

In this unpleasant hotel, I remained three days, treating my pneumonia as best I could and waiting for the Italian ship to come and liberate me. And for the waiting I was charged ten American dollars a day. Each

morning a state "doctor" called. He could have grown
geraniums under his fingernails. He wore no collar,
and his shirt had not been changed since the Bolsheviks
took charge of the common welfare.

When the steamer arrived, Fritz managed to get me
down to the dock. The customs officials, seeing that my
visa had been canceled, imagined that I was an especially dangerous character, and that they must be unusually careful in handling my case. While I sat in the
pier-shed with one hundred and four degrees of fever,
my clothes were searched in every seam. My baggage
was examined with a microscope. Every paper and letter I possessed was scrutinized by an English-speaking
agent. Every article I had bought in Russia for which
I could not produce a "valuta" receipt (proof that I
had *not* bought it with Soviet roubles, but with capitalist money) was confiscated.

But I was too sick to care.

The boat remained at the dock two days, un-
loading and loading; and I lay, little more than conscious, in my stateroom. In spite of the delay, I was
happy to be in a clean bed, to be attended by a clean
steward with clean hands, to have heat and light and
sanitation.

Finally, we were due to sail in an hour. In three days,
if I could hold on, we would be in Istanbul. . . .

But just when I was listening for the anchor to be
raised, I heard a knock at my door. The Captain entered, with my old friend, Dr. Fingernails, and announced that he could not allow me to sail on his ship:
I was too sick, and it would be very embarrassing all
around if I died. I must get ashore at once.

My most strenuous protestations were so feeble that they only confirmed the Captain's apprehensions.

So back I went to my old room in the Lilac Bower.

Meanwhile, Fritz, who had been acting as bodyguard and interpreter, having seen me safely on the boat, had returned to Moscow.

The next four days were grim indeed. I found only one consolation for being sick under Soviet care—I had the satisfaction of knowing that I must be hardy to live through it.

A second steamer, also bound for Istanbul, at last came by, remaining in port fortunately only a few hours. This time I took no chances. I forced myself, pneumonia or no pneumonia, to walk aboard alone, and sit fully dressed on a couch in the salon until the ship had sailed and left the U.S.S.R. far behind. Then I tottered into my cabin, fell into the bunk . . . and three days later, already improved, was able to stand on deck as we anchored off the Golden Horn.

A week in the hospital, and I was walking around again. What a progressive, civilized country Turkey seemed! Clothes — food — warmth — cleanliness! I found myself gazing in the beautiful shop windows for the sheer pleasure of it, or sitting in the cafés just to see the people enjoying an idle hour without fear or shame.

I could get a pair of *gloves*—think of it! And everyone was carrying a handkerchief—imagine! I didn't need my squares of Tiflis bed sheet any more. The shops even had fountain pens, and cameras, and the clerks didn't look like refugees.

And all these things I could buy without fear that

they would be confiscated if I failed to show proof that they were *not* purchased with Turkish money.

And my hotel, though it was modest enough, seemed like a palace of luxury. It had a *bathtub* with hot water; and electric lights that actually lighted. I could pass the toilet without fainting. I could buy a newspaper with *news* in it—including more accurate news about Russia than the Russians are allowed to read . . . and in the bookstores, I could survey the newest books on any subject, from New York, Paris, London or Berlin. I saw a moving picture, and to my delight it was not one of those Bolshevik propaganda epics in which the workers take over the factory, but simply a charming, superficial little romance where the boy won the girl.

And most wonderful of all, I began to realize that my letters were not going to be opened; that I was no longer to be spied upon; that I could travel about Turkey whenever and wherever I cared to, and depart when I chose.

Freedom! I'd never known what it was before, because I'd always had it and taken it for granted. But my adventures in the U.S.S.R. made me, for the first time, fully realize the meaning of the word. Unconcerned heretofore with politics and social problems, I now found myself *very much* concerned, for fear that I, and those I cared for, might some day be forced to live under such a régime as I had observed during the past two months.

However, on second thought, I realized that so far as my own country is concerned—with all its social injustice, its economic ills, the blundering and sometimes brutal way we muddle along—I could put aside any apprehension that the Russian brand of Communism was going to overwhelm us. For I knew that not until the Statue of Liberty does a back-flip off her pedestal into New York Harbor, will Americans ever submit to such despotism and such deprivation as exist under the Red Flag of Russia.

CHAPTER XX

THE SULTANA OF TURKEY—FROM MARTINIQUE

FROM the top of the highest hill in Istanbul, dominating every corner of this dramatic old city, soar the domes and minarets of the Mosque of Sultan Mohammed II. In the courtyard of this mosque, in a secluded and unfrequented corner, stands a tumble-down kiosk that encloses the hundred-year-old tomb of a woman whose life-history makes one of the most extraordinary stories I have ever read.

This woman, having lived a life more eventful and more fantastic than anything in *The Arabian Nights,* having upset an empire with her beauty and ruled it with her brains, having controlled armies, humbled conquerors, and altered the history of the world—this woman is all the more remarkable in that so few people know that she even existed.

For having heard of her myself I am indebted to Benjamin A. Morton, now vice-president of a New York bank, who after years of patient and scholarly research has pieced together this obscure but highly important chapter of European history. The record of his investigation he turned into a biography called *The Veiled Empress,** a book I held under my arm as I disembarked at Istanbul from Batum.

---

* *The Veiled Empress,* published in 1923 by G. P. Putnam's Sons.

Back in 1917, Morton made the first of several visits to the island of Martinique, in the French West Indies. Since history was his avocation, he naturally took an interest in the early chapters of the life of Josephine, Empress of the French, who was born on Martinique and lived there all during her girlhood. Pursuing this subject he stumbled upon a few obscure legends about one of Josephine's cousins, Aimée Dubuc de Rivery, and on inquiring further, turned up a story more romantic and more marvelous even than Josephine's.

I had read *The Veiled Empress* before leaving America. And I knew, once I had put on my seven league boots and started out again to see the world, that I would return to Constantinople and make a humble pilgrimage to the tomb of this infinitely fascinating woman.

The astonishing story that Morton's research gave to history, he collected from a hundred sources—family traditions in Martinique, old letters preserved in Paris archives, a few dim and dusty records at Constantinople. But when the mosaic was put together—what a startling clear picture it made!

In the year 1763 Josephine Tascher de la Pagerie and Aimée Dubuc de Rivery, both destined to be empresses, were born on Martinique sugar plantations not far apart. The parents of each were French of pure and noble blood. In fact it was Aimée's striking *blonde* beauty that was to raise her from a Martinique sugar plantation to the throne of Turkey.

As children the two little girls were very good

"No woman's land" is the peninsula of Mount Athos in northern Greece. Here no woman nor any female animal or fowl is allowed to set foot. Scattered about the peninsula are twenty monasteries, all from five hundred to a thousand years old. The monastery pictured here, called Simopetra, is one of the most spectacular of the group.

Many of the monks of Mount Athos occupy themselves with the arts and crafts, and many of the holy pictures found on the walls of Greek Orthodox churches were painted in monastic studios of this holy community.

The interiors of the monastery chapels dazzle one with their Byzantine glory. Gold and silver have been used in extravagant profusion, so that on special occasions, when the hundreds of candles are lighted, the chapels look like treasure houses.

friends. Closely associated, they grew up in the happy, idle, comfortable society of colonial Martinique.

When they were about twelve years old, according to a story which Josephine herself often told in later years, they went, just to be amused, to a famous Negro soothsayer on the island, and eagerly asked to have their fortunes told. For Josephine the fortune teller predicted two marriages. Her second husband would fill the world with his glory and conquer many nations. Josephine was to become greater than a queen, but this great dignity she would outlive, and yearn for the sweet peaceful life once led in Martinique.

For Aimée:

On a sea voyage her ship would be taken by Moslem pirates. She would be conducted into a seraglio, and have a son by a great sultan. All the rest of her life she would occupy a vast and magnificent palace *where she would have command.*

Both little girls probably giggled on hearing such thrilling fortunes prophesied for them. They probably departed gayly from the soothsayer's home to make mud pies or put their dolls to bed—and forgot all about their shining future. But every single word the old fortune teller spoke came to pass. Indeed, in Aimée's case the prophecy was not half spectacular enough.

When Aimée was thirteen she was separated from Josephine, and sent off to France to complete her education in a convent at Nantes. For eight long years she remained there, prevented from visiting her native island by the wars raging between France and England.

But at last in 1784, when Aimée was twenty-one— now an arrestingly beautiful young woman with pale gold hair—she started for home, for her beloved Martinique which she had not seen in so long.

Aimée neither then, nor ever again, reached Martinique.

Her ship was set upon by Algerian Corsairs, as fierce and daring a race of pirates as ever lived. At that time they were at the height of their power, the scourge of the Mediterranean and eastern Atlantic. The unarmed passenger ship was easily captured, and everybody aboard taken prisoner.

Among the captives Aimée stood out. She was more than beautiful. She had extraordinary charm and a distinguished manner as well. At once the Corsair Captain, realizing that he had found a rare prize indeed delivered her over to the Dey of Algiers himself.

But not even here did Aimée's story-book adventure end. The Dey happened to be under great obligation to the Turkish Sultan, his overlord, for money and munitions. (At that time Algeria was still, nominally, a part of Turkey.) In this beautiful Christian captive he saw a chance not only to pay back, but to win for himself new and special favors from the capital.

So Aimée was bundled up again and placed on a Corsair ship that sailed eastward through the Mediterranean, past Greece, into the Ægean, past ancient Troy, through the Hellespont, landing at Constantinople on the shore of the Seraglio Hill.

Here the Sultan took one look at her—and his heart stood still. He had a score of wives already, Greeks, Armenians, Circassians. But they were mostly untutored slaves. *This* girl could read and write. She came from the great world. In fact, she was by far the most intelligent wife he had ever had.

Aimée immediately became the Sultan's favorite, and in due time bore him a blond son.

She had long since given up all hope of escape, all hope of ever seeing Martinique and Josephine again. No woman of the Seraglio had ever found freedom. So since she was doomed to reside the rest of her life "in a vast and magnificent palace," completely cut off from all she once knew and loved, she decided that "she would have command." Was that not what the fortune teller had foretold?

Meanwhile cousin Josephine was having a few adventures of her own. She had married Vicomte de Beauharnais and borne him two children. But during the French Revolution her husband went to the guillotine. Not long after, she married again, this time a wild young genius from Corsica named Napoleon Bonaparte, six years her junior. Life became very exciting for Madame Bonaparte. Her husband was winning one military victory after another for France, and as his wife she was receiving honor equally with him.

But Aimée, a Sultana in Constantinople, found herself even more occupied. Here the question of royal succession had arisen. She and her son, Mahmoud, who was the third in line, were becoming involved in the deadly intrigues that seemed to be the natural order of things in Turkish seraglios. The first and second Princes were sworn enemies, and their respective mothers even more hostile. Each mother tried to poison her rival's child, to undermine the other's influence by fair means or foul. Aimée had the best wits of the three.

Consequently, she managed to keep *her* son away from the poison cups being handed around.

The Sultan died in 1789, and Prince Selim, the rightful heir, succeeded to the throne. But the mother of Prince Mustapha, the next in line, never wavered from her ambitious designs. And so persistent was she that she actually succeeded in having Selim dethroned, and Mustapha crowned.

But this high-handed business infuriated a certain faction of Turks. They stormed the Seraglio, meaning to murder Mustapha and replace Selim. The palace gates were hurriedly closed. As the rebels pounded upon them, Mustapha's mother rushed assassins to slay not only Selim, but Aimée's son too. *That* would settle the question of succession!

The assassins, spurred on by the shouts and fighting at the gates, found Selim first, and stabbed him to death. But the defense he put up gave Mahmoud time to escape up the chimney and onto the roof. And before the murderers could overtake him, the palace gates crashed down, and a crowd of Mahmoud's friends ran in to save him.

Prince Mustapha was in turn executed, leaving Mahmoud—and Aimée—to rule the Turkish Empire from the Indian Ocean to the Adriatic Sea.

At last, in her vast and magnificent palace, Aimée "had command."

Mahmoud, from childhood, had more than loved his mother. His regard had amounted to worship. She had been his wise and devoted counselor throughout all the dangerous days of his youth. Now that he was Sultan—and only twenty-three—she became his entire ministry.

Consequently, because Aimée, the real head of the government, was thoroughly French, and because her beloved cousin Josephine had become the Empress of Napoleon's empire, "Mahmoud" threw all his political weight toward France in that country's wars against the rest of Europe. French officers came to train his army. French seamen manned his warships. French gunners drove off the British fleet from Constantinople. French fashions, French schools, French language, took possession of the Turks. (To this day French is the common foreign language in Turkey.) Napoleon himself must have been puzzled by Mahmoud's devotion. England was completely baffled. Even the Turks thought it strange. Everybody had forgotten that Mahmoud's mother, wearing a Turkish veil and sitting quietly and unobtrusively behind the curtain of the seraglio, was a French woman—a *patriotic* French woman—still dreaming, despite her years of exile, of Josephine and Martinique.

This curious situation lasted until 1809, when Aimée was forty-six and Mahmoud twenty-four.

Then suddenly dramatic news came from Paris— news that caused an explosion in the Seraglio.

Napoleon had divorced Josephine!

Aimée's lovely eyes grew hard. She clenched her hands together. Such injustice! Such ingratitude!— and to the most lovable and unresentful of women! Napoleon would pay for this. Aimée had been a secret ally who gloried in his glory. Well, that was ended.

She would face about, instantly. All she had done for him she would now do against him, and revenge her cousin.

Had it been Aimée herself who was scorned she could not have released a more calculated fury against the French Emperor. For three years she bided her time. She waited until 1812—probably the most eventful year in modern history up to 1914. She now perceived, with a far-seeing vision that was inspired, that her opportunity to strike Napoleon was at hand.

For some months Russia had been at war with Turkey, and had the major part of its army in Turkish territory. Napoleon, well aware of the fact, chose this moment to make his celebrated march on Moscow.

For the undertaking he assembled the largest and best equipped army ever known until then. It numbered over six hundred thousand men—this vast military Juggernaut that was to roll relentlessly to Moscow and make Russia one more subject nation. France marshalled the last of her resources to back up her Emperor for this one great gamble.

For Napoleon it was no gamble. Who could withstand his might? Anyway the main Russian Army was far to the south, well occupied. He offered Mahmoud extravagant rewards in return for even more vigorous action against the Russians.

Mahmoud said nothing, promised nothing. But the day Napoleon's Army left Dresden, headed for the Russian border, the Sultan, though he had every reason to believe that Russia was on the brink of destruction, signed a secret treaty of peace with the Czar giving him everything he asked for. The treaty released fifty thousand Russian veterans, who at once started north to cut the French lines of communication with Paris.

But Napoleon, believing his path was clear, marched on deeper and deeper into Russia.

He was by no means unopposed, for Russia was capable of raising more than one army to resist the invaders. Battle after battle had to be fought. Thousands of men perished on both sides. Napoleon, regardless of cost, continued to drive before him Russia's defenders. Week after week the French Army, growing ever smaller and hungrier, plowed its way forward—sixteen hundred miles eastward from Paris. And simultaneously the Russian Army that had been fighting the Turks, miraculously released by the inexplicable peace treaty, was racing north by forced marches, straight toward the middle of Napoleon's over-extended life-line.

When at last, still unaware of the impending blow, Napoleon *did* reach Moscow, over two-thirds of his forces were gone.

Gone too was the population of Moscow. The French captured an almost deserted city.

Napoleon established himself in the Kremlin, in the apartment now used for Stalin's offices. But hardly had he made himself at home, ready to spend the winter preparing for further conquests in the spring, when Moscow was set on fire by the Russians themselves. In two days more the French held nothing but a sea of smoking ruins.

And now came the last, the final blow.

On September thirtieth a messenger reached Napoleon's headquarters with the disastrous news that the fifty thousand Russian soldiers, supposedly in Rumania fighting Mahmoud, had appeared four hundred miles west of Moscow, cut the French supply line, and established themselves on the west bank of the Beresina River . . . waiting.

When Napoleon read this terrible dispatch he is said to have sat speechless with bewilderment and despair, for he knew that the message was a death-sentence to what was left of his campaign. Already the melting of his forces had made his position extremely precarious. Why had such a thing happened? Why had the Turks, apparently his staunchest allies, played so treacherously?

He never thought to look to Josephine's Cousin Aimée for the answer.

There has not been discovered, in all the archives of France, Russia and Turkey, a single document that proves Aimée's commanding part in this deadly maneuver. No one ever overheard her instructing Mahmoud to strike Napoleon in the back, or witnessed any such order being signed by her hand. The evidence that she surrendered to the Russians in order to revenge Josephine is circumstantial. And yet, in this case, the testimony of the facts themselves leaves no doubt as to the source of the destructive move. Aimée worked secretively, hidden behind her veil; but for that very reason she worked all the more effectively. She received no public official other than her son—but through him she ruled Turkey.

It is not to be supposed, however, that personal revenge was the *sole* motive for the maneuver. Aimée no doubt likewise felt that there were possible political advantages to be gained.

If the release of the Russian Army *was* Aimée's strategy—and who can doubt it?—the move succeeded beyond her wildest hopes. Napoleon, trapped and defeated, knew there was nothing to do but retreat, to run for his life, for there would be no more food, reinforcements or munitions. Everything was cut off by the exultant Russian Army waiting for him four hundred miles away.

One hundred thousand French soldiers (all that remained) began the retreat from Moscow, the middle of October. Seventy thousand more perished from cold and starvation before the Russian blockade was even reached. There at the Beresina River, as the French tried to cross into the teeth of the enemy's artillery fire, the final slaughter took place. The merest handful of Napoleon's followers broke through. Napoleon himself escaped capture only by a fluke.

Aimée—and Josephine—were revenged.

Shortly after landing at Istanbul, I climbed the Seraglio Hill with an interest I had never known before. I passed the Mosque of Santa Sophia, now a museum, in the dark recesses of which I had once spent a night (watching the ancient ghosts parade). I stepped inside again to note the changes that have taken place, to admire the glorious Byzantine mosaics, hidden for centuries and only lately uncovered. But not even Santa Sophia could long delay my visit to the Seraglio where Aimée de Rivery had ruled.

The Seraglio since Turkey deposed the sultans, has

likewise been opened to the public. It is built on the slopes of a point of land that juts out into the Bosporus and is a maze of throne rooms, courts, apartments, baths, stables, galleries. In recent times this vast confusion of buildings, which once housed twenty thousand people, has been conscientiously restored to its original condition. The extravagant oriental furnishings, the carpets, the thrones, are still there; and anyone with the price of a ticket can be conducted by guides through the entire place.

My guide, a very special and valuable guide, had accompanied me from the city outside. He had been recommended by a curator of the National Museum as the one man in all Istanbul best informed about the history of the Seraglio, as he was an old eunuch who had lived most of his seventy years in the midst of the imperial household, guarding the harems of the sultans. He spoke French, had a good memory, and apparently a keen sense of historical values. In his soft voice he talked entertainingly about the harem days before the World War—and to my delight knew something about "the French Sultana."

Images of the past rose up as we entered the front gate of the Seraglio. Through this gate the blonde and beautiful Aimée, arrayed in all the riches Algeria could provide, had been conducted. In the cypress-shaded courtyard the Sultan had come to greet her, the loveliest girl he ever laid eyes on.

We reached the Seraglio itself. Each sultan had added a new apartment, new gardens and fountains, built new pavilions and new throne rooms, in the various styles of the moment. I saw the rooms of the seventeenth-century rulers and the rooms of the last one. Here in this suite in the women's quarters, my guide declared, Aimée had given birth to Mahmoud. Over there was the famous courtyard gateway which the partisans of young Sultan Selim had broken through at the time they tried, too late, to save his life. In this corridor was Selim slain by the assassins sent by Prince Mustapha's mother. And up this enormous chimney Mahmoud had escaped to the roof where he was rescued. The building has not been materially changed in one hundred and twenty years. With a little assistance from confederates I could have climbed up the same chimney myself, even without the shouts of pursuing assassins to give extra energy to my efforts.

The section of the great palace where Mahmoud lived is clearly marked by placards. In a part of it one finds today a small but exquisite flagstoned garden looking over the trees and down upon the harbor. There is a marble fountain here, and marble benches. Perhaps on one of these benches the Veiled Empress had often counseled her son the Sultan; had told him of her idyllic childhood on the tropical French island with her playmate Josephine; had taught him in his secret heart to put great value upon his relationship with the Empress of the French, to love this kinswoman married to the unconquerable Napoleon. Through the Turkish ministers in Paris, Aimée and Mahmoud were kept informed about Josephine's dazzling career, and rejoiced as her triumphs mounted. From these same ministers had come the fateful news of Josephine's divorce.

That Josephine was not likewise kept informed about Aimée is one of the most curious features of this story.

No letters ever passed between them. There is certainly no indication that Josephine, or for that matter Napoleon himself, ever knew that the deadly treachery of Mahmoud had been urged by his revengeful mother.

One instantly asks: Why did Aimée keep her position so secret from Josephine? Why has this chapter not been in all our history books? How has Aimée, with her marvelous career, escaped attention from the hundred writers who have combed Europe looking for every scrap of information about Napoleon and his associates?

The explanation is obvious enough. To escape attention, even from Josephine, was Aimée's deliberate and undeviating policy. For only by keeping out of sight, hidden behind her veil, invisible to all ministers of state, unknown to all foreign ambassadors, could she—a foreigner, a Christian, a French woman with strong French sympathies—hope to counsel and control Mahmoud without interference from the government and hostility from the people. In her obscurity, in her inaccessibility, in her very imprisonment, lay her strength.

And this is why Napoleon went to St. Helena still wondering what had caused Mahmoud to betray him to the Russians—a betrayal which, as much as anything else in his career, brought about his ultimate downfall. And for the same reason the name of Aimée Dubuc de Rivery, before Morton resurrected it, was known only to tradition in Martinique, and to a few old eunuchs in the Constantinople Seraglio.

It was sunset when my guide and I turned to leave the palace. At the gate I thought to ask him if it were known where Aimée was buried. He replied that it was very well known, and directed me to the place.

Alone in the twilight, I climbed up the city's highest hill. On the summit stood the Mosque of Mohammed II. In the courtyard was a wooden kiosk, built about 1800 and locked fast for the last eight or ten years. A coin secured the key from the caretaker, who brushed away the dust and cobwebs from the door and conducted me inside.

There in the dim light I found two dozen wooden tombs, each covered with a green brocade and enclosed by a railing of mother-of-pearl. These tombs contained the bodies of Sultan Mahmoud's various wives and children. And in the exact center stood the tomb of Aimée Dubuc de Rivery, his mother. Her tomb is larger and richer than the others, and tilted (though she never accepted the Moslem faith) toward Mecca.

Across the end of it I found an inscription in Arabic. Morton has translated it carefully as follows:

> May the beauty of Sultan Mahmoud's mother
>   never be forgotten.
> May her fame and glory never be unveiled.
> Of her, the majestic Emperor, the Sultan of the
>   World,
> Mahmoud, of soul shining as a cloud in heaven,
>   was begotten.
> The Beautiful One, her name. The Queen
>   Mother, she was,
> When this crown of earth was placed upon her
>   head.

Outside in the courtyard stood a row of flower shops. There I bought an armful of roses and chrysanthemums, and, groping my way back through the darkness, placed them respectfully on Aimée's tomb, in memory, not of the great Sultana who ruled an empire and thwarted Napoleon, but of the little girl from Martinique, neglected and forgotten, faded to a fragrant memory . . . and so far from home.

CHAPTER XXI

NO WOMAN'S LAND

THERE exists today in southeastern Europe a little country, washed by the Ægean Sea, so fantastically different from all other countries in the world that when I first heard about it my credulity was strained to the utmost. So let me assure you at the outset that every word of this story is strictly true.

This country is almost a thousand years old, and has a government which has functioned uninterruptedly over a longer span of time than any other government on earth. But in all this time it has never introduced a single new idea in politics, education or science. The four thousand people who inhabit it occupy the same venerable buildings, read the same parchment books, wear the same style of clothes, lead the same kind of lives, as their country's founders in the tenth century. In the midst of progress and evolution it has remained a medieval world, frozen but still living, where we can return to wonder at the past.

When we examine it we find, to our astonishment, that *every inhabitant is a male*—as all the inhabitants have been since the state was founded.

Since 1345, when a Serbian King dared to bring his wife to visit this place, only one woman has ever set foot upon its soil. And she remained just fifteen minutes. No child has been born within this country's boundaries in nearly a thousand years. Baby boys may have been brought here to grow up, but never once a baby girl.

This country is located entirely on a narrow peninsula. At the point where the peninsula joins the mainland the inhabitants have stationed special police whose sole duty is to keep "wolves and women" from crossing the frontier. Some of the older inhabitants have not even seen a woman for fifty years.

Not only are all females of the human race rigorously barred—females of any sort are barred as well. There are large flocks of roosters in the country, but not one single hen—plenty of rams but no ewes—herds of steers and bulls but not one cow. There are numerous cats, all tom; plenty of dogs, all male. Only winged creatures have been able—to the state's great annoyance—to bring their wives across the border. Consequently it is necessary for the monks from time to time to travel abroad and bring back fresh supplies of male animals.

All the inhabitants wear long beards. Hair-cutting is not allowed. Instead, the men's tresses are gathered into a big knot at the back of the neck and secured with hairpins. Baldness is almost unknown.

In this curious country, all games and sports are prohibited; singing and dancing and love-making are strictly banned; there is a tabu against bathing and fighting; and dying is almost unheard of.

The capital is called Karyes, which when translated into English gives the lovely and mellifluous name of Nuts.

And I assure you I'm not making this up. I'm writing only solemn facts—about the Holy Communities of Mount Athos.

If you will look at a map of Greece and the Ægean basin you will see, eighty miles east of Salonika, three long narrow peninsulas extending like crooked fingers into the Ægean Sea. Of these Athos is the eastern-most—thirty miles long and five wide. Its isthmus, however, is so flat and narrow that King Xerxes of ancient Persia, bringing his fleet to Athens for the conquest of Greece, easily cut a canal through to save his ships having to round the stormy point. Rising above the southern point is an abrupt and spectacular peak six thousand feet high, of pure white marble. The crown is treeless so that the peak seems to have a perpetual diadem of snow. Between the peak and the isthmus stretches a range of the wildest steepest mountains imaginable. Where the rocks and canyons permit, dense forests grow.

And on the rugged sea-slopes of this peninsula, placed from one to three miles apart, are twenty lonely and isolated communities. Each is enclosed within a huge medieval stone building, walled and battlemented, built around a court. These communities are monasteries. Several of them were founded between the years 900 and 1000. Several more in the 1100's. One, the baby of the family, was already one hundred years old when the Pilgrims came to America.

The monasteries are giants in size. The largest measures nearly a third of a mile around its walls; another is eight stories high. Fortress, castle, college, church, all in one, they were built in beauty and in grandeur by the outpourings of riches from the emperors of old Byzantium.

It is in these vast crag-crowning refuges overlooking

the sea that the entirely masculine population of Athos—at present about four thousand monks — has been burying itself since the tenth century, wearing long black gowns, never shaving, piously idle, and sworn to poverty, chastity and obedience. And it has been their abbots who have passed the unique laws forbidding any creature of the female sex from profaning the holiness of this long-bearded heaven.

The origin and endurance of this monastic state is one of the marvels of history.

Byzantium—now Istanbul—was in the year 900 the most zealously Christian city ever known. The Eastern Orthodox Church dominated it completely. But for many of the citizens in this excessively religious metropolis, Byzantium was not half pious enough. These fanatics, protected and supported by the government, retreated to the wild and uninhabited—and dramatically beautiful—peninsula of Athos. Here, as monks, they turned their zeal to the construction of monasteries which for splendor and size had never been equaled before and certainly will never be again.

In the center of each monastic courtyard the monks built a church in the form of a Greek cross. Into these churches were poured the gold and silver and jewels that Byzantium, then mistress of the Western world, had wrested from a hundred conquered nations. Not pounds but wagonloads of gold were spread across the altars. Huge gold chandeliers hung from the domes; gold candelabra, higher than a man, lit the holy treasuries. From Byzantium the greatest artists and craftsmen came to paint and carve the walls and ceilings.

Once these churches were finished, the monks held

gorgeous services, conforming strictly to the ritual fixed by church laws but embellishing every traditional rite with the most sumptuous trappings.

That was in the year 950. And what remains today of all this glory?

Everything!—or at least everything not lost before 1350, at which time the attacks on the monasteries by pirates and foreign invaders came to an end. Every ornament, every treasure, every ikon, every slightest detail in the services, exists now almost the same as then. On occasions of special ceremony, such as Christmas Eve, one may see the exact same splendor and color, the same rich priestly robes, and hear the same prayers and chants, that Emperor Justinian saw and heard in ancient Byzantium when he dedicated the Basilica of Santa Sophia to the glory of God. This endurance of tradition and ritual is all the more wonderful when we remember that for over four centuries—right up to 1912—Athos, along with all northern Greece, was part of Turkey and surrounded by a sea of Moslem civilization and Moslem faith.

The first generations of Athonian monks rendered an incalculable service to humanity, for they possessed cultural as well as spiritual strength. Into their monasteries they brought all the books they could lay their hands on. Sixth-, fifth-, even fourth-century manuscripts, collected from as far away as Egypt, Syria and Arabia, found their way to Mount Athos.

And with classical Greece and Rome long since crumbled, and with Italy, France and England still sleeping through their centuries of barbarous darkness, the peak of Athos, with its bald white marble summit, shone like a lighthouse in the night, attracting to it most of the scholarship and learning of the age. Whatever historians, poets, musicians, scientists there were in southeastern Europe during the Dark Centuries were nearly all gathered in the monasteries of Athos, laboriously and patiently recording their knowledge into parchment books. And these precious documents, every page a hand-drawn masterpiece, were stored away in the libraries where they were to be protected by crags and battlements through the centuries.

And what has happened to these thousands of scholarly books? Have they been saved?

Many of them have been—again, that is, in the monasteries which survived the invasions of the fourteenth century. Today these precious books, yellow and fragile with age, rest safely on the shelves—all too safely, for the monks are jealous guardians and disinclined to show them even to scholars. Only as a special favor was I allowed to hold in my hands a parchment gospel written, one letter at a time with ink and brush, in the year 450— a thousand years before printing was invented. Another time I was allowed to examine a dozen pages—all that remain—of a duplicate of the famous fourth-century Codex Bible which the British Museum acquired at the bargain price of half a million dollars. One monastery had twenty-five hundred parchment books all written before 700; books on music, medicine, surgery; and, most marvelous and beautiful of all, a sixth-century text book on botany, with two hundred hand-illuminated illustrations of flowers and plants found in the Byzantine empire.

But the monks themselves who have imprisoned all

these ancient treasures—what sort of people are they after thirty generations without women and without children?

To answer that question we must first understand what sort of men come here, and why. They come mostly because the Eastern Orthodox Church in Greece, Russia, Serbia and Bulgaria, has so emphasized the literal bliss of a physical heaven and literal torments of a physical hell, that the simple and susceptible-minded have been left to believe that only by a life of abstinence and self-mortification can they hope to escape from eternal frying.

There are other monks, with romantically inclined natures, who have had their souls slain by the infidelity and inconstancy of some woman. With broken hearts, seeking refuge in religion and solitude, they flee to Athos, vowing they never wish to see a woman again.

There are many, too, who are philosophers, whose whole mind and heart are taken up with life, death and immortality. They aspire to the completely spiritual existence, and feel that their bodies only shackle their souls. Consequently, eating and drinking and mating— the whole physical world—they shun as much as possible. And the absence of all women is supposed to help clear their path in the quest for spiritual truth. Further to protect this type of monk against the distractions of the flesh, all female animals are likewise uncompromisingly kept out. The Lord's injunction to "be fruitful and multiply" is considered shockingly improper by the saintly fathers.

This all seems highly ridiculous to us—but not to the monks. They take their soul-saving with desperate seriousness. In his excellent book about them, Michael Choukas,* assistant professor of sociology at Dartmouth, tells the story of one monk who when sick refused to see a doctor because, for an examination, it might be necessary to undress. Another monk confided to me, on my own visit to Athos, that he never allowed himself more than four hours' sleep each night for fear that if he slept too much he might dream worldly dreams. Hearing such stories, one can better believe the absurd lengths to which the monkish mind can go to maintain virtue.

Absurd or not, the law against women has been successfully enforced. Cases where this prohibition has been defied are so few that the entire mountain remembers them and talks of them for years after with as much interest as other countries talk of past wars and revolutions.

Four thousand men—and no women! Holy or unholy, Christian or pagan, such a situation is abnormal and conducive to more sins than it prevents. Disrespectful journalists with a preconceived hostile attitude, visiting Athos and observing critically whatever came to their attention, have accused the holy men of sins unmentionable; have declared their piousness only a pose, that they ate and drank gluttonously and, beyond their mechanical lip-service, had precious little spirituality left.

Well aware both of the tradition and of the cynical accounts, I had long wanted to visit Athos and decide for myself what I thought about this curious world. On

---

* *Black Angels of Athos,* published in 1934 by the Stephen Daye Press, Brattleboro, Vermont.

three previous trips to Greece, I had made an effort to
reach the Holy Community; once, from the summit of
Mount Olympus, I had even seen the bald dome of
Mount Athos shining one hundred miles across the
Ægean. But each time something had prevented my
going.

Now, prepared to leave Istanbul, and with Greece approaching again, I meant to take no chances, but go
straight to the peninsula before the siren city of Athens
distracted me. I determined to go even though the
season was the most uninviting of the year—early January. No one who could help it ever went to Athos in
mid-winter, so I was told, for the snow was piled four
feet deep on the mountain trails, blocking for days at
a time all communication between monasteries. And
nearly always in January the waters around the coast remained in such a continual torment that boats were unable to land passengers, or, more to the point, to take
them away. If I went now I would soon learn that the
guest quarters all had tenth-century heating, that the
churches were gold-plated ice-boxes, that the fog hid
the beautiful marble mountain and killed the splashing
colors in sea and sky which make Athos such a glorious
place in summer. Besides finding Athos at its very
worst I would probably be forced to spend a week or
two imprisoned by snow and tempests in whatever monastery I happened to be visiting when the storm broke.

Even this possibility didn't discourage me. Rather,
I found the idea amusing. But it wouldn't have been
amusing had I known how completely the imprisonment
prophecy was coming to pass.

I said good-by to Istanbul—and Sultana Aimée—

and took a boat through the Dardanelles (past the point where Leander, Byron, myself, and three Smith College girls had swum the Hellespont!) and landed at Salonika. Another smaller boat, struggling and wallowing through the wintry Ægean, took me back along the coast and deposited me, with considerable difficulty, on the shores of the Holy Mountain, at the little port of Daphne, where for a thousand years men fleeing from women and from the world have entered this land of refuge.

CHAPTER XXII

THE INVOLUNTARY MONK

ON REACHING the dock I was immediately asked tↄ show my special passport which gave me permission to visit Athos. Though included in Greek territory, this little state considers itself absolutely independent, and allows no one to cross its borders without the authorization of its own officials in Athens or Istanbul. Nor could I call upon a single monastery till I had first gone to Karyes, the capital, five miles away, and received from the mayor a letter stamped with the Great Seal of Byzantium instructing all monasteries to give me food and shelter.

Karyes is a town unique in the world. From all outward appearances it is just like any other ancient town of provincial Greece. Orchards and gardens surround it. Pack mules and their drivers move along its crooked cobbled streets. Church bells ring at any and every hour; the cocks crow at dawn; and in the spring birds by the thousand build their nests in the village trees. Karyes has shops, inns, dwellings, schools, a bank and a postoffice.

But for one thousand years no woman, with the one historic exception I have mentioned, has ever set foot in Karyes!

A single day in this weird town, and I began to have

the jitters. I passed a barnyard containing perhaps half a hundred chickens—all roosters; and a dozen head of cattle—all bulls. Shepherded for the day into a court-yard was a flock of sheep—all rams. I entered a dozen shops to look at the goods on sale and get acquainted, and I saw only monks—monks—monks. There is a lit-tle department store; the salesgirls are graybeard monks. Everything for the monks' and the muleteers' clothing needs is there, but not one article of feminine apparel. The village laundress is an old monk; the ser-vants are young monks. There is not a baby in all Karyes. I could not find one child though I walked up and down all the streets. I began to wonder if I was dreaming and having a nightmare . . . sentenced for my sins to some place enchanted by an evil magician where only one sex existed, where no woman's voice would ever speak to me, where no woman's sympathy would ever comfort me, where there would never be a pretty girl to love . . . a world without a mother or a child. . . .

I could not believe that in such an empty-hearted village there could be any true Christianity, any godli-ness worth while.

I was happy to move on, with my interpreter-guide, along the rocky path to the first monastery. We had no time to lose for in January the night came early. Also the monastic doors are closed inexorably at six o'clock, and no matter what the emergency the devil himself cannot get them open again till morning.

My first night's goal was one of the smaller monas-teries, built three hundred feet sheer above the sea on the top of a rocky promontory. A storm had begun to blow across the Ægean and to drive huge waves with a terrible roar against the building's rock foundations. It looked as if the weather I had been promised had arrived.

About thirty monks lived there. They greeted the two of us most cordially, since visitors in January are almost unknown. The guest-monk, fat and dirty and amiable and wearing the usual heavy beard, led us through the courts and corridors and up rickety stairs that had been worn hollow long before Columbus discovered America. Our bare cell-like room had harbored guests like ourselves for seven centuries, and so, I fear, had the beds.

We ate a supper of octopus, a dish that tastes like nothing so much as boiled linoleum, and is less easily digested. As we worked away on the long horny tentacles, half the monastery stood around to watch. They were mostly old men, for Greek youths of today yearn toward Hollywood more than Heaven, and scorn to join the holy orders. Of the fifteen beards surrounding us, twelve were white or gray. We all had several drinks of *oozu* together, whereupon the monks laughed easily and explained readily, almost eagerly, why they had renounced the world and come to this monastery:

> Women.
> Unemployment.
> Passport to Heaven.
> Fear of Hell.
> Atonement for a life of sin.
> Desire for spiritual peace.
> Refuge from the police.
> Women.

One had come as a boy to visit relatives, and been persuaded to remain. Another, the liveliest of the lot, had wronged two Greek girls on the same week-end, and by their respective fathers had been brought to judgment. To escape having to marry *both* girls, he fled to Athos, became a monk, and hid behind a wild red beard.

All night long, wooden gongs sounded and monks tramped into the church for endless services in the freezing chapel. Their chanting came faint and far away, through the whistling of the January wind and the pounding of the waves at the foot of my sanctuary.

Next day, departing with many blessings from these men of God, my guide and I moved on twenty miles down the storm-lashed coast to the tip end of the peninsula where stands the monastery of Lavra, the oldest, largest, holiest and most powerful of them all.

That night, January sixth, was Christmas Eve on Mount Athos, for their calendar is thirteen days behind ours. To be present at this climax of the church year, in the richest and most venerable of the monasteries, was good luck indeed. No other non-Greek had come to Lavra at this snowy and tempestuous season during the last thirty years.

At sunset the special service began in the church. It was suggested that I delay my attendance until one o'clock in the morning, when the Bishop would appear amid a burst of glory.

When the time came I felt my way in the darkness through the maze of steps and galleries leading to the courtyard. There it was snowing and the bitterly cold wind that had been increasing in violence all day whipped the snow into my face so that I could hardly see ahead. Only the chanting in the church directed me. Plowing through drifts I groped my way into the front door—a door that had admitted worshipers since the year 960—and beheld a sight more dazzling and more gorgeous than King Midas' treasury.

The small church, perfect and polished as a cut jewel, was ablaze with hundreds of candles all mirrored by the masses of gold plate that gleamed from wall and altar, ikon and chandelier, candelabra, candlebrackets, candle-crosses. Gold, gold, gold. I had been wondering what had become of the riches of Byzantium, one of the wealthiest and most extravagant cities in history. I had my answer in the Lavra monastery: much of the riches had come here to this glittering church.

I had not witnessed, as had the monks, the gradual increase in the brilliance of the service. I had just plunged from the wintry murk outside into this flaming pageant of tenth-century Byzantium. I found a seat in one of the wooden stalls, in the middle of a hundred monks, and sat there about as wide-eyed as I ever hope to be.

Brilliant as the coronation of a king, the ceremony rolled on. Two acolytes, dressed in robes of cloth of gold, brought forth a fourteen-hundred-year-old Gospel, bound in gold and adorned with pearls. From this the white-bearded Bishop, in his cope of gold and purple that had been worn on Christmas Eve throughout ten centuries, read in a chanting voice. The litany was caught up by other priests, and the reading and the response tossed back and forth across the chapel. Endlessly they repeated holy phrases beginning in quiet tones and swelling to a shout and dying off again . . .

kyrie eleison—*kyrie eleison*—KYRIE ELEISON—KYRIE
ELEISON—KYRIE ELEISON—*kyrie elesion*—kyrie eleison . . . God have mercy on our souls, over and over
again a hundred times.

At four o'clock the culmination came, for out from
under many locks and keys was brought a gold and
jewel casket containing, supposedly, a large piece of
the True Cross. The fact that the cross was found
(thanks to a vision) three hundred and fifty years after
the crucifixion, and is of the most dubious authenticity,
meant nothing to this credulous congregation. Each
holding a candle, the hundred monks formed a line and,
chanting hosannas, passed by the sacred box. And each
stopped to touch his lips to this fragment of hallowed
wood.

Dazzled as I was I did not lose sight of the most wonderful fact of all, the fact that in this ceremony I was
looking back through the ages and beholding a glimpse
of old Byzantium. The monks themselves were tenth
century, their garments, their beards and faces, their
faith, and most of all their unskeptical and childlike
minds.

On Christmas Day snow two feet deep covered the
trails, and still continued to fall. Even so I was determined to move on to the monastery of Simopetra—the
Rock of Simon, another twenty miles farther around
the sea-slopes of the great peaks. The first day we made
only ten miles, and slept that night with a hermit-monk
in his cave cut into the face of a towering cliff that
reared above the Ægean. Next day, sinking up to
our knees in snow at every step and struggling
against a storm that was developing into a blizzard, we

reached the shore below Simopetra, and saw twelve hundred feet above us the most spectacular, most audacious monastery building in the world outside Tibet.

It climbs on wings into the sky, from the pinnacle of a perpendicular rock, seeming to aspire, like the Tower of Babel, to reach the gates of Heaven. For the first hundred and fifty feet of its buttressed base there is not a single opening. Then in circles around the top are four wooden hoop-like galleries jutting out from the surface of the wall.

The other monasteries I had visited had seemed solid and immovable. This one soared and sang. Its colossal mass has heroic harmony with the rock it stands on. It commands all eyes to gaze at it—and marvel.

We followed the steep trail that zigzagged up the cliff—still beaten by the snow which had not ceased now in thirty-six hours. The monastery became more swelling and more overhanging with each new and closer view. We reached the wall. But we had to continue climbing another two hundred feet, up endless tunneled stairs and spiral passages to the reception gate.

From the highest balcony, looking down at the chasm that fell away nearly a thousand feet on two sides of us, I could half believe the legend about Simopetra's founding:

A hermit living on the rock had a vision in which he saw a monastery rising from the rock-peak. He tried to promote his vision and get the monastery built. One of the first architects to examine the possibilities of this outlandish and impossible site was accompanied by a water boy. The boy, climbing upward with his water pitcher, slipped and fell eight hundred feet . . . only to be seen five minutes later climbing back up again with his pitcher still unharmed and water-filled. It seems an angel, dressed in a monk's black gown and hat, had caught the boy as he fell and landed him like thistle-down upon the path below. This was obviously a sign from Heaven that the site had divine approval. And so Simopetra rose.

One hundred monks now live in this flying fortress, detached from the earth in fact as well as in spirit.

And for six days and nights, with my interpreter, I had no choice but to live there too. The fall of snow had been unprecedented. Every trail, either to Daphne or back to Lavra, was now completely buried. And the storm-churned sea, hurling its waves savagely against the rocky coast, made it impossible for any res-cue boat to come for me. I simply had to resign myself to being a prisoner, an involuntary monk, until the sea subsided or until the monastery's mulcteers could clear the ten miles of trail that led to the port.

This imprisonment might easily have become irksome. But on the first evening, while my clothes were drying, I had put on a monk's woolen robe. Next morning, I decided to keep it on. I had nothing to read, not being able to understand a Greek menu, much less tenth-cen-tury manuscripts. The monks were too busy praying and fasting to play with me. Out of sheer desperation I decided to adhere strictly to the routine of the monas-tic routine, asking no favors except to be allowed to work and worship beside the monks, eating only what they ate, and sleeping only when they slept. I had no hope that my many sins would be redeemed by one week

of piousness, but it would be an adventure—which was
more important.

For the first two days I was allowed to wear, along
with my robe, a monk's stiff fez-like black hat. But when
I walked on the balcony the wind snatched the hat from
my head, and carried it out of sight into the abyss—
and no angel returned it. So the monks refused to
furnish me with another. And my beard, even after
six days, was still not very flowing, merely stubby looking, so that I did not present a very holy appearance.

The hardest work I did was getting up every morning in the January weather at two A.M. and going to
religious worship for three hours. Simopetra was no
Lavra. The church, while rich and gold-plated, was
only a poor imitation of the Lavra church . . . and the
Christmas season had passed. Nor could I understand
one word of the service—partly because it was in Greek,
and partly because it was read at such breakneck, slap-
dash speed. The desire to "get it over with" seemed to
be in everyone's mind. Michael Choukas tells in his
Black Angels of Athos of asking one of the chanters
why he read so fast. "We've got some other work to
do besides reading hymns," was the answer.

This boredom, this weariness, is a sample of the
monastery's modern tendency. The old religious passion that once consumed the monks is almost dead. Their
holiness has in most cases become mere routine without
meaning, their prayers just rigmarole babbled out
mechanically.

As for the old scholarship among the monks, which
once made Athos a symbol of learning and culture, almost nothing remains, judging from my observations

at Simopetra. During the six days' visit I saw only one of my holy brothers reading—a movie magazine left behind by a previous visitor. And I was the only monk who ever went near the library. True, there was a good excuse in this particular monastery, for the books available were not very exciting, if the pictures were any indication of the texts. Simopetra had lost its original collection when fire gutted the building in 1893. The present library is less than forty years old, of little value and interest.

A number of the monks, even though they were not great scholars, were certainly great talkers. Seeing that I was more than willing to listen to any story about the Holy Mountain, the fathers turned on their endless supply. The stories which they remembered with the greatest relish, and told with the most gusto, chiefly had to do with the age-old battle to keep women from the monks and monks from the women. The narrators, animated by a bottle of wine, would chortle with glee over the success—or failure—of the people concerned, especially if the misdemeanor brought embarrassment to a rival monastery.

One story I remember, concerned two German artists who, the winter before, had been snow-bound like myself in Simopetra. Hoping to rescue them from the direction of the sea, their two adventurous wives, waiting impatiently on the mainland just beyond the frontier, hired a powerful motorboat, drove it southward along the stormy coast, dared approach the inviolable shore, and actually steered the boat in behind a small private breakwater used by the monks. There the ladies, having sounded their horn loudly to attract the attention of their husbands in the monastery above, climbed out onto the dock.

The horn caught the attention of the monks as well as the husbands, and the apparition of two females on the shore below caused unprecedented excitement and anger among the holy men. As the German painters ran recklessly down the path to greet their wives, the old Abbot, followed by a score of his black-garbed disciples, came racing after, screaming at the top of his lungs, "Throw those damned demons out! Throw those damned demons out!"

The damned demons stood their ground and got their husbands safely away.

The episode rocked Mount Athos like an earthquake.

Another damned demon who broke the law happened to be (so the story goes) a famous Queen—Elizabeth of Rumania, who died in 1916. Her country had contributed so generously to the support of the monks that she was given a special permit to land on the shore and approach the front door of one of the largest monasteries—the only woman ever to be invited to the Holy Mountain. The door was to be left open in order that she might look inside the sacred courtyard without entering.

All went well, up to a certain point. The Queen gazed for several moments into the forbidden area. Then, to the horror of the assembled monks, she suddenly walked resolutely and quickly through the doorway—just because she wanted to—into the courtyard, straight toward the entrance of the church itself— the *church*, the very heart and sanctuary of this community of godly bachelors. The monks were almost paralyzed with consternation. They couldn't seize the woman bodily—she was a Queen and their benefactress. But every step she took, further wrecked the accumulated holiness of centuries. The monastery would be cheapened and desanctified in the eyes of all the other monasteries. While the poor abbot, in despair, was frantically wondering what to do, the Queen, having seen all she cared to see, calmly walked out again, and down to her boat, and away.

For seven days and seven nights the monks of the profaned monastery didn't stop praying to God for absolution for the disgrace they had allowed to befall His sacred courtyard.

The most disconcerting of all such intrusions happened the summer before my visit. After six months it was still the subject of violent, almost physical, contention throughout the community.

In June, three young Danes came with proper passports to the peninsula to make a tour of the monasteries. Two of them were in no way conspicuous, but the third member of the party, though wearing man's attire and purporting to be a male, immediately aroused suspicion. At the first night's stop the monks looked scrutinizingly at this particular guest. Was he really a youth—or a girl in man's clothing? As the suspected visitor walked about, into the church and library and every sacred corner, the monks' alarm grew. Most of them had not seen a woman in five—ten—twenty years, and couldn't be sure whether this was one or not. The "boy" had short hair, but it was strangely soft and fine. His voice was like a girl's, and there was no sign of a beard . . . and yet the figure was a boy's figure.

The poor puzzled monks did not wish to humiliate their visitor if he *were* a boy by expelling him for being a girl. But neither did they wish to be made fools of, or to have their monastery lose caste, by sheltering what might possibly be a female. They tried every conceivable ruse, every trick, that might reveal the sex of their guest. They even set spies to watch the most intimate moments of the troublesome visitor. But the visitor was on the alert, remained as enigmatic as ever, and left the monastery before the distracted monks could come to any decision.

The excitement continued from one night's lodging to the next. It even began to precede the arrival of the three Danes. The boy-girl became the scandal, the sensation, the consternation of the entire peninsula. The battle over the sex of the girl-boy raged up and down the slopes of the peak of Athos. The monasteries where the disturbing enigma had set foot swore in self-defense it was a boy. The monasteries not so honored, in a holier-than-thou mood, swore it was a girl in disguise. As long as the Danes remained on the mountain, the monks all dropped theology and concentrated on biology.

Mount Athos still smokes with the controversy. But to this day nobody knows the truth.

Twice a day, though on holy days only once, we hundred monks gathered in the refectory for our frugal meal. Having only a small fraction of their once generous income (nearly all the monastic estates on the mainland have been taken away by the Greek Government and given to refugees from Asia Minor), the

monks must eat accordingly.   Barley soup, black bread
and salt fish—and octopus—make up the daily menu, a
menu so unvarying that had I remained in the monastery longer than I did I'm sure I would have found the
diet fatally monotonous.   Each of us had a pewter
plate and a wine mug, and a steel knife and fork.   We
stood while grace was said, before and after meals.   We
took turns serving one another.   God knows what we
talked about, once the scandal had been exhausted, for
nothing ever happened (except more snow), and no
news ever came.   Nevertheless, there was a buzz of conversation.   I spent most of my meal hours looking at
the lurid mural paintings of devils torturing sinners in
Hell's fire and of saints floating around Heaven on pink
clouds.

Changelessness.   That one word sums up the monks
and every feature of the monasteries. They have learned
nothing new and thought nothing new in ten hundred
years.   For example, the early monks did not wash
either their clothes or their bodies, and so the present
generation follows the example.   Outside the kitchen I
did not see a piece of soap in Simopetra.   But the early
monks were never sick; and, as Professor Choukas has
remarked before me, neither, apparently, are their suc-
cessors in modern times.   Nobody *ever* dies.   Modera-
tion, no work, no worry, seems to be the explanation.

Their superstitions and relic-kissings are other examples of the monks' fixed mentalities.   As a favor, on my
first day's visit, the Abbot got out from the treasury
vault the mummified foot of one saint, the skull of another, the hand of a third, the girdle of Mary Magdalen,
more splinters of the True Cross.   One is supposed to

tremble in awe before such sacredness. The monks accompanying me kissed each relic in turn, and kneeling before each, touched their foreheads three times to the ground. I was glared at threateningly because I would not, could not, do either. In fact, the whole picture of ignorance, superstition, dirty bodies, long lank hair, all groveling on the floor before boxes of ancient flesh, made me feel slightly sick.

Obviously I was not one to enjoy or appreciate monastic life. Six days of unwashed, unshaved, octopus-fed piousness had in no way profited my soul. Quite the contrary. I'll admit that when on the sixth day the trail to Daphne was open, I leaped at the chance to escape from the monastery's physical and spiritual stagnation, and seek out at once all the pagans I could find, and breathe fresh air again.

Perhaps I have given an unkind and one-sided picture of Mount Athos. Perhaps I have failed to sense the true value of holiness and solitude. Most of the men who enter the monasteries do so because they feel deeply that they will be happier in their hearts, leading a pious life, and they are accepted only after a long novitiate which tests their sincerity. But I believe my picture of the final result is generally correct. The fire, the faith, the scholarship, the spirituality, the passion for learning and teaching have, with notable exceptions, gone out of these men of God. Only dried up and sterile husks remain.

It is no wonder the peninsula fails to attract new blood. And without it, how can the Holy Community endure? Inevitably, before many years have passed, the monasteries of Athos, vigorous, commanding, magnificent for a thousand years, must close their doors for lack of occupants, and become romantic ruins like the castles on the Rhine.

When this day comes the spiritual loss will be less than negligible. But the gain to the world's knowledge of Byzantine art, learning and literature, when the hidden treasures of Athos are distributed among public museums and libraries, will be beyond computation.

But what will become of the Holy Mountain itself if it reverts to private ownership? Will Heaven blight the peninsula when this last stronghold of anti-feminism falls?

I doubt it. In all probability Mount Athos, with its unspoiled and indescribably beautiful scenery, its marble mountain and its purple seas, will develop into one of the most ideal summer resorts in Europe. Think of the girls who would come here looking for romance! Bathing beauties would animate the beach of the little port of Daphne; and lovely hostesses would bring some liveliness back to old Lavra at ten drachmas a dance. And as for that particular skyrocketing monastery where for nearly a week I prayed all night and pursued celibacy and piety and poverty all day—I'll not be surprised to see, before many Junes have passed, a rash of posters in every travel bureau, with the behest:

"Bring your brides to Simopetra for that heavenly honeymoon!"

CHAPTER XXIII

THE CITY OF THE MINOTAUR

ON REACHING Athens I found Greece on the verge of civil war. The political party led by ex-Premier Venizelos had been out of power for three years and was determined to get back again. And the opposition that happened at the moment to be in power was just as determined to go to any lengths to protect itself from being overthrown.

Venizelos himself was living in Canea, on his native island of Crete, protected by armed guards. It would be doubly interesting if I could meet him under the existing circumstances. So I wrote from Athens, asking for an audience. A response came back at once from Madame Venizelos, inviting me to Canea. Twenty-four hours later, having crossed to the island by boat, I was lunching with the greatest of living Greeks and his wife.

And all afternoon I stayed on, for never had I been so close to a revolutionary firing line. Political bombshells were already set to explode; the house was full of agents and couriers. Back in Athens a group of hired murderers, who had almost succeeded in assassinating both Venizelos and his wife just outside the capital, were at that moment being given a half-hearted trial by the government-controlled courts—a crisis which had brought the antagonism between Venizelos' followers and enemies to the boiling point.

Less than a week after my visit to Crete the explosion came. In Athens a company of anti-government guards mutinied and fought a pitched battle against loyalist troops. The whole city shook from artillery fire. In northern Greece several army corps joined the revolution. Simultaneously pro-Venizelos naval officers seized the Greek fleet and ran off with the four biggest battleships. And all this was already in the air the afternoon I spent in the grand old statesman's company. Consequently for me it was a sensational visit, made doubly so by the character of my host. With all his seventy-odd years Venizelos impressed me as the most forceful, most determined-to-rule statesman I'd ever met. And I found his own fighting qualities well matched by those of his wife, who shared with him, moreover, a deep and real appreciation of Greece's ancient greatness.

When, after tea, I was about to make my departure. Madame Venizelos asked me what else I planned to see, since I was in Crete.

"Anything else would seem a bit flat now," I suggested.

"But surely," she said, "you're not going to miss Knossos."

I looked none too comprehending.

"You know the story of King Minos' Labyrinth where Theseus killed the Minotaur, don't you?"

"Oh, of course—I've known *that* story from childhood."

"Well, it all took place at Knossos, just outside of Candia, ninety miles down the coast from here. Sir Arthur Evans has been digging there since 1900, exca-

vating the Labyrinth, and is still at work. Why don't
you go to see him?"

I did go, at once, by the next steamer. Sir Arthur
was not at home. But I saw Knossos, and felt a
double debt to my hostess back in Canea, for it was hard
to decide which I found more exciting—the Revolution
or Labyrinth.

Knossos, the site which four thousand years ago included both the palace of King Minos and the city surrounding it, is four miles inland from the port of Candia.
From a great mound of half-buried debris, Dr. Evans
has completely disentangled the original plan of the
palace-labyrinth, finding much of it still intact (even to
the paintings on the walls) and skilfully rebuilding
other parts with the original stones.

The place was almost deserted when I arrived on foot,
for in mid-winter Candia sees few visitors. Only one
caretaker was in evidence. He turned me loose to wan-
der wherever I chose through King Minos' courts and
corridors, in one of which the terrible Minotaur, half
bull and half man, had died at Theseus' hand. And as
I wandered, I tried to fit into the scene all that I had
by now learned of King Minos' superlatively romantic
history.

Crete lies where the Ægean Sea meets the Mediterranean, half way between Greece and Egypt. It is
now a poor and generally barren island, and considered
of small importance (except as Venizelos' stronghold)
by the motherland of Greece to which it has belonged
politically for forty years. But back in the remotest
ages of ancient history, long before Greece itself had

emerged from barbarism, Crete was the center of an amazing civilization. Under the leadership of Minos, its King, Crete conquered all the neighboring states, and ruled the Mediterranean with a mighty fleet. Knossos, the capital, was the greatest city in the Western world, and the royal palace the wonder of the age.

Around King Minos the Greeks of a later time built up a marvelous legend which has been handed down through the millenniums, and will continue to be told as long as our civilization, sprung from Greece and Rome, endures:

Minos was all powerful at home and successful abroad; but in his private life, according to the legend, he knew only the most bitter tragedy. First of all, his young wife, Queen Pasiphaë, who had borne him a son, Androgeos, and a daughter, Ariadne, developed an insane passion for a sacred white bull. The fruit of this relationship was a ferocious monster—the Minotaur. In an effort to keep this hideous domestic skeleton in the darkest and securest possible closet, King Minos had Dædalus, his renowned artificer, build a labyrinth so complicated that the Minotaur, once imprisoned in it, could never escape and reveal the black secret to the people of Knossos.

But hardly had Minos suppressed this private tragedy, when another arose. His son, famed for athletic prowess, had gone to Greece to contend against the barbarians in their sports. In the town of Athens he easily defeated all the local athletes in every contest. This so enraged the Athenian King, Ægeus, that he caused Androgeos to be treacherously slain.

Thirsting for revenge King Minos swept down upon

Attica with his great war fleet, ravaged the country, burnt Athens, and forced the Athenians to pay him a yearly tribute of seven maidens and seven youths. On arriving in Crete these fourteen ill-fated hostages were thrown into the Labyrinth to be devoured by the Minotaur.

Two years of this ghastly tribute had been paid. A third group was being collected in Athens, when young Theseus, the son of the guilty King Ægeus, offered himself as one of the victims, hoping to kill the Minotaur and put an end to the misery being suffered by his countrymen.

Ægeus was loath to see his only son so sacrifice himself. But Theseus, feeling he must redeem the family name, refused to yield. He asked his father to watch for the return of the hostage ship. If it came back to Athens with black sails, this would indicate that the desperate plan had failed, and that Theseus was dead. If the ship returned white-sailed, Ægeus would know that his son had conquered the monster, that the hostages had escaped, and that all was well.

Once more the fourteen maids and youths set out for Crete, where the Minoans seized them and led them straight to Knossos. There they were not fed at once to the Minotaur—King Minos, for the moment, had other plans in mind. The annual bull-fighting and bull-vaulting season was at hand, and the King decided to send the seven male Athenians into the ring as a feature of the spectacle.

Theseus fought the wild beasts sent against him with such courage that Princess Ariadne, the King's only daughter, fell in love with him. The thought of the fate awaiting Theseus made her so unhappy that she decided to risk her father's anger, and help the Greeks escape.

Into Theseus' prison-cell the Princess managed to smuggle a ball of finest thread, and a sword. The sword Theseus hid in his tunic, and the thread he unwound behind him as he and the other thirteen hostages were driven into the Labyrinth. Far away, through the dim and twisting corridors, they heard the hungry Minotaur bellowing, and they shook with terror. But when the monster rushed upon them, Theseus stabbed it to death and by following the thread back through the intricacies of the Labyrinth managed to escape. And he took with him not only his own Greeks but Ariadne as well, since she feared that if she did not follow her lover she would be slain by her father.

Sailing once more for Athens, Theseus, in his joy over the escape and in his impatience to be home again, forgot to change the sails from black to white. And King Ægeus, watching anxiously day after day for his son's returning ship, saw it at last—black-sailed. Frantic from grief and remorse he flung himself into the sea, and was drowned. From that time to this the sea has been called the Ægean.

In Knossos, King Minos' own heart was heavy too. True, the Minotaur was dead, but the manner of its death had revealed the royal family's shameful secret. And as if that were not enough, his only daughter had deserted him for the very Greeks who had murdered her brother. Such crushing events turned Minos into a tyrant. Bitter over the Minotaur scandal and hating everyone connected with it, he locked up Dædalus and his sixteen-year-old son Icarus in the Labyrinth just because Dædalus had built it.

This turned out to be a futile gesture, for Dædalus, the greatest mechanical genius of his age, turned his inventive mind to fabricating a means of escape. He had already built the city's port and bullring, and given to his countrymen a weaving machine, the plumb-line, the auger, and the carpenter's level. He had even been experimenting with *wings* of feathers and wax by which he himself could fly. Perfecting this device, he fixed wings first to Icarus' shoulders and then to his own, and together they flew out of the Labyrinth and away from Crete, high above the fleet of the despot King. Icarus, as we all know, went too close to the sun. The wax that held his wings melted, and the boy fell into the sea—the Icarian Sea. Dædalus did not come to earth till he reached Sicily, only to find that he was being pursued by King Minos who was determined to recapture the cunning fugitive.

The King of Sicily pretended to receive Minos cordially (though actually hating him and greatly admiring Dædalus) and promised to surrender the famous runaway. Pleased with his reception, Minos, weary from his long sea voyage, asked for a hot bath. A huge vat of boiling water was prepared, and into this the Sicilian King's three daughters pushed their royal guest and scalded him to death.

This legend is one of the immortal stories of the world. Theseus, in succeeding generations, became the foremost hero to the Athenians who never tired of telling the story in poetry, in song, in marble and bronze. The alleged hostage ship in which Theseus was said to have returned, black-sailed, from Crete, his grateful countrymen preserved as a national relic for centuries. On dozens of Greek vases seen today in the Athens museum, one finds pictures of the famous combat—man and Minotaur. School children, for four thousand years, have been told the story and never forgotten it. In my own childhood I was one of these.

And yet this glorious legend was merely grouped in the general collection of fabulous Greek myths, along with the stories about the gods on Mount Olympus. The Labyrinth was supposed to be as fanciful as the flying feats of Dædalus, and the love affair of Queen Pasiphaë. No great Cretan metropolis, such as tradition described, had come to light. The entire story was remembered as a marvelous fairy tale.

And then, in 1900, Sir Arthur Evans, the British archeologist, came upon a huge mound near the present city of Candia. It was covered by trees and small farms. Even so, to Evans it looked suspiciously man-made. He bought the mound, dug furiously into it with a hundred laborers, cleared off twenty feet of earth and rubbish— and behold!—the foundations and walls of a colossal palace such as only a great and civilized king could have built and occupied! As the excavations spread, the size and complexity of the palace unfolded; corridors and courts, various levels, secret passages, water tunnels, hidden entrances. And still standing in the Throne Room was a great Double-Axe, known to be a sacred emblem of the Minoan religion corresponding to the Cross in Christian countries of today.

The Greek name of the Double-Axe symbol is *Labrys,* a word come down to us in the form of Labyrinth. The connection between this name and the intricate plan of the palace led Dr. Evans to write that "there can be little remaining doubt that the vast edifice which we call the Palace of Minos is one and the same as the traditional Labyrinth. A great part of the ground plan, with its long halls and blind galleries, its tortuous passages, its bewildering system of small chambers, does in fact present many of the characteristics of a maze." *

The Theseus story, on the announcement of this discovery, began to shift from the realm of fancy to the realm of fact. . . . And Dr. Evans, with increasing excitement, dug farther. He next found that a city large enough to shelter a hundred thousand people surrounded the palace. But nowhere could he find the city's walls. That failure only gave further proof that this was Knossos, for it is known that King Minos depended for defense entirely on his "wooden walls"—his warships. His fleet ruled the Mediterranean, and no enemies, so he reasoned, could even land on the island.

Nor did they, for centuries. Then, about 1400 B.C. a storm destroyed the fleet, or a race of superior seamen overcame it, and Knossos was left defenseless. Enemies poured in, and pulled the mighty palace to the ground. For centuries more the ruins remained uninhabited, as they were considered haunted. Sand and debris slowly covered the site, buried the urns, statues, coins, jewelry, the storehouses and theaters and baths, the Throne Room with the sacred Labrys, and preserved them all

---

* From *The Palace of Minos*, by Sir Arthur Evans. Used by permission of The Macmillan Company, publishers.

for *thirty-three hundred years,* until Dr. Evans unveiled them again at the beginning of this century.

To reach King Minos' palace I had followed, out from Candia, the oldest road in Europe, a road used for fourteen hundred years before the founding of Rome, the road along which Theseus was led from Candia Harbor, and along which he fled with Ariadne. Unearthed along with Knossos—it, too, was hidden beneath twenty feet of soil—the flagstone pavement was discovered to be in excellent condition. But the archeologists were surprised to find the harbor highway only four feet wide, until they remembered that horses were unknown in King Minos' capital. Everybody walked or was carried in a palanquin, so that a four-foot road was wide enough.

On reaching the palace itself I soon realized what an enormous amount of care and labor Dr. Evans had put into its reconstruction. Dozens of the curious Minoan columns, bigger at the top than at the bottom, now stand in place again. The more important rooms are all walled and roofed. On every side one is reminded of the Minotaur, for bulls were the favorite subjects of Minoan artists and sculptors. Bronze bulls, stone bulls, painted bulls, carved bulls, dominate the scene. Rows of huge bulls' horns made of stone line the balustrades and rise from the cornices. Elaborate wall paintings indicate that bull-fighting and bull-vaulting were the favorite sports of the people of Knossos.

With all this resurrected testimony of ancient power and glory surrounding one, no special imagination is necessary to visualize the vast palace as it was—magnificently built, splashed with color and animated by King Minos' highly civilized subjects.

To me, one of the most interesting features of the huge building was the olive oil storehouse. It consisted of twenty parallel subterranean lanes filled with enormous earthenware jars six to nine feet high. There must be *two hundred* of these giant jars still intact, indicating that olive oil was the chief item of commerce and the chief source of income for the Minoan princes. Considering the tons upon tons of oil stored in the palace at the time it was pulled down and burned, the wonder is that with such quantities of fuel for the fire, anything survived the conflagration.

Every visitor who comes to Knossos is impressed by the superb frescoes. One, the most famous of all, represents a Minoan Priest-King walking through a garden of fleurs de lis. His figure is moulded in the classic Minoan ideal, massive shoulders, waist so abnormally slender as to appear almost deformed, and long graceful legs. From his crown, peacock feathers wave; around his throat is a necklace of white flowers. And all about him are the butterflies of a Minoan paradise.

The colors of this picture are as bright as they were four thousand years ago. The fleurs de lis are still purple, the Priest-King's eye still bright, the breeze still blows through the tall green flower stems.

On another wall I found a perfect portrait of a Knossos debutante. She wears a fashionable hair-dress with a small curl trickling over her forehead. At the back of her head is bunched a loose knot of ribbon that

was undoubtedly the last word in style in the year she
"came out." Her lips are cherry red, and obviously
plastered with rouge. She has heavily penciled eyes.
Yet you have the feeling that despite her fancy make-up
she's no dumbbell, but a smart and altogether modern
gal, and something of a beauty, too.

Last of all, I found the Throne Room.

Only twenty-five feet square, this room rather re-
sembles a council chamber. The walls on three sides
are covered with brilliant frescoes of pink griffins (*pink*
after four thousand years!), fabulous creatures half
lion, half bird. And placed close to one wall is the
high-backed stone throne of King Minos himself. No
more ancient throne exists in Europe, or perhaps in the
world—forty centuries old. It was the seat of kings at
a time as long before the birth of Christ as our present
date is Anno Domini; then buried amid the ruins of
Knossos for thirty-three hundred years, and brought to
light again just yesterday.

The throne is carved from a single block of gypsum,
not unlike alabaster. It looked more delicate than it is.
I touched it with my hand. It was immovable. I
tried sitting down upon its hard stone seat and leaning
against the high stone back. Perhaps it was the long
walk out from Candia, but I found the throne exceed-
ingly comfortable. Sitting there was in no way out of
order, for nothing could have been more proof against
damage than this durable block of rock. And so, for
a few moments, waiting for the winter rain to slacken
outside, I continued to rest there.

What marvelous scenes this room had witnessed, what
immortal heroes had stood arm's length away!

Seated on this throne, the King had directed his ministers and his admirals, and had governed his people, and made his empire a great power in the world. Seated on this throne he heard the news that his wife, Queen Pasiphaë, had given birth to a monster, half man and half beast.

Here too word had come of how his son was slain by the jealous King of Athens. And from here he ordered his captains to assemble the fleet in order that he might ravage Attica in revenge.

In this room he had inspected three shipments of the fourteen Athenian hostages, and ordered them fed to his wife's voracious offspring. Here, perhaps, Ariadne had first seen Theseus.

While seated on this throne King Minos heard that Theseus had killed the Minotaur, and escaped, and carried off the faithless Princess. Here, in that moment, the King's soul turned to vinegar, his benevolent reign to tyranny.

And when he learned that his famous artificer had flown away on wings, it was from this very throne that the King rose up, swearing that he would bring Dædalus back—and set out in pursuit—and never returned.

Outside, in the Great Court, the rain had ceased, and the early winter night was approaching. At this hour, in ancient days, the Minotaur would have been bellowing in the depths of the palace for his supper, and the King would have been leaving his throne, followed by his courtiers, to prepare for the evening's banquet.

I rose to depart also, from the Throne Room, from

the palace, and from Knossos, where the myths began to seem almost too real in the half-shadowy solitude. Once more I found the ancient flagstoned harbor road and followed it back to Candia, as it wound through four thousand years of Cretan history, down to the Ægean Sea.

CHAPTER XXIV

THE DEADLIEST SPORT IN HISTORY

WE MODERN Americans like to think of ourselves as having tried every sport, old or new, that can offer a new thrill to our souls and bodies. Skiing, gliding, bronco-busting, bob-sledding, auto-racing, stunt-flying, and a hundred more—we have mastered them all. But anyone who visits the ruins of Knossos will soon learn that in comparison with the sensational sports the ancient Cretans enjoyed, our own seem like so much knitting.

There is no American athlete today, nor athlete of any other country, capable of standing directly in the path of a charging two-thousand-pound bull, waiting for the beast to lower its head to gore him, then seizing the horns, and as the bull tosses its head in fury, doing a backward somersault over the animal's neck, to land right side up on the galloping haunches—all executed at full speed.

But this was the national sport of the subjects of King Minos. Nor did they have any sort of protection whatsoever—no sword, no shin-guards, no horn-proof corselet, not even a red cloak. Just their two hands, and eyes quick as lightning, and superhuman agility, and the courage of demons. And if any harm came to the bull, the toreador was expelled from the ring! What's more, the toreadors were as frequently women as men.

This sport, which for danger and difficulty has never been matched before or since, until recent times was not even known to have existed. The Romans with all their inventiveness for gladiatorial contests and animal spectacles, never thought of trying this one, for it never occurred to them that it was humanly possible.

We are indebted to the archeologists for revealing to us this spectacular daredeviltry, popular in Knossos around 2000 B.C. Evidence that it *was* popular is all over the place, in complete detail—on the walls, on vases, in the statuary, even in the carvings of precious gems. It is perfectly clear that the Minoans took a great delight in this particular form of bull-baiting.

Lacking horses and possessing a magnificent breed of cattle, the young people of Knossos were forced to concentrate on bulls for sport. The uncovered ruins have brought to light the most graphic representations of every possible form of contest between bulls and men: youths roping wild bulls with lariats, fighting them with nets, wrestling with them, in rodeos just like ours.

But it was the bull-vaulting that gave Minoan sportsmen their supreme thrill. And the spectacle found no less favor among artists. Thanks to them (and to Dr. Evans' spade) we know everything that can be known about this desperately dangerous game.

One particular, brightly colored picture painted on plaster, called the *Toreador Fresco,* tells the whole story.

The picture is about three feet long, and portrays a charging bull and three toreadors, each human figure

being about a foot high. Of the performers, two are
women. Though these two are dressed much like men,
their sex is emphasized by the jewelry they wear, the
curls across their forehead, and by the whiteness of their
skin in contrast to the dark red skin that always char-
acterizes a man in Minoan art. Nor is it in this fresco
alone, but in numerous others also, that we learn how
frequently women took part in the suicidal sport.

In this picture we are looking into the arena at
Knossos. With all the city watching, the toreadors
stand, almost naked, and calmly wait as a huge bull
charges at them. Then as the beast lunges forward to
impale its victim, one toreador, instead of leaping aside
as is done in Spanish bull-fights, seizes the flying horns
and raises himself to a hand-stand upon them. As the
bull tosses its head upward, the toreador is lifted from
the ground and does a complete backward spin, heels
over head, landing feet first on the bull's body. The
acrobat then jumps—or does another somersault—over
the animal's tail onto the ground where a second performer stands with outstretched arms to catch the tumbling figure when he lands, feet first, on the ground.

In the fresco we see the performer, still in the air, up-
side down over the bull's back. And ready to catch him
is one of the girls. The other girl has seized the onrush-
ing horns, and is at the point of making the somersault
in the same manner as the boy.

The fact that as many girls as men entered the bullring indicates that skill in bull-vaulting did not depend
on strength but on timing and speed and agility, with
which the girls were as gifted as the boys.

Unquestionably there must have been many frightful

accidents, for the horns of all the Minoan bulls were like long daggers sticking straight out from their heads. One smallest mistake, one mistiming, and the toreador would be overturned and ripped open by the enraged animal. That the unprotected vaulters were often gored to death, the records of Minoan art prove. There are vases showing the toreador-girl who has missed her grasp, impaled on the uplifted horns with the points piercing her back and protruding through her stomach. On carved stones are pictures of a youth lying between the bull's front feet where he is being gored and trampled.

Because of the frequency of fatalities each bull-vaulting team, consisting of three performers, was kept apart from the other teams and prohibited from watching them in action, lest they be unnerved by seeing one of their fellows torn to pieces. This bloodshed, however, as in the modern bull-fights, was part of the show. It was a dull day indeed if at least one girl vaulter was not disemboweled before the eyes of the grandstand.

Modern rodeo champions have stated flatly to Dr. Evans that the Minoan bull-vaulting feat transcends human ability, that it is now, and always has been, physically impossible; that no acrobat however agile and daring could have had eyes quick enough and feet sure enough to seize the bull at just the right split second; and that the terrible impact of a two-thousand-pound animal rushing at a man, head on, would prevent him from keeping any semblance of balance.

Nevertheless, no matter how suicidal the feat seems to us, the Minoans definitely accomplished it. The details are too minutely, too graphically and too fre-

quently found among the ruins of Knossos for the sport
to be merely an artistic convention.

While bull-roping, bull-fighting, and bull-wrestling
could be enjoyed by everyone, bull-vaulting itself was a
sport indulged in exclusively by the nobility. In this
most dangerous game of them all only young Minoans
of the highest social rank could participate. The fash-
ionably curled locks, the elegance of the ornamented
loin-cloth and the jewels worn by both sexes of toreadors, reveal gentle birth.

Not only have the excavations at Knossos given us
a perfect picture of the contests in a Minoan arena, but
also a picture of the spectators in the grandstands. The
crowds there did not hesitate to demonstrate vehemently
their approval or disapproval. Everyone in Knossos
knew the fine points of the sport, for bull-vaulting was
of ancient origin and had been developed through generations. Many attending the games had been toreadors
themselves. Consequently a bungle, any sign of cow-
ardice, any evidence of inexpertness, brought down
jeers from thousands of voices.

One beautiful and brilliant fresco depicts the arena's
royal box in which the first row is filled entirely with
noble ladies. How human they appear, dressed in their
flounced skirts and puffed sleeves! In 1900 when the
fresco was unearthed, the latest Paris style in women's
clothes was such a perfect reproduction of this four-
thousand-year-old costume that the discovery caused a
sensation among the couturiers.

The ladies in the box, obviously, are taking advantage of this social gathering to talk scandal, to gossip
about parties and styles and flirtations. You can see

it in their eyes and attitudes. Yet below them, in the arena, we know that bull-vaulters of their own class and own sex are being impaled upon the gilded horns and dying in horrible agony.

Comparison has often been made between Spanish and Cretan bull-fighting. Scholars have tried to trace the Spanish *corrida* back to a Minoan origin. But actually they have little in common. The Spanish system, as Dr. Evans notes, is to exhaust the bull's energy and finally kill him, whereas in ancient Crete any toreador who caused a bull to fall, or in any way injure itself, was in disgrace. In Spain the bull-fighter has every advantage—in Crete all the advantage was the bull's.

If there are any athletes in America who suffer from ennui because there are no more sports to conquer, or if any rodeo cowboy feels he needs a new sensation to rouse fresh response from the public, I suggest that they stand, unprotected and empty-handed, in the paths of charging, murder-minded bulls, and do back-flips over the tossing horns. And if they lose enthusiasm for this feat as the furious beast plunges down upon them, let them take courage in remembering that this was the favorite pastime for fashionable young ladies of Knossos, forty centuries ago.

CHAPTER XXV

HORROR ISLAND

OFF the coast of Crete, near its eastern end, lies a small island called Spinalonga, upon which the Venetians of the Middle Ages built one of the most complete and beautiful little cities to be found in the Mediterranean basin. But today, though this island-city is still more or less intact, and still beautiful, it has gained such a sinister reputation among Greeks that they speak of it in fearful whispers, and cross themselves whenever its name is mentioned. No Cretan would consider accompanying me there; and once I had made the journey alone, and returned to Candia, people shrank from me when I confessed where I had been.

Their fear and their revulsion I can fully understand, since I myself, for several nights after setting foot on that evil place, suffered from nightmares.

In my sleep I saw people with hideously disfigured faces grimacing at me; I saw blind men crying piteously to be led; I saw women with both hands missing, trying to wrap their rags about them with their raw stumps. I saw ghost-like figures completely hairless, with skin as white as this sheet of paper, sitting motionless, like corpses propped up in the sun. I saw specters with noses eaten away, breathing through artificial tubes protruding from their lungs, and making a sighing whistle-sound whenever they exhaled . . . the sickening music of this orchestra pursued me in my dreams. I saw three hundred damned souls, imprisoned, though they were innocent; shunned, though they were helpless; waiting for a merciful death to come and release them from this horror island, from Spinalonga, the habitation of the lepers.

Back in Canea I had first heard about Spinalonga from Madame Venizelos. At the moment of my departure from her house, after she had urged me to visit Knossos, she had added that I might be interested in seeing Spinalonga too. She told me a little about its beauty, and its misery, and of the charitable work she was trying to do among the lepers to mitigate their helpless lives. She personally had been collecting books and games to send them, and hoped soon to install a radio, to give them once more a link with the world. I promised her I would go to the island, and write a story about it for the Athens papers, in an effort to help her bring the tragic situation there to the attention of the Greek public.

And I kept my promise, and spent one long and heart-sickening day with these three hundred pitiful victims of humanity's cruelest and most horrible disease.

Greece has gathered up all the lepers within her borders and sent them, regardless of family ties, of social position, of age, sex or color, to Spinalonga. It is a one-way traffic, for the leprosy-cures lately effected elsewhere have not yet been tried successfully here. About fifty new prisoners arrive each year, and each year fifty die. The average length of life is about six years.

This was by no means the first leper asylum I had

seen. Anyone traveling in India, China or the Pacific islands, learns to accept the disease as commonplace. (There are today over *three million* lepers in the world.) But the concentrated anguish, the hideous evil existing in the midst of the beautiful and romantic Venetian setting of Spinalonga, will make the Greek colony stand out in my memory always. And (though this is an uncharitable reaction) the fact that the lepers in Greece are of a Western race like oneself makes their condition seem particularly disturbing.

On my journey from Candia to the island I accompanied one of the newly condemned men and his guard. A motorbus had taken me to a little port at the eastern end of Crete. From there to reach Spinalonga I had to travel in a public launch down the coast another ten miles. Aboard this launch was the leper, a simple young peasant from a village near Mt. Olympus.

The diseased man had been suffering several years before the district medical authorities found out., Leprosy inflicts no pain and in the early stages causes no special inconvenience. He had gone about his work in a normal way, paying no attention to the raw spots slowly growing on his hands and face. This continued until his appearance became so frightful that children ran from him in terror. Then he was seized, separated from the only associations he knew, and led off to Spinalonga.

And now the last stage of the last journey was before him. His head and hands swathed in bandages, he sat listlessly, unconscious of the glorious snow-clad mountain range behind him, or the dancing sun-shot waves beneath. Primitive and passive though he was, he realized now that he was an outcast, a pariah, to be imprisoned away from society and left upon a little island to rot slowly and relentlessly away.

Unclean! Unclean!—the leper's cry of despair that has been heard in Eastern countries from prehistoric times. In Babylon, in Egypt, in Palestine, in Greece and Rome, there has always been the same cruel intolerance and persecution of those who suffered with this hideous malady. No aid or sympathy was ever given them. Regardless of their station they were driven outside the city walls to starve and beg. And if a stranger unwittingly approach too close to them, they must announce their untouchable state—unclean! One of the very rare instances of charity toward a leper is recorded in Biblical history: "And, behold, there came to Jesus a leper and worshiped Him, saying, Lord, if thou wilt, thou canst make me clean. And Jesus put forth his hand, and touched him, saying, I will; be thou clean. And immediately his leprosy was cleansed."

Our launch sped on. Presently we rounded the corner of a promontory and saw rising abruptly before us the infamous island, one thousand feet long, five hundred wide, and one hundred high.

Whatever stories I had heard about Spinalonga along the way, had emphasized its horrors and told nothing about its striking beauty. The Venetians seem to have been incapable of building anything that was not beautiful—and their houses still cover the island. They also built a great wall around it at the water's edge, to protect the city against every attack. With Spinalonga as a base their ships dominated the eastern end of the Mediterranean, and brought there the riches of the

East. As the city prospered rich dwellings rose in tiers up the steep rock slopes, huge stone battlements frowned out upon the open ocean, and a castle and church rested close behind them. Probably fifteen thousand people inhabited the islet in its great days during the fifteenth century.

But when, about 1670, Crete finally fell before the Turkish onslaughts, Spinalonga fell too, and all the inhabitants deserted it. Since then many of its houses have crumbled, though many still remained intact when in 1890, Greece decided to repopulate it with her lepers.

This then, this Venetian sea-fortress, was where the unhappy launch-passenger and I landed.

I was prepared to see horrible sights—but not prepared enough. As our boat touched the dock three snow-white men, their beards, hair and eyebrows missing, caught our gunwale with a hooked pole. Their skin was unbroken, but nothing could have been more repellent than its ghastly color. A person first meeting them in the dark might well have died of fright straight off, for no imaginary ghost was ever as ghostly white as these three lepers.

The newcomer climbed ashore to greet his fellow victims, to see how horrifying leprosy can become, how horrifying he himself would some day look.

I walked through the beautiful Renaissance gateway, and found a group of inmates seated in the tiny square. I hardly could believe that human beings could be so disfigured, yet live. One man's face, lips and ears were so swollen he no longer had a human aspect. Another held a cup of tea between fingerless hands. Another whistled through the artificial breathing tube.

Sea-sick and a little faint, I looked away from this tableau of horrors, and moved on down the ancient street. I came to the outdoor café and found a dozen prisoners, drinking beer and being served by two of the living snow-men. As in every group there were two or three whose affliction was scarcely noticeable, who would easily have passed, unsuspected, in the world outside. I wondered how they, who seemed more or less normal, could endure the constant company, year after year, of their foul and pestilential comrades whose disease was more advanced. The answer was that their own clean appearance would not last long. One year, two years, and the diabolical corrosion would creep across their faces, and leave them horribly white, or swollen into knots.

And women—there were women too, and children; one woman for each three men. Mutilated and distorted, they dragged themselves about their little Venetian houses, trying to cook meals for their menfolk. Many of the women had become so gruesome in appearance I could not bear to look at them. One woman, ill with the white variety, put her ghastly, completely hairless head suddenly out a window as I passed . . . and at the sight my own blood ran cold.

There is no attempt at segregation. Every person in Spinalonga has the same disease except the guards, the doctor and the priest. Everybody is slowly dying from it—there is no escape. Nothing that the medical department has done seems to check it. Like a rust, its progress is imperceptibly slow but inexorably sure.

If a man and woman wish to marry, and have children, it is permitted. Indeed over one hundred chil-

dren have been born on Spinalonga in the last twenty
years. It would seem a criminal offense against the
child, to give it birth with such an inheritance. But
strange to say, oftener than otherwise, the child—if removed to a healthful atmosphere at once—grows to
maturity *entirely uninfected*. This is not always the
case, however. Sometimes a child of lepers does inherit
or contract the fatal germ—and back to Spinalonga he
must go, the most horrible of homecomings.

The fact that the offspring of lepers so frequently escape the disease, only adds confusion to the understanding of it. Is leprosy inherited? Is it contagious?
Where does it come from? People have worked closely
with lepers for a life time—and died of old age. Others,
so exposed, have caught it in short order and joined the
awful procession.

In Hawaii, the Philippines, and in the British hospitals in Palestine, the age-old enigma of this disease
has been partly solved. Taken in time, cases of leprosy
have been definitely healed . . . after three thousand
years of study. Doctors have always known this much:
that leprosy and squalor generally go hand in hand.
Soap and sunshine are its deadly enemies. Of the three
hundred victims on the island fully nine-tenths had been
living in the most primitive and unhygienic conditions
when infected.

But not always. One leper I talked with spoke excellent English, having worked ten years in America.
It was in New York that his "health began to fail," he
told me. His face swelled, his hands would not heal.
Perhaps the cold climate was to blame. Perhaps his
own Greek sun and wine would cure him. So he re-

turned home, and sat in the sun for days. Still
his ulcers spread. He visited a doctor . . . he's been
four years now on Spinalonga. His eyesight and his
hands are gone, his voice weak and tired. "I have
only another year," he said. "I've chosen my grave.
From it you have a nice view of the sea."

In the forty-five years since lepers have been sent to
the island, not one has tried to escape. The rowboats
to the mainland are carefully guarded; it's over half a
mile to swim. And once ashore only barren and uninhabited mountains face the runaways. Also they have
no money. But more discouraging than these things is
the attitude of anyone to whom the leper might apply
for help. If his disease were obvious he would be
shunned. If it were not obvious, his own sense of shame
would be so strong that he would probably shrink from
any helping hand with a cry of *"Unclean,"* just like the
ancient victims. And if he got home again he would
only be shipped back a second time. On first arrival
the lepers think about escape, but as their strength fades,
as they see themselves growing slowly more and more
hideous, they lose interest. Their desire becomes *not* to
live with healthy men, but to hide in the deepest shadow
of their prison house.

No lepers on Spinalonga are cold or hungry, both of
which they probably were in their own homes. The
Greek Government gives them twenty-five cents a day
for food, which in Crete is enough. And as for shelter
there are more lovely old Venetian houses standing than
there are people to occupy them.

Still wandering up and down the partly ruined
stair-stepped streets, I could not help comparing the

scenes that once animated them with the scenes one witnesses today. In the sixteenth century, when Venice
held sway here, rows upon rows of bright-hued galleys
lined the water front. Merchants in velvet cloaks,
women in embroidered farthingales, soldiers wearing
shining breast-plates, happy children; silks and silver-
wear from Syria, dates and oranges from Egypt, wine
from Italy, marble statues from the mainland of Greece,
and fifteen thousand people buying and selling and enjoying this luxury, all filled the streets with life and
laughter.

And now, even the houses that still stand seem as
leprous as the people, for many of the roofs have fallen
in, there are holes in the walls, and patches of white
lime show on their scarred faces. In the old Venetian
shops leprous hands sell cheap and scanty merchandise.
The great ladies are disfigured now, and noseless. The
streets are still as death, for of the three hundred inhabitants who live in the ghostly city fully half are unable to leave their beds. Those who do appear on the
streets move so slowly, so painfully, they scarcely break
the tomb-like hush that prevails; the eerie sigh of their
breathing-tubes is almost the only sound. In Venetian
times all streets led to the harbor, to the ships, to the
wide world. But now they lead only to the grave.

Standing before one of the island's houses, examin-
ing its carved façade, I was approached by the most
neatly dressed Spinalongan I'd seen. Marks of leprosy
were clearly evident upon his face, but not in an advanced stage. To my surprise he spoke to me in French,
and seemed to have pleasant manners.

"Do you like our happy little city?" he asked.

"It must be a bit dull—for you," I answered, sensing his superiority to his fellow prisoners. "Have you anything to read?"

"Only the books Madame Venizelos sends. But my eyes are already so weak, reading is painful. This is especially hard to bear—I was a student in the Athens University."

When I expressed surprise he told me his story. He had been studying law, and was in the best of health, when his face began to break out in swollen patches and his knuckles to grow stiff. The shock almost killed him when he learned the truth. He had never seen anyone or known anyone who had the disease. Even so, the age-old feeling of "unclean" came upon him. He loathed the thought of Spinalonga, but he loathed much more the necessity of having to shrink from the "clean" world. He came here unresistingly, and cut himself off from his friends. He allowed no members of his family to visit him lest they be made miserable by seeing the horrors he had to live with.

"I try not to think," he said, "try not to remember. The doctors took a special interest in my case when I first arrived. They tried everything they knew for me. But nothing has helped. They've become indifferent now. I realize what I must look like, and be like, someday—but by then I hope my mind too will be so feeble I shan't care."

"But don't you want me to show you the island?" he said suddenly changing the subject. "It must be beautiful to a stranger."

First of all my escort took me to the chapel, Venetian-built. The Greek orthodox lepers have a "clean" priest officiating here who baptizes them, and marries them, and buries them. About forty lepers attend his services on Sunday: a congregation of mutilated, ulcerous, revolting figures, who try to believe that having suffered such hell in this life, they surely will attain salvation in the next.

With the law-student I next climbed to the topmost rampart of the great stone fort from which Venetian cannon had often fired upon Turkish pirates. Carved in the middle of the fortress-wall I found a huge Lion of St. Mark still standing defiant in the midst of the degradation into which the once-proud city had fallen. As we rested on the parapet, surveying all about us the magnificent panorama of sea and snowy mountains, the launch bell rang in the harbor below, summoning me back to a happier world. The student, to say good-by, put out his hand to shake mine. There was a painful silence . . . but rather than see the friendly fellow drop his eyes in shame, I stifled my repugnance and clasped his outstretched hand.

As I walked down to the dock again, some twenty of the lepers followed close behind. Visitors were so few and far between; and it gave them a mild excitement to see other men departing; since they could not. They hobbled, limped, groped their way through the entrance gate and onto the end of the pier. And there they stood—the most cursed, the most ghastly sight one could possibly behold. How could anyone comfort them? What could I do for them other than leave money? I couldn't think of anything except to wave my hat feebly as the launch rushed out to sea. And then I saw the twenty lepers turn, and hobble, limp and grope their way back through the beautiful Venetian gate. Above this gate, in large letters, I had seen the name of an imperial Venetian Doge carved in stone. But to these living dead-men now passing painfully beneath that portal, those letters spelled out the terrible sentence: *All hope abandon, ye who enter here.*

That these conditions should endure indefinitely at Spinalonga is unthinkable. American doctors in charge of the Philippine and Hawaiian leper asylums are curing the disease right along. Of the four thousand patients who have entered the Manila colony, over six hundred have been discharged. Chaulmoogra oil, the known remedy for the ancient curse, is being adopted, however slowly, on the Cretan islet. I like to believe that Spinalonga, as a pest-house, has served its day, that in another decade the sense of doom will be dispelled, and above the gateway will be engraved for future sufferers to read: *Leper—do NOT abandon hope—Here shalt thou be made clean.*

CHAPTER XXVI

"AND Salome, the daughter of Herodias, came in and danced, and pleased Herod. And the king said unto the damsel, Ask of me whatsoever thou wilt, and I will give it thee.

"And she went forth, and said unto her mother, What shall I ask? And she said, The head of John the Baptist.

"And immediately the king sent an executioner, and commanded the head to be brought.

"And he brought the head and gave it to the damsel: and the damsel gave it to her mother."

This story of Salome, as told by St. Mark and St. Matthew, I underlined in a copy of the New Testament, as I sat on the deck of a ship sailing on eastward through the Mediterranean from Crete to the Holy Land.

Three times in previous years I had enjoyed long visits in Palestine. But since the last visit, I had developed a new and special interest in one feature of its past which I had overlooked before. I intended, this time, to go to Machærus, the site of the castle of King Herod Antipas, the castle where Salome danced the most famous dance in history and received as a reward the head of John the Baptist.

Throughout Christian countries there are few stories
better known than that of Salome. It has been unfail-
ingly popular with artists and preachers since Christianity began. No doubt I learned it first from the
huge and somewhat lurid picture-Bible that was a
cornerstone of my grandparents' house. Since then innumerable paintings, plays and ballets dealing with the
subject had elaborated the meager Biblical account and
increased my interest. But above all I had been impressed by Strauss' opera, *Salome,* given at the Metro-
politan not long before my departure from New York.

Salome's deplorable reputation had drawn such
crowds to the opera-house that police reserves were
called to control the jam. Fortunately I had bought
a ticket days in advance, and had a splendid seat.
The performance was not flawless; the full moon kept
slipping from place in the canvas night-sky, and the
large Scandinavian soprano who sang Salome's part
superbly was more grotesque than enticing during her
dance. Nevertheless the thrilling story surged forward
irresistibly to its gruesome climax on the waves of music.
I sat enthralled as Salome, swathed with veils, appeared
in the banquet hall to dance; as Herod, in an ecstasy of
delight, made his reckless offer; as Herodias, hating and
fearing John's loud denunciation of her private life,
prompted her daughter to demand his head; as the black
giant, with curved scimitar and silver charger, disappeared down into the dungeon. . . . A moment of dramatic suspense while the orchestra rasped out a sawing
sound . . . and then we saw the charger slowly rising
out of the pit, lifted up by the executioner's huge black
arm, bearing the horrible gift Salome had asked for.

On the way home that night after the opera, I began to ask myself exactly *where* this bloody chapter from Biblical history had taken place. Could one go and explore the spot today? What was there left to see of the palace and the prison? Why was it that during all the months I had spent in Jerusalem, mixing continually with students of religious history, I never had heard one of them mention the name of the place where Herod's drama-drenched palace had stood; nor met, so far as I knew, anyone who had been there?

Next morning I went to the library in an effort to learn, from authoritative books on Biblical geography and archeology, the answers to these questions.

And what I found astonished me. I found that the scene of this sensational episode was perfectly well known—the tip-top of a terrible, lonely mountain peak, one of the highest in the Holy Land, hanging cut off from the world, four thousand feet above the Dead Sea. And I found that the name of the castle, and the ancient city around it, was Machærus; that the ruins are still very much in evidence; and that the dungeon which was in all probability John's execution chamber, is intact today. I was particularly indebted to H. V. Morton's *In the Steps of the Master* for enlightenment on this subject.

I learned however that despite all these tangible remains of the castle, hardly one foreigner a year, out of the hundreds of thousands who visit the Holy Land and seek out its storied ruins from Dan to Beersheba, ever goes to Machærus.

The explanation for this neglect is simple: Though Machærus is only twenty-five miles from Jerusalem as the angels fly, it is the most inaccessible of all the historical sites in Palestine. One needs several days, special military permission, an armed escort, considerable physical endurance and mountain-climbing skill, to reach the banquet hall where Salome danced, and the cell where John was slain.

Herod Antipas, son of Herod the Great, inherited from his father, as the historian Josephus tells, among other legacies the crown of Moab, a rather barren state bordering the east bank of the Dead Sea, today a part of Trans-Jordania. Always fearful for his life in those violent times, Herod Antipas built for himself, at about the time of the birth of Christ, a strong citadel on the pinnacle of the highest and wildest mountain he could find along the Dead Sea's eastern ramparts. Close by, he also raised a palace and a town. The citadel later came to be called in Arabic *El Mashnaka,* the Hanging Place. No name could be more appropriate, for the mountain stronghold is indeed poised on the edge of an abyss almost as deep and awesome as the Grand Canyon.

The chief features of this lofty refuge were several enormous towers, each two hundred feet high, which rose from the topmost rocks. From those towers Herod could look across the vast blue void that fell away below him, across the mountains on the other side, and see, fifteen miles beyond them, the domes of Jerusalem silhouetted against the horizon. From the Mount of Olives, just outside Jerusalem, the towers were clearly visible in return. Today, however, they have disappeared.

Absorbed with my new interest in the story, I reached

Jerusalem from Crete late on an afternoon, and went at
once to climb the Mount of Olives, to locate the Hanging Place. When I reached the crest of the hill, the sun
was low in the west, sending its level rays full upon the
mountains of Moab that rose in the east, straight across
the dark shadows of the Dead Sea's bottomless chasm.
And there, soaring higher, glowing more brightly than
the other pinnacles, was Machærus.

But to get there was another matter.

I had to take a motorcar through Jericho, cross the
Jordan, and travel deep into Trans-Jordania; spend the
night at Amman, and continue on south across the dreary
hills and canyons of Moab, back toward the shores of
the Dead Sea—one hundred and fifty miles to reach a
point twenty-five miles away from my Jerusalem hotel.

The last ten miles I had to scale precipitous cliffs,
upward from the depths of the Dead Sea depression.
My Arab soldier-guide and I had horses, but riding was
impossible, so we climbed on foot and pulled the horses
after us.

As I clambered over the rocks, where the road has disappeared centuries ago, I looked up ahead at the barricades we had yet to conquer, and behind into the
chasms from which we were ascending. And I wondered why on earth Herod chose this fearful and desolate mountain top for his residence. No doubt he felt
more secure in such an impregnable position. No doubt
it gave him great satisfaction to be able to look down
upon his enemies and rivals in Jerusalem. Also, he
must have loved the sensational drop into the Dead Sea,
four-fifths of a mile below his terraces.

There is still another likely reason why Herod chose

this place. He was probably a victim of the afflictions
that penalize a debauched life, and would certainly have
sought relief in the hot sulphur springs which gush out
of the canyon near the foot of the mountain. One
spring, big as a river, leaps half-hidden in sulphurous
steam over a precipice two hundred feet high, a boiling
waterfall whose sinister appearance belies its healing
power.

On the day of my visit, Arabs were bathing in the
curative waters. I bathed too, and was led into a cave
through which the hot stream bubbled, filling the cave
with scalding vapor. In five minutes I was completely
cooked, and fled back into the comparatively cooling
desert sunshine.

Herod could easily have commanded his slaves to bear
him in a litter down the mountain side, to bake himself
perhaps in my very cave, and then gone back, refreshed,
for more banqueting on his peak-top.

I envied him his litter now, for it took three long
hours of climbing, of slipping and sliding, of zigzagging
up the cliff-face, to bring me to my goal.

There is nothing one can do, on first reaching the
Hanging Place, except stand and stare and marvel.
The entire map of the Holy Land is stretched out before
one: the towers of Jerusalem on the ridge across the
abyss; the winding River Jordan and the Sea of Galilee
to the north; and the great sink far below, paved in blue
of such an intense shade that no conscientious artist
would dare to reproduce it for fear of being gaudy—
the matchless blue of the Dead Sea.

Of the famous citadel that once stood here, only bits
of the foundations remain, and a dungeon-like chamber

hewn out of the solid rock. The palace itself, of which
more extensive portions exist, was built upon a near-by
ridge, separated from the citadel by a narrow valley,
but reached by a stone causeway which is still there.
Judging from the few walls which the earthquakes
have not tumbled down, this palace was a vast structure
of innumerable rooms and courts and halls, all of cut
stone. About it spread a stone city to house the court
and the garrison of soldiers, all of whom were forced to
share the King's self-imposed exile upon this spire of
rock.

I found the stones of the palace so jumbled together
that it was hard to distinguish one apartment from another. But I did come upon one hall of especially large
dimensions, with two of its side walls standing—just
such a hall as might have served Herod when he feasted
on that tragic night. And here, as anyone must do who
stands upon this spot, I tried to reconstruct the scene
that made the place immortal.

John's martyrdom was not the result of a momen-
tary whim on the part of Herodias. According to
Josephus, the Jewish historian who wrote before the end
of the first century, the motivation of her deadly plot
had been developing for months, and not without
reason.

Herod's father, Herod the Great, had been one of the
most violent men in history, maintaining his power by
torture and murder. It was he who commanded the
slaughter of all the infants in Bethlehem when it was
prophesied that one of them, Christ, would become
King in his stead. His wives, his brothers, his sons, fell

likewise before his murder-mania. On his deathbed he heard that the Crown Prince was already giving himself kingly airs. So Herod ordered him killed too, one day before his own death.

None of the three sons who managed to save their lives was much improvement on their father. One of them, Herod Antipas, inherited Galilee and Trans-Jordania, and married the daughter of the King of Petra, the neighboring state to the south. His half-brother Philip married Herodias, the daughter of another half-brother, and resided most of the time in dissolute Rome.

Herod, on a visit to Rome, became infatuated with Herodias, his own niece as well as Philip's. And Herodias returned the passion. The fact that each of them was already married was easily waved aside. Herodias left Philip, taking their daughter Salome with her, and ran off with Herod. Meanwhile Herod's legal wife, hearing of their approach to Machærus and fearful that she would be divorced with a sword-stroke, escaped south to Petra.

Immediately Herod married Herodias, and brought her and Salome (both daughters of his half-brothers) to his mountain-top citadel. There the young Princess became a favorite in the court of the man who was at once her uncle, her great-uncle, her stepfather—and her admirer.

But no sooner were they established there than two bitter enemies began to harass them. One was the King of Petra, whose daughter Herod had cast aside. The other was John the Baptist.

John, although he enjoys a high place in Christian

tradition, would undoubtedly be considered something
of a nuisance by the privileged classes if he were to re-
appear today with his same manners and prejudices.
The facts of his history attest that John was a half-clad
and half-starved hermit, who wandered out of the wilderness from time to time to thunder denunciations at
everyone whose reputation did not meet his standards of
righteousness. One sees his type in Jerusalem at the
present day, hungry, wild-eyed, in rags, vehemently de-
nouncing sin and prophesying the coming of a new
Messiah. But John, to his contemporaries, seemed inspired, and we know that he had a compelling religious
genius. It was John who announced that "One mightier
than I cometh. . . and every mountain shall be brought
low"—a message which Herod, on high Machærus, must
have heard with some alarm.

John's great hold on the masses in Moab was easy to
understand. He kept telling them that the New Day,
the New Kingdom, was at hand: no more Herods, no
more taxes, down with the capitalists, away from cor-
ruption, back to the poor man's pleasures of repentance
and prayer.

It can well be imagined what this zealous country
preacher thought of the goings-on at the Royal Palace.
And with his outcries against the incestuous King and
Queen, he had no end of success in stirring up excitement. The fact that intermarriage among the ruling
families of the Roman world, at that period, was so frequent as to be almost the rule, did not matter to John.
For Herod to have divorced his lawfully wedded wife
and to have taken in her place his own niece, whom he
stole from his own half-brother, was in John's eyes an

abomination to the Lord. And he climbed up on the housetops to say so.

Herod endured this agitator for a time; but he was disturbed by the unrest John was causing with the promise of a new kingdom in which Herod was the *last* person likely to be King.

While Herod's dislike of John was political, Herodias' dislike was personal. John, with his inflammatory talk about the monstrous sin Herodias was living, continually made her feel guilty for having left a husband she hated in favor of a man she loved.

In short, for the royal couple, the shag-haired preacher had become a menace who sooner or later would have to be put out of the way. So it is not surprising that Herod seized the prophet from the midst of his worshipful followers, and cast him into a dungeon in the citadel of Machærus, there to await the time when the King would make up his mind how to dispose safely of a fellow who quite possibly might possess miraculous powers. For the truth was, that for all his resentment, Herod was himself a little in awe of the prophet.

And so the situation stands on the night of the King's birthday party in the year A.D. 29. . . .

The hour turns toward midnight. Outside the palace, the stars seem entirely to encompass the soaring mountain top. Only the citadel across the causeway breaks the skyline—the citadel beneath which is the dungeon where John the Baptist is in chains. Down from the walls of the fortress the world falls away into unfathomable blackness, into the bottomless void of the Dead Sea.

Within the palace, the rich banquet hall is thronged.

All the officers of the army and the nobles of the country are on hand. When the meal is over, musicians come to entertain the guests. This is the moment for which Salome has been waiting. She gives a signal to the orchestra. From it comes a burst of rhythmical music . . . and Salome, in a dance costume that makes no pretense of concealing her lithe brown body, glides through the doors onto the center of the floor.

We do not know what has prompted Salome to dance, at this particular moment, before the King and his lords and captains. Perhaps it is just that she wishes to honor Herod's birthday in this very special manner . . . or is it possible that Herodias has forced her daughter to this act, as a maneuver which only Herodias understands?

As a dancer Salome is superb. At first her movements are languorous and restrained. But soon the music quickens; the drum-beat swells; the cymbals increase in tone; and Salome's body responds, whirling faster about the hall, until with a concentrated crash of all the instruments, she hurls herself into an utterly abandoned frenzy of motion, and spins to her knees at the feet of King Herod with the last wild note.

The King is dazzled by her beauty and roused by her passionate performance. He bids Salome come to him; he puts his arm around her slender waist, and before all his guests—since an extraordinary birthday gesture deserves an equal return—he offers on his oath to give her whatever she may ask for. "Ask of me," he said, "whatsoever thou wilt, unto the half of my kingdom, and I will give it thee."

Has Herodias, waiting in the women's apartment, not counted on Herod's making just this promise? . . .

has she not instructed Salome to consult with her before answering?

Salome leaves the banquet hall to take counsel with her mother. Now Herodias will have her revenge against that scandal-crying hermit whose insolence has been rankling in her heart. . . .

With crafty, narrowing eyes, she tells her daughter to demand the head of John.

And Salome returns to the hall and asks Herod to give her, in a charger, the head of John the Baptist.

According to St. Mark, "the king was exceeding sorry," but felt he must make good his public oath.

Political commentators, however, do not agree that Herod was exceeding sorry. They insist that in the nature of things, he must have been, at least secretly, exceeding glad, and that his show of remorse was only for his guests' sake.

Whatever his secret feelings were, he summons his executioner, and gives the fatal order.

Holding a torch, the executioner leaves the palace and crosses the causeway that leads to the citadel on top of the Hanging Place. The guards unlock the dungeon door, and force John to kneel and to bare his neck. Then with one blow the executioner decapitates the gaunt and unresisting prisoner, seizes the bleeding head by the long hair, places it on a silver platter, and bears it back to the banquet hall.

Herod, grim, silent and somewhat afraid, sits slumped in his chair. The guests wait, tense and apprehensive, not knowing quite what to do. The executioner enters with his horrible burden. He hands the charger to Salome. The guests, unable to endure this gruesome and shocking scene, melt from the hall, wishing to take no part in the death of a man whom the common people claimed could raise the dead.

Salome, repelled by her gory gift but forced to accept what she has asked for, takes the charger, bows toward Herod, and flees from his presence, to deliver the head to her mother.

There is no fear, no remorse, no revulsion, on the part of Herodias. She takes the charger in her hands, looks mockingly at the silent tongue protruding from the distorted mouth—and smiles. . . .

He would denounce her no more!

It was six o'clock in the afternoon when I walked from the ruins of this historic palace, down the path to the stone causeway, and across to the fortress—the same path over which the executioner fetched his ghastly trophy some nineteen hundred years ago.

I climbed to the top of the Hanging Place, and standing there, watched the sun set behind the Holy City, twenty-five miles to the west. Jerusalem's spires rose up black and sharp against the glowing sky. The abyss of the Dead Sea changed from blue to black as the twilight deepened . . . and all about, a dead world faded into shadows, leaving me lost on this wild and awesome summit, a summit fitting for the terrible scenes it has beheld.

When the last blood-red rays of the sunset left the peak, my Arab guide and I found our way into the cavern hewn out of the solid rock on the site of the citadel. Forty feet long by fifteen feet wide, it was obviously used once as a prison, for the holes are still in the walls where the spikes were fixed and the chains attached. It is the only dungeon to be found on the hilltop, and was beyond any reasonable doubt John's prison place.

In this cave, we built a fire and spread our blankets on the bare earth for the night.

But I could not sleep. I kept remembering that perhaps on this very spot where I lay, John's head had been struck from his body. Somewhere close by, this ground had been stained by martyr's blood.

By the light of the candles I had brought along, I once more opened my copy of Josephus, the book that had already told me so much about the history of this mountain top and the violent and passionate people who once dwelt here. There was a postscript to the Salome story:

Herod did not live out his life in Machærus. And Herodias was to blame for his final downfall. Seeing neighboring kings under Roman control being more greatly favored than her husband, she prevailed upon him to accompany her to Rome to demand redress. But the Roman Emperor, covetous of Herod's provinces, instead of granting him more favors exiled him to Gaul; and Herodias, proud to the end, chose to follow her luckless husband into oblivion.

As for Salome, she had her one superlatively dramatic moment, a moment immortalized in art and literature throughout the centuries. But what happened to her after that, no one knows; there is no further mention of her in history.

It was getting cold on the wind-swept peak, and I had to pull my blanket close about me to keep warm.

The fire was out; my candle burning very low. But just as I put my book aside, I came across a sentence the historian had written around the year A.D. 90—a sentence that made a startling ending to the story of John, who had seen visions of Heaven in the wilderness, and come down to the River Jordan to baptize Jesus, and roused the people throughout the land to prepare for the coming Kingdom. Josephus, sixty years after the beheading of the Baptist, reconsidered the prophesying hermit's wild utterances, checking them with the developments he himself had seen, and gravely declared of the Messiah whose forerunner and announcer John had been: "He was the Christ. And the tribe of Christians so named from him *are not extinct to this day.*"

CHAPTER XXVII

HADJI HALLIBURTON

Ever since the time I first read books of history and geography one of my ambitions has been to make the pilgrimage to Mecca.

The fact that non-Moslems are rigorously excluded from this Sacred City, and are likely to forfeit their lives if caught there, has not discouraged me. Neither have I abandoned my dream because of the knowledge that each non-Moslem who has managed to reach Mecca possessed qualifications I completely lack—an intimate knowledge of Arabic speech, customs, mannerisms, prejudices, that turned away suspicion.

I am speaking strictly of non-Moslems. Quite a number of Europeans—perhaps fifty—who have renounced Christianity and embraced Islam, have made the pilgrimage without special difficulties. Sometimes their conversion has been only skin-deep, but at least they have had sufficient familiarity with the outward forms of the Mohammedan religion to convince the authorities that they were sincere.

So far as I know there has not been a single case of a non-Moslem, lacking all linguistic and religious background, who has just walked into Mecca because he wanted to see the sights.

Well aware of these facts, I nevertheless thought I might be the exception. The Hejaz—the Moslem Holy

Land of which Mecca is the capital—was only five days' travel from Jerusalem (to which place I had returned from Machærus). The temptation to go on to Suez, run down the Red Sea and try to have a look at the Forbidden City, grew too strong to resist. My chances of seeing it would be better at this particular time than at any other, for the pilgrim season, lasting a month, would be in full swing when I reached there.

The Mecca pilgrimage dates back to A.D. 622. In that year the Prophet Mohammed was forced by his idol-worshiping enemies to flee for his life from Mecca (his native city, where for ten years he had preached his new religion) to Medina, two hundred and fifty miles north, where a large band of his followers gave him shelter. The Mohammedan calendar, containing only three hundred and fifty-four days to the year, is dated from that event, just as ours is dated from the birth of Christ. For some two hundred million people spread from the Philippines and Java to Nigeria and Morocco, this is the fourteenth, not the twentieth, century.

From 622 until today, upon the anniversary of this flight, thousands of Mohammedans from every Moslem country in the world make a pilgrimage to Mecca, to worship for a special period of three days at the sacred shrines, and gain absolution for their sins. Up to 1914 the pilgrims never numbered less than two hundred thousand. Today, due to economic depression, there are only one-fifth that many.

Once a Moslem has attained the Holy City on the exact date of Mohammed's flight, and performed the necessary ceremonies, he has the right to carry the title *Hadji* before his name (one who has made the *Hadj*—

the pilgrimage), a title that gives him honor and distinction the rest of his life, no matter what his social caste may be.

This anniversary does not fall at the same season every year, since the Arab year is eleven days shorter than ours, being pegged to twelve lunar months of exactly twenty-nine and one-half days each. Consequently the date of the pilgrimage moves back eleven days each time; and in thirty-three years makes a complete circuit of the seasons. The year of my visit to the Hejaz, the three holy days came in March. For the past fifteen years the pilgrims have been traveling to Mecca in the six hottest months. Disease, flies, contagion, scarifying heat, have had to be endured. But for the next fifteen years the date will slowly revolve backward through the six cooler months—a prospect for which all the Moslem world is grateful.

The pilgrimage, as an international party, is an unqualified and assured success. People from a hundred races, speaking as many tongues, gather annually at this one place to honor the same Prophet and the same God. Their national dress is put aside in favor of a uniform consisting of two huge Turkish towels, called the *ihram*. All the pilgrims look alike in this humble costume. Rank, wealth, race, are forgotten. King and beggar, saint and sinner, rajahs from India, donkey-boys from Morocco, half-naked Negroes from the Sudan, are leveled to the same common denominator. Only the unbelieving infidels are scorned and excluded.

No other infidel ever marched on Mecca as badly prepared as myself to overcome the barriers ahead. I did not speak or understand one word of Arabic. In Arabian costume I looked as if I'd been rigged up by a cheap costumer for a fancy-dress ball. And as for the Mohammedan religion, I'd once been in a movie in Hollywood in which I had to kneel on the floor of the "Delhi Mosque" and say my prayers—say them so badly that the "orthodox Moslem" Mexican extras kneeling beside me, saw through my disguise and chased me into the streets where I ran for my life to the end of the hand-painted scenery. Other than this one lesson in Islamic ritual, I'd had no training in how to act like a pious Mohammedan.

My hopes of reaching Mecca should have been infinitesimally small. On the contrary they were absurdly great. A little ingenuity, a little audacity, a little luck, and a cigarette offered to the right guard, would take me, I fully believed, to the center of the great Mecca Mosque.

So I traveled by train to Suez, via Cairo, and there boarded a tiny Red Sea steamer, along with one hundred other pilgrims, and headed for the Hejaz.

After four days Jedda, the port for Mecca, rose over the horizon—a tightly clustered town clinging to the beach, surrounded by a mud wall, and topped with minarets. Out from the shore a fleet of Arab *dhows* came flying to meet us. Into these the pilgrims, all shining-white in their Turkish towels, piled with their baggage.

Jedda seethed with Moslems preparing for their journey to the Holy City, forty-five miles inland. Each one had been met at the dock by his Arab agent, called a *mutawwif,* and was being shown about, or packed aboard a motorbus or a camel.

Straightway I tried to find a *mutawwif* to facilitate my own pilgrimage. Only two or three of them spoke any French or English, and they, on learning that I had no pilgrim passport, wasn't a convert, and didn't know the first thing about the Moslem religion, refused even to consider helping me. Cigars, money, a bottle of Scotch—nothing could move them. They admitted that in the old days such a project might have had some chance of success. But now, under the present fanatical Wahabi control, each entrance to Mecca was blocked by grim and incorruptible soldiers who scrutinized and cross-questioned everyone who passed. And I was assured that in Mecca itself every man, woman and child was a spy eager to denounce any suspicious-looking stranger. There was only one thing for me to do if I was determined to make the pilgrimage: Go back to Jerusalem or Cairo, study Arabic, learn the fundamental teachings of the Koran, pass an examination before the elders in the Mosque, and thus become, officially, a Moslem. Then I would be given a passport, and conducted to every sacred corner of both Mecca and Medina at the pilgrimage season. But any effort to reach Mecca by stealth would be madness.

Definitely I could not expect any help from the *mutawwifs*. So I decided to see what I could do alone.

First of all, going into the native bazaars, I bought an *ihram*. I'd never get to Mecca in my sky-blue shirt, mail-order flannel clothes and beret. I wrapped the *rida* towel about my shoulders, and the *izar* towel around my waist and legs. I also bought regulation sandals, and a string of prayer beads. Hats are not allowed, but I found an umbrella (white for purity) which is entirely orthodox. A satchel on one shoulder held my food, money and camera.

This pilgrim uniform I found very comfortable. But this comfort had to be paid for by the acceptance of a rigid behavior-code that goes with the *ihram*. Dressed in the uniform, one may not quarrel no matter what the provocation, one may not use violent language, all carnal thoughts and actions must be abhorred, one must not take any form of life . . . mosquitoes, fleas, lice, especially become inviolate. One must not scratch one's self for fear of disturbing some of Allah's little creatures. There is no law, however, against sprinkling one's body with insect-powder and allowing the fleas to die of acute indigestion.

Arraying myself carefully in this garb of piety, I could not see that my costume deviated in the smallest detail from all the rest of the forty thousand pilgrims. In other respects, however, I wondered if I were not about as inconspicuous amid a crowd of Arabs, Javanese, Indians and Sudanese, as a fire engine going to a funeral; for my hair after several hatless weeks in Palestine and at sea was burned almost white, and a new brick church is no redder than the color my face had become.

To offset this I carried two pounds of silver *bakshish* and twelve packs of cigarettes. I also had a partway passport. Soon after my arrival in Jedda I had presented to the police a letter of introduction given me by the Hejaz consulate in Cairo, and received from them a card that allowed me as a very special favor to make "one trip by motorcar and under escort" as far as the village of Bahia, the half-way point between Jedda and Mecca. Fifteen miles beyond Bahia and eight from Mecca lay Shimayse, the carefully guarded gate to the holy area. I would try to use my special card as a pilgrim-passport as far as Bahia. After that I would have to trust to luck and my guardian angel. It seemed so unreasonable that the Moslem sentries should know—or hold against me—the fact that as a child I had once been sent, very much against my will, to a Presbyterian Sunday School.

In Jedda, the Mecca Gate was obviously the place to start for Mecca. Just outside this gate I found a scene of the wildest confusion. All the world seemed to be going to the Holy City. Several thousand camels, resenting their heavy loads, groaned and snarled; countless donkeys brayed; and motorbuses bursting with passengers honked frantically for their right of way through the chaos of men and animals.

I debated long and earnestly whether a camel or a motorbus would be best for the forty-five mile trip to Mecca. True, my card said "motorcar and under escort" but there probably would be no one to examine the card until I got to Bahia, so I was free to choose my own transportation that far. I first considered a camel. This is the more meritorious conveyance, but it takes two nights and a day, against three hours for the bus. Also the camel's howdah, called a *shugduf*, didn't appeal to me. It's a double-basket business swung on both sides of the hump. The baskets are made of cane and wicker, and will hold one passenger each; and both baskets must be occupied, and abandoned, simultaneously, else the heavier basket, unbalanced, slips to one side. If the

camel stumbles, the passengers are often pitched violently to the ground.

Perhaps half the pilgrims, especially the poor and the
pious, travel this way. A mile of it might have been
good sport, but two nights in such cramped and swaying
quarters seemed excessively adventurous.

So, arrayed in all my holy whiteness, I took a bus that
held twenty pilgrims. The Arab bus-drivers, before
leaving Jedda, are required to examine every ticket and
passport. But my driver's anxiety to be off (in order to
hurry back for another load) was terrific. He looked
at my card, saw Bahia, a way station, and in the hurry
and bustle didn't bother to note the "escort" provision.
In fact, as things turned out, I doubt if he could read
anything at all except the names of villages along the
Mecca road.

We twenty pilgrims were packed almost on top of
one another in the bus. More than half the passengers
were Javanese who spoke no more Arabic than I did;
and the three Syrians aboard were light enough in color
to have passed for Spaniards or Sicilians. Consequently
in this particular group I did not stand out as much as
I might have; and whatever infidel aloofness I may
have felt was soon lost, when after a few miles over the
bumpy desert road we were all, with our bundles and
umbrellas, tumbled together into almost inextricable
confusion.

We passed streams of traffic. Mecca had swelled
overnight from twenty thousand to sixty thousand. All
this mushroom population, with its animals, had to be
fed, and this could be done only from Jedda and the
sea. Truck-loads of grain and canned goods struggled

by; and the camel caravans, still the chief transports, extended in an unbroken line all the way to Mecca and back again. There were hundreds of pilgrims walking, too—those unable to pay even for the camel hire. They trudged along, carrying their baggage in bundles on their heads, their white towels turning yellow with dust.

The country between the two cities is an endless sand waste unrelieved by a single tree. On every hilltop is a ruined stone blockhouse, once occupied by Turkish troops to protect the pilgrims from bands of robbers, who in former times preyed unmercifully upon the travelers. Oddly enough, a previous ruler of the Hejaz, King Husein (whose army Colonel Lawrence and Husein's son, Prince Feisal, led so successfully against the Turks during the Great War), is accused by the people in Jedda of having set spies to watch the pilgrims and learn which ones were rich. The King, so the local gossip runs, then dispatched his own private plunderers to attack them.

But under the present orthodox and high-principled King, Ibn Saud, any sort of molestation of pilgrims is unheard of. Not a pilgrim but has far less fear of losing his money on the road to Mecca than in any country from which he came.

My bus pushed on, finding its way through the sand hillocks, and bouncing about, despite its heavy load, most uncomfortably. The wind blowing across the desert scorched one with its very touch. (And this was March! What must the heat be like in July?) In a great cloud of dust we drew up at Bahia. This village is just a string of shacks along both sides of the road, mostly food shops and "hotels" for the pilgrims who

Pilgrims leaving Jedda for the forty-five-mile march to Mecca.

Ibn Saud, the giant King of Saudi Arabia, makes the pilgrimage to Mecca.

The King's private secretary and five of his twenty-seven living sons.

King Ibn Saud poses for a photograph with the author. This picture was taken eight miles outside the walls of Mecca near the tomb of the mother of the Prophet. Ibn Saud, six feet six inches tall, is the most important figure in the Arab world. Beside him stand the French and Italian consuls at Jedda.

travel on foot or by camel and wish to break the journey. For ten months in the year it is half deserted, but when the pilgrims begin to arrive it overflows with activity.

Before the guard-house, we passengers were directed to get out and have our passports stamped by an official, otherwise we would not be allowed to travel beyond Shimayse.

This was a hazard that had been explained to me before I left Jedda. I knew that if I showed my pass-card I'd be turned back. So instead of going into the bureau I walked across the street, through the crush of people and donkeys, into a bread-shop where I was immediately lost in the confusion of white-*ihramed* bodies. And when the other nineteen pilgrims piled aboard the bus again, pocketing their stamped passports, I piled aboard pocketing my biscuits. The driver, seeing me in a regulation pilgrim garb, if he noticed me at all, probably supposed that the guards had given me permission to go on. In any case on I went.

That, I thought to myself, was absurdly easy. But I hardly hoped to have such luck again.

Another fifteen miles in the crowded bus, still passing the endless traffic of pack animals and pilgrims, brought us to Shimayse. This is the deadline for non-Moslems, and is marked by two huge stone pillars. The tomb of the mother of the Prophet is just beyond.

To my great disappointment I saw there was no village here, no seething crowd of white-garbed people in which I could lose myself—only a guard-house such as one finds at any other frontier station.

This was my front-line trench. And I didn't have

the vaguest idea how I'd get beyond it unless some direct assistance from a Christian Heaven came to help me.   Perhaps a Presbyterian angel would swoop down and distract the heathen guards, and allow a good ex-Sunday-School student to walk through.

The bus stopped and once more we all got out for inspection.

The moment I saw the guards at this station I feared for the worst.   They were Wahabi soldiers of the sternest possible visage.   I knew at once there was no hope of trying to use my pass-card, nor could I get back in the bus undetected as at Bahia, for this time each passenger was being carefully checked.   The guards took no chances.   If the Mecca police caught an infidel inside the holy area, these frontier sentries would never hear the last of it.

My only hope was to let the bus go on without me (since I could not do otherwise) and try to deal with the soldiers alone.   There would be no chance to "reason" with them if the other pilgrims were standing by . . . and it was only eight miles to walk into Mecca in case I got past the boundary.

With the bus on its way, the Wahabis turned their entire attention to the curious-looking pilgrim who had been left behind.   They asked for my passport, and I surrendered all I had.   They looked at the card . . . "permission is granted the bearer to travel by private motorcar and under escort, once only, along the Mecca road as far as Bahia"—and then, with some surprise, at me—and then, with still greater surprise, at my pilgrim costume—and then at each other, perplexed.   Never before had they encountered anyone all dressed up for the party, white umbrella and all, with no invitation.

They bombarded me with questions, in Arabic. I answered with cigarettes. They telephoned headquarters to ask what to do. I suggested taking some *bakshish* and sending me on to Mecca.

Both my offers were indignantly scorned. Wahabis were holy men; what did *they* want with my bribes! And for them to smoke a cigarette, at the very border of the holy territory, was sin unspeakable. For smoking, along with playing music, or taking photographs, or singing, or committing adultery, is sure to send a Wahabi straight to the nearest Hell.

With tobacco and treasure both angrily rejected, I had no further ammunition. But it was already eloquently clear that the guards' reply to any plea whatsoever that I might make (in English) for a pass to Mecca, was going to be a vigorous and outraged NO.

I looked to Heaven for some sign, some aid. Not a cloud appeared, and no angels. But then I really wasn't counting too much on heavenly intervention, and wasn't *too* disappointed. . . . I'd had a pleasant ride, and seen more of the country and more of the pilgrims than if I'd sat stolidly in Jedda.

When the guards saw I'd given up my intention of descending on Mecca, they told me I could use their shelter till a Jedda-bound bus came along to take me home again. So, since wait I must, I gathered my Turkish towels regally about me, and sat on the floor of the guard-house, and surreptitiously smoked one of my cigarettes.

But what of my fellow passengers? What did they see that I didn't?

On reaching Mecca they hurried straightway to the great Haram—the Central Mosque in the middle of the city. Here they found an enormous open court, surrounded by colonnades. In this court rises the Kaaba, a cubical granite structure fifty feet square and seventy high, kept completely covered at all times with a veil of black cloth. Abraham was the original builder of the Kaaba, according to legend, and it was venerated by the idol-worshipers long before the lifetime of Mohammed.

Around this Kaaba, every pilgrim, dressed in his *ihram,* must march seven times, chanting special prayers.

Next he must run a special half-mile course between two sacred points—seven times. This running commemorates the anxiety of Hagar who ran all over the neighborhood looking for water to give her little son Ishmael, dying of thirst. When she returned empty-handed to the place where she had left him, she found a beautiful spring flowing from the earth by Ishmael's side. Allah had gone to the rescue of the child.

Today this spring is called Zem-Zem, and its waters are incomparably holy. Pilgrims all drink it, and carry bottles of it home.

But these ceremonies can be done at any time of the year. Observing them does not make a *Hadji.* The *real* pilgrimage is not to Mecca at all, but to a special holy hill called Arafat, fifteen miles from Mecca. And to win any merit the pilgrim must be beside Arafat at sunset on the first of the three holy days. On the year of my pilgrimage—to Shimayse!—forty thousand gathered on Arafat. In 1927 two hundred and fifty thousand. This hill is where the Angel Gabriel taught Adam and Eve their prayers, and where our first parents met again after being driven from the Garden of Eden and separated for long years.

Just at sunset every pilgrim must break camp and rush as fast as his legs will carry him to another place called Muzdalfa, to sleep. For this is the place where Adam and Eve spent the first night after their reunion.

The second of the three holy days the pilgrims spend casting stones at devils. They must throw seven pebbles three times at each of three special posts, on the road back to Mecca, which mark the places where Abraham, Sarah and Isaac, tempted by the devil, threw stones at him and drove him away.

The third day of the pilgrimage is given over to the sacrifice of animals. Every pilgrim, no matter how poor, must sacrifice at least one animal. The rich may have hundreds killed. In 1930, when there were one hundred and fifty thousand pilgrims, over one million sheep, goats and camels were slaughtered. The poor are allowed to take away all the meat they can carry. But ninety per cent of this vast food store is left untouched and has to be burned, not as a religious rite, but for sanitation.

Such ceremonies do not impress us in the West as being very spiritualizing or uplifting. But Moslems *are* uplifted. A pilgrimage for them washes clean the sins of a lifetime. To die in Mecca and be buried in the Holy Area assures one of Paradise.

In times past, before modern medical precautions

were taken, thousands upon thousands gained this privilege, for cholera and smallpox, breaking out on the plain before Arafat, have been known to kill *one-third* of the pilgrims in a week. Between the epidemics and the bandits, they had to feel a great urge indeed to brave the dangers of the road to Mecca. The pilgrimage is much safer now, but for many it is still an ordeal. Each year pilgrims arrive who have walked from the middle of India; or from the heart of Nigeria, twenty-five hundred miles away, taking four or five years to make the round trip.

My own round trip took exactly six hours. I returned to Jedda feeling not a little annoyed at my lack of success, and determined, at the first opportunity, to embrace Islam with both arms, and return to the Hejaz and go to Mecca, and walk seven times around the Kaaba, and watch the sun set at Arafat, and throw all the pebbles in sight at the holy posts, and sacrifice whole flocks of sheep. And thenceforth, clothed in sanctity, and forgetting my rejection at Shimayse, I'll proudly sign my name forever—Hadji Halliburton.

CHAPTER XXVIII

THE GIANT

TODAY, in a palace in Mecca, there lives one of the mightiest men in contemporary history.

Fifty-five years old. Six feet six inches tall. Two hundred and twenty pounds of toughness.

Married *one hundred and sixty times.*

A Moslem puritan who says his prayers five times a day, a dictator who rules a nation according to the commandments of the Koran.

A fighter whose courage and audacity have created the legend that he is the reincarnation of Alexander the Great.

A conqueror who has subjugated, united and tamed one of the oldest, wildest and most romantic countries on earth.

The greatest figure in the modern Arab world, who may well be capable of uniting all Islam into a single formidable power and of reviving the once glorious empire of the Caliphs.

Ibn Saud, the fabulous King of Arabia.

Ibn Saud, outside Arab countries, is almost unknown. But in his own country, or wherever Arabic is spoken, the very mention of his name causes Arab eyes to shine, and imaginations to leap, and patriots to rejoice, and the unrighteous to tremble.

While America and Europe since the World War have been preoccupied with the vagaries of their own statesmen, this ruler has been quietly, steadily growing in political stature, until he now looms across the Eastern skies like a fairy-tale jinn of monstrous size. For he personifies not only the power of the state within his own borders, but also the far greater power of the Moslem faith, which transcends all national boundaries and sways millions of devotees in three continents.

And likewise, Ibn Saud has not merely conquered and governed Arabia. The Turks did that. He has touched off a spark that promises to grow into a great Arab renaissance in all Arab lands, a rebirth of self-confidence and self-control that may restore the character and vigor of a people who once dominated the earth from India to Portugal and enriched it with a superb civilization that endured for seven centuries.

Naturally, residing in Jedda I heard much about this giant King of the country, since he is the Guardian of the Holy Cities and Allah's chief advocate on earth, as well as head of the state. To make his acquaintance was a hope that had been in the back of my mind since my first arrival in the Hejaz. It would have been a feather in my cap if I could have called upon him in his Mecca palace. But having found that an infidel couldn't attain the Holy City simply by dressing himself up in Turkish towels and taking a bus, I realized such a plan was out, and tried to think up some other way to get an interview.

I was well aware of the fact that the King holds himself aloof from foreigners and sees as few of them as possible (a policy which explains why his extraordinary career and régime are so little known abroad). He divides his time between Riyadh—a town in the heart of Arabia to which non-Moslems may go only on the rarest occasions—and Mecca which is completely barred. Even in Jedda non-Moslems are not permitted to land without very special permission from the Foreign Office; and when they have landed, the King keeps them practically prisoners. The entire foreign colony consists of only some twenty-five Europeans. More are not welcomed.

But perhaps this anti-foreign policy is well reasoned. Ibn Saud has observed how England has absorbed Egypt, Palestine and Iraq, and how France has taken Syria. Now that he has fought so long and so hard to win control of Arabia, he is determined that no European nation is to wrest it from him—and the best way to keep out Europe is to keep out Europeans.

These were all very interesting facts, but they certainly didn't give me and my interview-project much encouragement.

Not knowing what else to do I went to the King's Foreign Minister, an English-speaking Syrian, and explained that I was an American journalist eager to have the privilege of interviewing His Majesty.

"But His Majesty almost never gives interviews. And moreover, he is in Mecca, and will be remaining there indefinitely. You realize, of course, that makes him inaccessible to Christians."

(*How* inaccessible, my ridiculous "pilgrimage" had proved, though if I had tried to enter in earnest, I would undoubtedly have been taken before him—had I lived that long.)

Then I made a suggestion which was, I fully realized, an unparalleled bit of impertinence:

"Would the King come to Jedda to see me?"

And before the Minister could speak I rushed on to explain that America knew so little about Ibn Saud's marvelous career and his ambitions for his race; that I only wished an opportunity to help project him more definitely upon America's consciousness in order to increase the great interest we already had in his country. . . .

No one had ever before had the effrontery to make such a request of the mightiest man in Arabia. The Foreign Minister lost his diplomatic poise for a moment; then the boldness of the idea seemed to amuse him. He picked up the telephone and called the King in Mecca, stating my case, conveying with I know not what Oriental circumlocutions my suggestion that since the reporter could not go to the mountain, the mountain might come to the reporter.

The conversation was in Arabic, which I could not understand. I waited for the inevitable refusal, thinking meanwhile what a strange compromise a telephone in Mecca represented. I was close enough to hear a rapid stream of Arabic coming over the wire. Obviously the King, with his state policy and personal antipathy against any foreign contact, could only be telling what he thought of a wandering infidel journalist who expected him to come trotting forty-five miles down to Jedda as an accommodation.

I reached for my hat, prepared to thank the Minister for his amiable gesture and to make my departure. As

I stood waiting he hung up the receiver. There was a twinkle in his eye.

"The King will come to meet you eight miles out from Mecca at four o'clock tomorrow, near the tomb of the mother of Mohammed."

I think the Minister was almost as much surprised as I was. Such a royal favor had almost never been granted to anyone since Ibn Saud became master of the Hejaz.

I thanked the Minister for his courtesy. He proceeded to give me instructions for the trip. The conference place the King had designated was, ironically enough, Shimayse, the very point where his soldiers had ended my unofficial excursion a few days before. He must have known about the unorthodox "pilgrim's" march upon Mecca, but whether he connected me with the escapade, I never learned. This time there would be no difficulty with the road guards, as I would have a military escort, an interpreter, and the most incontrovertible passport in all Arabia.

Early next afternoon my party left Jedda, and arrived at the rendezvous well before the appointed hour. The Wahabi guards, who recognized me at once, were nonplussed to see me ride grandly past their bare little guard-house and on to where the royal pavilion was already set up—a large square tent made of camel's hair cloth, dyed brilliant shades of orange and purple. Rich carpets covered the ground inside, and chairs— probably a graceful concession to my foreignness—lined the walls.

Before long the advance scouts of the King's bodyguard arrived in motorcars, bristling with guns and swords. I looked down the road and saw an endless caravan of other motors following—six cars, ten, twenty—all filled with soldiers, and rushing forward in a cloud of desert dust.

Somehow I had expected that the King, with a secretary or two, would gallop over the desert from Mecca on a racing camel—and instead, here came this motorized army, that seemed like half the garrison of the Forbidden City. Had the Minister by any chance misunderstood my request, and arranged a review instead of an interview?

Presently a long limousine drew up. Standing on the running boards were four enormous black slaves, dressed in flamboyant scarlet uniforms, carrying great bright scimitars, the bare steel blades glinting in the sun. In the back seat, alone, was the King, his handsome brown face framed in a muslin head-shawl, his colossal body enfolded in a white Arab gown devoid (in accordance with his puritan principles) of any luxury of silk or gold.

His calm, distinguished countenance struck me as remarkably fine . . . a nose thin and slightly hooked; straightforward eyes, wrinkled at the corners so that his gaze seemed concentrated and domineering; a thin black beard pointing the chin; and a full, strong mouth that combined cold serenity with a hint of cruelty and sensuality. As he stepped from the car, I noticed his serenity first of all; in fact, I thought that this famous fighter, whose iron grip was felt from the Red Sea to the Persian Gulf, was wearing a notably gentle expression.

He stood straight and tall—six-feet-six—a great

proud bear of a man, a figure right out of the mythical age of gods and heroes; and when I advanced with the interpreter, he greeted me warmly.

At the entrance to the tent he took off his sandals and walked barefoot to his chair . . . the barefoot King, conscious of his Arab heritage, scornful of alien customs, majestically disdaining to import his manners from abroad.

As the King took his seat, his entourage assembled. He motioned me to a chair beside him, then gave a command, and out from the crowd marched five of his six oldest sons, the Emirs of five provinces of his empire—Feisal, Fahad, Mohammed, Abdulla, Khalid, all dressed in the same simple dignity as their father. Each was the ruler of a state, but they stood respectfully until their Olympian father bade them be seated.

And then outside, the bodyguard of two hundred fanatically loyal Wahabi tribesmen, wild and lean, ranged themselves in a great circle, completely walling us in with a fence of steel rifles and daggers. At the tent entrance, the four scarlet-uniformed black giants stood rigidly with curved swords drawn.

The stage was all set for the interview. But I was so bedazzled by the pageantry and so overwhelmed by the honor the King had paid me that it was difficult to rally my wits enough to ask the question I'd prepared.

Fortunately, one possible opening was very obvious.

A few days before, the name of Ibn Saud had been on the front page of every newspaper in the Moslem world, for an attempt had been made to assassinate him. The assault was still the talk of the land, the more so because of the outrageous circumstances under which it had been committed.

Having expressed my gratification over his escape, I asked him to tell me what had happened.

He talked easily and well. Even through the interpreter, I could feel that he is a master of the art of speech.

As is their annual custom, he told me, he and his oldest son, Crown Prince Saud (not present at the interview), both dressed in pilgrim costume, had been making the seven sacred circuits around the Kaaba, the holy shrine in the center of the great Mosque courtyard at Mecca. They were part of a vast throng, for it was the height of the pilgrimage. On the fifth circuit, as they passed the Zem-Zem Well, three assassins in ordinary Arab dress suddenly rushed at Ibn Saud with daggers drawn.

The crowd, pressing thick about, were too horrified to interfere. The very idea paralyzed them with shock— murder, here before the sacred Kaaba, of the chief of pilgrims himself! And at the holiest of seasons!

The assassins were almost upon the King. His bodyguard, heavily armed even in the Mosque, were so pressed by the crush of pilgrims they could not intervene in time.

But with lightning swiftness, Prince Saud flung himself between his father and the murderers, and received the blow of the leading assassin's knife.

This brave self-sacrifice delayed the onslaught for one precious second—just long enough for the bodyguard to reach the King. Two of the assassins were hacked to pieces in the shadow of the Kaaba, an enviable place

to die, but not an enviable manner. The third, breaking free in the confusion, fled across the Mosque courtyard; he too was overtaken and struck down.

Saud's knife wound was painful, but proved to be not
serious. When the bodies had been removed (probably
the first victims of violence the sanctuary had ever seen)
the King's party, Saud included, continued on their
ceremonial march and completed the seven circuits that
had been interrupted.

Subsequent investigation proved that the would-be
assassins were religious zealots of a minor sect whose
creed differed from that of the Wahabis. In their eyes
Ibn Saud was a heretic whose guardianship of the Sacred City was intolerable, and they were prepared to
commit murder—even suicide—to express their resentment. One charge against him, the King explained to
me, was that several times during the last few years he
had permitted himself to be photographed, a breach of
Moslem convention which was unforgivable in the eyes
of the fundamentalists. I was surprised to hear that
there were Arabs more puritanical than the King—and
I promptly took advantage of his confession to ask him
to pose for me, a favor he granted.

Memories are long in the desert, and there, where
"Iskander" is a common name and the great general's
exploits are a vivid memory, Ibn Saud has frequently
been compared to Alexander. There is indeed coinci-
dence in their life stories.

At twenty-one, Alexander the Great was routing
every opposing army and driving Persian kings before
him.

At nineteen, Ibn Saud, an enormous vital lad standing a head taller than his comrades, began *his* conquest of an empire.

During Ibn Saud's early childhood in Riyadh, his family's tribal capital in central Arabia, where his father was ruler, the Sauds had fought an interminable war with a more powerful neighbor, the Rashid. When Ibn Saud was about twelve years old, the Rashid won an overwhelming victory, captured Riyadh, and drove the Sauds into the southern deserts.

There for several years the young Prince had to endure hardships and privation, living without shelter, raiding and fighting and sleeping on camelback, and subsisting for days at a time on a meager ration of dates.

At nineteen he could endure this exile and humiliation no more. With forty followers he returned by secret marches to Riyadh. Spies told him that the city, newly walled and fortified, was garrisoned by several hundred soldiers and commanded by one of the Rashid's best officers, named Ajlan.

Nevertheless he determined to attack.

At midnight, by means of a palm-trunk, Ibn Saud and his men scaled the walls and hid themselves in a house opposite the entrance to the fort. When dawn came, Ajlan, hearing from the sentries that the night had been quiet, ordered his horse for an early ride through the town. As the gate of the fort swung open and Ajlan emerged, Ibn Saud and his company burst upon him.

For a moment the commander was frozen with amazement; then he called to his guards, and a real battle ensued. He and Ibn Saud fought ferociously, hand to hand, across the courtyard of the fort. It was an un-equal struggle. Who could stand against the fury of this young lion?

Ajlan went down, and the rest of the garrison, help-less before the suddenness of the attack, surrendered. The young Prince proclaimed that he had regained his birthright, and the city rejoiced.

Inspired by this amazing success, Ibn Saud became imbued with the self-confidence, the will-to-victory, that he has never lost.

That was in 1900. Far and wide across Arabia the story of the capture of Riyadh spread. Ibn Saud became a hero. Fighting men, especially young ones, found in him their romantic ideal—a leader brave, strong, free-handed—and flocked to his standard. As his army in-creased, he struck out in wider and wider circles, sub-duing one after another of the restless warring tribes of central Arabia.

Each year he added a new province to his growing empire.

By 1924 only one Arabian state still defied him—the Hejaz itself, the Moslem Holy Land, with the cities of Mecca and Medina. On the throne sat King Husein, who enjoyed English support as a reward for his ac-tivity against the Turks during the Great War. Ibn Saud knew better than to attack this combination.

But at the end of 1924 England, compelled by home influences to alter her foreign policy, withdrew her sup-port and told Husein to shift for himself. Ibn Saud had no illusions as to what had been the real power in the Hejaz. In a flash he swept upon Husein, drove him out of Mecca, pursued him until he fled by boat from

Jedda—never to return—and had himself crowned King of the Hejaz and Guardian of the Sacred Cities.

Meanwhile, as his victories increased and his empire spread through the favor of Allah, Ibn Saud, a devout Moslem from childhood, grew ever more religious, searching the Koran for counsel in all his actions and following that counsel with grim fidelity. His fighting men understood such a leader, being themselves the most inflexible puritans. Alcohol, tobacco, music, luxury, entertainments, were immoral to them; and the things that we call immoral, they abhorred. Their greatest self-indulgence was to plunge themselves into the pleasure of chastising heretics, by which they meant anyone whose interpretation of the Koran differed from theirs. And five times a day, whether they were fighting or resting, they never failed to prostrate themselves in prayer.

Ibn Saud commanded the very souls of such followers as these. Like most puritans, he was militantly honorable, scrupulously just according to his prejudices, undeviating in his character, industrious, God-fearing, and able to inspire like qualities in his army of pious killers.

But this was only the stern side of his Mohammedan character. There was a softer side, too.

Matrimonially Ibn Saud and his Wahabis ran wild. Wild according to our customs, that is; for of course, their multiple marriages were strictly according to the rules set forth by Mohammed. "Thou mayst," said Mohammed, "take two, three, or four wives, but no more." A good Wahabi husband, however, may divorce his wives simply by saying, "I divorce you"—and marry four more, as often as he chooses.

And in the accumulation of wives and ex-wives, Ibn Saud, as tremendous a lover as he was a fighter, led the field.

At fifteen, when he was already six feet tall, he married his first wife.

At eighteen, he had three.

At thirty-seven, he had married and divorced an even hundred women.

Now, at fifty-five, the number has reached eight score, and the King has given no sign that he intends to relinquish the active championship.

He has twenty-seven sons, and a great many daughters too, but he doesn't think them worth boasting about. If they are merely as numerous as his sons, the total would be fifty-four. Ibn Saud said he hadn't counted the family lately, so I cannot report exactly.

It is his policy to have only three wives currently on hand. The fourth bed he keeps vacant, in order to fill it instantly if a new damsel takes his eye, or if reasons of state make it wise to cement a new alliance with some powerful or hostile tribe by marrying into it.

Probably half his marriages have been primarily diplomatic. His divorces, I might add, have been effected with equal diplomacy. As each woman in turn becomes an ex-wife, she is established in a fine house with a retinue of servants, where she resides in dignity and no doubt happiness, supported and honored by the state. One of the heaviest drains on the Arabian treasury is the colossal bill the King's hundred and fifty-six erstwhile mates manage to run up for sweetmeats and millinery. When I heard the details of this expense, I reflected that the much-maligned Bluebeard of the fairy tales was probably not bloodthirsty, but simply trying to balance the budget.

During my conversation with the King, when we were discussing his many marriages, I told him about the schoolboy who described King Solomon as being a great ruler because he had three hundred wives and seven hundred *cucumbers*. I asked Ibn Saud if along with his one hundred and sixty marriages, he had any cucumbers. The humor was all lost when translated into Arabic, and had to be explained. The King laughed and said no, he had no cucumbers. They were forbidden by Moslem law . . . and he is a stickler for law. He tolerates no form of extra-connubial alliance, either for himself or for his subjects. True, he has fifty-four children, but not one is illegitimate.

I do not wish to give the impression however that Ibn Saud's time is monopolized entirely by women. Quite the contrary. His empire is a one-man show—*l'état, c'est lui*—and the administration of it keeps him busily engaged. Every smallest detail of government he must check. He sleeps only five hours a day, and works sixteen. It is easy to understand why his country is called *Saudi Arabia*—Saud's Arabia.

He realizes that, being Guardian of the Sacred Cities, he holds a position of immense responsibility and immense power in the Moslem world. He can reach out and touch all the two hundred million Moslems, in no matter what land. And touch them he has—no, *seized* them—with his idealism, his courage, his ability, his majesty, his piety. Ibn Saud's personality sheds its rays of inspiration over India, Egypt, Syria, Iraq, Palestine.

Algeria, Morocco, Java, and even as far as the Mohammedans in the Philippines.

What the international results of this religious Arab
renaissance may be, one scarcely dares prophesy. There
is sufficient gunpowder in the possibilities to blow up the
map. If Ibn Saud lives long enough (and one cannot
prophesy this either about a ruler whose subjects are
of such a wild temperament) he may easily become the
most disturbing figure that the East has known in modern times.

Ibn Saud answered all my personal questions with
gracious patience; but toward the end of the audience,
when my questions touched pointedly on his foreign
policies, he asked to be excused from answering.

So I changed the subject, perhaps a little startlingly.

"Sir, can you give me any hope that some day I may
enter Mecca?"

In an instant the King's composed features altered
into a Moslem frown. He gazed at me narrowly, to
see whether I had asked the question flippantly. Then
his face relaxed into a smile.

"Each pilgrim season," he replied, "at least one new
European convert enters the sacred precincts. In every
case, we have satisfied ourselves beyond the slightest
doubt that the conversion is sincere and unreserved. We
do not proselytize, but we know that Mohammed's divine power to convert infidels to the true faith must
still be at work in the world beyond our borders; and
when we believe that a European honestly recognizes
the truth of the Koran, we welcome him. If you wish to
enter Mecca, you must become—from the depths of
your heart—a Moslem."

The King had begun to talk with me at four o'clock. It was now well on toward evening, and the shadows of our tent were long across the desert. In a moment more the sun sank beneath the hills. In Mecca and Medina the muezzins were chanting from the minarets, announcing that the day was done, that night was at hand, that the time had come to pray.

The barefoot giant, the great King, knelt down before the tent, facing the Sacred City, and bowed his forehead to the earth, and three times stood and knelt and bowed. Behind him his five sons assumed the praying posture of their father, and bowed when he bowed, and stood when he stood. Behind them, row after row, the armed Wahabis, the fighting, praying tribesmen, laid aside their daggers and knelt humbly in the sand.

And the King, acting as their Imam, quoted aloud from the Koran:

"In the name of Allah, the Beneficent, the Merciful.
Praise is due to Allah, the Lord of the Worlds.
Thee do we worship and Thee do we beseech for help.
Guide us, O Allah, in the right path. Amen."

CHAPTER XXIX

THE RHINOCEROS EXPRESS

FROM Jedda a ship took me eight hundred miles on down the Red Sea. I was on my way to Ethiopia.

If you look at a map of Africa, you will find Ethiopia at the northeast corner of the continent, near the southern end of the Red Sea. Cut off from the rest of the world by deserts and mountains, and by the war-like nature of its people, it remained, before the Italian invasion of 1935, completely and proudly independent, while all the rest of Africa was being colonized and annexed by European powers.

Ethiopia has ten million people, most of them black. The nobility, however, are much lighter in color and consider themselves Semitic rather than Negro. Surrounded by Moslem and pagan nations, they have continued to be, since the year A.D. 300, fanatically Christian. In fact the population is wholly subservient to the priesthood.

Ethiopia has no seaport—the only country in Africa without one. To reach Addis Ababa, the capital, travelers must disembark at Djibouti, a French colonial port at the entrance to the Red Sea, and take the French-owned railroad inland for five hundred miles. The trip takes three days of daylight travel. At night the passengers must sleep at rest-houses along the way. Bandits, wild animals, violent rains that sweep away the tracks, are some of the hazards that make night travel too dangerous. Also, the Galla and Danakil natives along the route are given to tearing up the rails, which they pound into spears, and to cutting down the telegraph wires, with which they make bracelets and necklaces. Consequently the train, though it is supposed to run on schedule, may be anywhere from a day to a week late.

A journey on this railroad is like a visit to the zoo. The entire country from the sea to Addis Ababa swarms with game: herds of antelope and gazelles, lions, leopards, monkeys, hyenas. At one glade near a waterhole, I saw a group of at least fifty deer, not two hundred yards away from the track. They bounded away, graceful and swift, when the engine's whistle startled them.

Until quite recent times the trains, on encountering such a herd, would stop, and the engineer, fireman, conductor and most of the passengers would seize their guns and go in wild pursuit. No one ever expected the train on time anyway, so another hour's delay wouldn't matter. Since the Italian occupation the crews' hunting instinct has been discouraged. However, if any prince or potentate is aboard and wants to bag an antelope, the train will stop to oblige.

Climbing steadily up from the sea, we passed several flocks of enormous coal-black hornbills, birds with bodies as big as condors, but with squat, duck-like legs. Awkwardly they waddled across the tracks, stretching out their long necks and ten-inch bills in the manner of hurrying geese. The pterodactyl, the extinct flying reptile of antediluvian times, must have looked, on a large scale, much like an Ethiopian hornbill.

Once my train was stopped by a huge two-hundred-pound turtle that had crawled over one rail but was too lazy to crawl over the other. So we found him paddling along down the track, headed for Addis Ababa three hundred miles away. And probably he would have reached there, too, in ten years, if we had not given him a lift over the four-inch barrier and thus enabled the train to proceed.

At the first rest-station the French station-master told me of an extraordinary lion hunt that had upset the railroad a fortnight earlier. A German wild-game collector had bought six magnificent lions in Addis Ababa and was shipping them to Hamburg. The train on which the animals were traveling to the sea stopped for the night as usual, near the station. When the animal-keeper delayed too long bringing them their supper, the lions, hungry and restless, managed to claw open the boxcar door; and all six were gone when the keeper returned.

The word spread quickly throughout the town. Every citizen seized his spear or rifle to join the lion hunt, hoping to recapture the animals for the sake of the reward. All night the search continued in the hills and ravines round about, but not one lion, or even so much as a trace of one, could be found. The most proficient lion-trackers in the party were baffled.

At dawn, exhausted and discouraged, the game collector returned to the train, accompanied by the engineer, the conductor and those of the passengers who had been willing to face wild beasts in the open country.

And there, fast asleep in the wide-open boxcar, were the six lions. After using the nearest sheepfold as a self-service restaurant, they had returned to pass the night in their private car, and gone peacefully to bed.

On my own journey, the greatest excitement happened at the half-way point where the ascending and descending trains met. On the Djibouti-bound train traveled a full-grown giraffe, en route, as the lions had been, to Europe. This gentle beast caused no alarms and excursions, but offered instead a unique engineering problem. For he was fourteen feet tall, taller than the numerous tunnels through which the tracks ran.

The giraffe's body could be squeezed into an open-top cattle-car—but what to do with his neck? An ingenious device solved the difficulty at last. A rope was fastened to the giraffe's head by means of a halter. The other end of the rope ran to a windlass. By turning a handle a black Somali boy would wind up the rope, and down came the lofty head willy-nilly for each passage through a tunnel. Out of the tunnel, the boy released the handle, the windlass unwound, and up popped the head again. Four sharp blasts from the locomotive was the signal for the attendant to start cranking down the poor giraffe.

I felt sure that the resourceful person who thought up this device must have worked on a tug-boat in the Seine at Paris and learned to haul down the smoke-stack in order to slide under bridges.

During the three days of my trip, there wasn't a moment's boredom. I could well understand how the train had come to be known among foreigners in Ethiopia as the "Rhinoceros Express."

The building and maintenance of this railroad have cost many a life. The original builders in 1916 had to be accompanied by a small army of guards to fight off the hostile Danakil tribesmen who actively resisted the construction of the line through their territory. And even now, in spite of years of suppression, these wild desert-dwellers have not been entirely quieted.

Just before my visit, two thousand of them, ignoring the punishment which they knew was sure to come, swarmed down the tracks and across the border to French Somaliland. They were just amusing themselves by stealing all the sheep, women and camels they could find, burning the villages in their path and murdering everybody who objected.

Near the border stood a small and lonely military outpost, garrisoned by one young French officer and eighteen native soldiers. This tiny force, armed with a single machine gun, dared block the passage of two thousand raiders. Against the machine gun the tribesmen charged, to be mown down. Again and again they attacked, with the same result.

And then the machine gun jammed. The tidal wave of half-naked Danakils, brandishing spears and swords swept over the little squad.

All nineteen of the defenders were struck down, butchered in accordance with the horrible battle custom of the Danakils, and left to die beneath the desert sun.

The triumphant raiders then swept on, until their
camels staggered with the loot seized from French territory.

There was a roar of indignation in Paris. Immediately
an Ethiopian army was dispatched to try to capture
the leaders. This army brought back the machine gun
and two elderly Danakil chiefs to the capital. The
chiefs confessed and were sentenced to hang.

While awaiting execution they were chained, in Ethiopian fashion, each to a guard and turned loose to amuse
themselves. After two days of this close association
with his guard, one of the old chiefs complained to the
court. His two wives had come to Addis Ababa with
him, he stated, and it was his custom to sleep between
them; but now that he was chained to a total stranger
his domestic arrangements were suffering no end of embarrassment and inconvenience. . . . Could he be un-
chained, at least for the night?

The court solved the old bandit's problem by speeding
up his execution and hanging him immediately, before
another embarrassing bed-time came round.

For five hundred miles of treeless plains and mountains, sparsely dotted with little round huts made of mud
and straw, and peopled by slender spindle-legged blacks
with buck teeth and wild frizzy hair, our train struggled
up the eight thousand feet to Addis Ababa. The arrival
of the Rhinoceros Express twice a week—if hunting and
Danakils permit—is an event. Several hundred natives had gathered to watch us emerge. They were
dressed exactly alike: long white cotton shirt, white

drawers tight around the knees, and a white shawl called a *chamma* thrown over the shoulders. Nine faces out of ten were completely black, though a certain beauty and refinement of feature distinguished these people from the full-blooded African Negroes.

Everybody pushed and screamed. I soon found out that the average Ethiopian, gentle and childlike when at peace, flares up into fierce excitement on the least excuse, and a throng of them can raise such a hubbub as almost to frighten a newcomer. The strong shriek at the weak; the rich beat the poor; yet nobody seems to mind. It's just the way of things in Ethiopia.

Addis Ababa is as large in area as Paris, though it has less than eighty thousand people. Built only forty years ago, the city sprawls up hill and down in a great forest of eucalyptus trees. Forty years ago even the trees were not there. They were planted by King Men-elik II, the conquering hero-king who shaped the modern state of Abyssinia and built Addis Ababa for its capital. The city is still only a big straggling village six miles in diameter, dominated by one of the palaces where Haile Selassie once lived. This "palace" is just a cluster of ramshackle tin-roofed wooden buildings, half suffocated by shabby outhouses. By far the most interesting sight in the place are the ex-Emperor's thirty favorite lions.

The lion, in a hundred ways, is the symbol of Ethiopia. Haile Selassie bore the title "The Conquering Lion of Judah." Before the Italian invasion it was the custom of the Emperor, as well as of all his ministers and provincial chiefs, to keep lions as companions. And there are still districts in the country where a man may not propose marriage to a girl until he can bring her the head of a lion he has killed with a spear.

Up to 1936, when Ethiopia lost her independence, one of the most deeply rooted institutions in the country was slavery. Of Ethiopia's ten million people, two million were slaves. In the capital itself, the proportion was one in four. It was difficult at first glance to tell who was slave and who was master, as all were more or less the same color. It took even a discerning eye some time to begin to notice the finer faces of the master class.

Under Italian control the importation of slaves is a capital offense. But the law is constantly broken, as in prohibition America, and bootleg slaves are easy to buy if you know the right bootlegger. As long as the importation of "black ivory" continues to be highly profitable, slave-running will persist.

Almost every townsman in Ethiopia owns one or more slaves. At the American Legation in Addis Ababa, the Minister employs half a dozen Ethiopians as grooms, chauffeurs, gardeners, office-boys. They may be paid no more than ten dollars a month, but each one owns a slave or two, and delegates to them any errand beneath the dignity of the master.

One of the commonest and most colorful sights in the capital is a provincial chief riding into town. He is always mounted on a mule richly caparisoned in scarlet cloth that floats out behind. As befits a chieftain, he is arrayed in a helmet of monkey fur and a purple coat, and protected from the sun by a white umbrella. And behind him, trotting swiftly and tirelessly, is his retinue of barefoot slaves—six, ten, fifty slaves, each carrying a rifle and a sword.   Some of the great chiefs own fifteen thousand and, on every public appearance, bring along as many of them as possible, for a man's station is indicated by the number of slaves he can display, and according to their number is honor granted him.

It was Haile Selassie's intention to abolish slavery (had he been allowed to continue his rule), but not by an immediate, general liberation.   He was well aware of the chaos and anarchy that rose in America when, after the Civil War, such a sweeping measure was effected. He insisted, wisely, that some occupation and economic independence should be provided for freedmen, before they were freed.   Otherwise, ex-slaves would be forced to resort to banditry in order to live—or return to virtual slavery.

It is a curious fact that in Ethiopia, which seems in so many ways a barbaric nation, the Christian religion is the most powerful of all forces.   The country has been completely dominated by the Coptic Christian Church for the last sixteen hundred years.   One man in four among the upper caste Ethiopians becomes a priest.

However, as always happens among Negro populations, the religion has been degraded until it consists chiefly of superstitions, fasts, incantations and the wearing of charms.   There certainly are no Christian moral standards.   Ethiopians take the championship away from the Bolsheviks and the Wahabis in the domestic sport of rapid marriage and divorce.   A youth begins marrying at fourteen, and by the time he is twenty it's a habit. But the marriage ceremony is a formality only the well-to-do can afford, so it's a rare Ethiopian who knows for certain who his father was.   It is surprising, in view of the prevailing carelessness, that the most profane oath a camel driver can hurl at his evil beast is to ask, "Who is your father?"

One would not expect prudery among such primitive people, nor does it exist. One of the sights of Addis Ababa is the public bath, an outdoor pool fed by hot springs, where at any hour of the day from fifty to a hundred men and women may be seen bathing together, not in the least self-conscious because of their total nakedness. I have seen the same freedom elsewhere; but in Addis Ababa, where only the lowest class uses the outdoor bath, the foreign colony has invented a ludicrous game in connection with the natives' innocent ablutions.

Carrying a pocketful of small coins, as my friends had instructed me, I accompanied two of them to see the baths. We tossed our pennies into the mud beside the pool. In a flash a hundred naked bathers—men, women and children—scrambled from the water and piled pell-mell upon the coins. We threw more money, until the struggling, shouting, steaming tangle of arms and legs was heaped up six feet high. I wondered how they could ever extricate themselves; but one by one they wriggled out, clutching their pennies and beaming triumphantly.

Pennies can buy considerable pleasure for the poorer classes in Addis Ababa, especially at the native bars which abound along the eucalyptus lanes. The shingle over the door of every bar shows the crowned Ethiopian lion holding a glass of beer in one paw. Excessive drinking is so much the rule that there is a law punishing any citizen found drunk on the streets after eight o'clock. But to evade it the gay blades choose to get locked up all night in one of the bars with a barrel of

The St. Bernard dogs are famous the world over for their great size, intelligence, heroism and fidelity. They are a cross between a bull-dog and a sheep-dog.

Dally and the author receive the blessings of St. Bernard. This statue of the Saint stands at the summit of the pass, where in the tenth century he founded the hospice.

The Pied Piper of Hamlin never attracted more children than Elysabethe Dalrymple collected on the Italian side of the Alps. They followed her in swarms from village to village. The author usually carried three or four of them behind him on Dally's back.

tedj, a fiddler and an amiable black barmaid.   It has been suggested that the curfew law is kept on the books at the insistence of the bar-keepers themselves.

At the first moment of my arrival in Addis Ababa, on descending from the Rhinoceros Express and crossing the platform, I ran in between two Ethiopians and was suddenly stopped short by a chain stretching from the right wrist of one to the left wrist of the other.   This sight I was to see twenty times a day, for it is one of the most familiar features of the city.

This chain usually links a debtor and a creditor, or any two people who cannot agree over a lawsuit.   If a creditor feels that his debtor is likely to run away before the debt is paid, he can have the borrower chained to him for safe measure.   In America, disputes over property, alimony, traffic accidents, slander, alienation of affection, and back-payments on the radio are taken to the law courts.   In Ethiopia, the two disagreeing parties are simply taken to the blacksmith shop, chained together and left to their own devices until they can come to some agreement.

They may be chained for days or even months.   They must eat, sleep, walk and work together, as inseparable as Siamese twins.   But instead of loathing each other as one would expect them to, those I saw appeared to be the best of pals.

In the days before the Italian conquest, one of the Emperor's most onerous duties in Addis Ababa was to conduct all murder trials.   The sentence for manslaughter and murder was death by shooting.   But fortunately for the murderer, he could usually avail himself of a legal alternative.   The murdered person's family was allowed to accept a cash payment as expiation of the crime. When the condemned was being marched to the execution ground behind the railroad station, his victim's bereaved relatives always went along to talk business. The murderer started off with an offer of a hundred dollars if they would spare his life. They spurned it as being too little compensation for their grief. Two hundred and fifty dollars . . . the procession was nearing the deadly field . . . the price increased with each step. Sometimes this auction sale went on right to the edge of the grave, the family accepting the blood-money only when they were sure it was every cent the murderer had. Sometimes he would refuse to offer anything, and die, rather than deprive his children of his property.

If the murderer did not have the price demanded and agreed to, he was allowed three days to raise it. Not infrequently one saw such a man chained to a guard, begging in the streets from everyone and explaining that he desperately needed another hundred dollars to finish buying his life. If in three days he had not managed to raise the money, the family either took what they could get, or else, if especially vindictive, demanded that the execution be carried out.

Sometimes the victim's family were the executioners and killed their man with the same weapon he had used. This savage system was discontinued by Haile Selassie, who also forbade the public hangings which, until his accession, entertained the populace almost daily in the market place.

But Haile Selassie knew the Ethiopian mind so well that he dared not adopt all the reforms he personally would have preferred. As head of the nation, he had to uphold a few of the theatrically cruel punishments that experience had proved to be most effective among primitive peoples. Especially in times of crisis did he have recourse to grim measures. When Italian aggression became a serious threat, this progressive ruler, the most enlightened that Ethiopia had ever known, issued a public decree that the punishment for treason to the state would be *anointment in honey and burning at the stake.*

CHAPTER XXX

THE KING OF KINGS

My visit to Ethiopia took place during the first months of the Italian invasion. Naturally I was eager to meet Haile Selassie, about whom the country was rallying all her forces of defense. With the affairs of the nation at such a crisis I felt especially fortunate when the Emperor, learning of my newspaper connections in America, offered to give me a series of interviews.

At this time, the King of Kings was holding court not in his palace in Addis Ababa, but at a small provincial city called Dire Dawa, on the railroad line half-way back to Djibouti. There he had gone to review his wild Somali troops and receive their oath of allegiance.

And it was at Dire Dawa that I alighted from the Rhinoceros Express and was met by one of the King's generals. Under his guidance I was taken to the Governor's Palace where Haile Selassie and his family were living at the moment. The palace crowned a hill in the middle of the town, and was approached by a steep flight of broad steps, some four hundred feet long.

As I neared the hill, I found it surrounded by a dense crowd of townsmen, slaves and tribesmen, all dressed in their usual cotton *chammas,* gathered there to witness some ceremony or other being held in honor of the Emperor's visit. The twilight had gone, and in the darkness this great crowd of black-skinned people seemed to be merely so many animated white *chammas* without heads, hands or feet.

Torches flared, barefoot soldiers lined the way, and down the steps came a most astonishing procession. A thousand barbaric Somali warriors, packed close together, naked but for a loin cloth, tramped down the great staircase. Their lean black bodies had been smeared with mutton fat and shone in the torchlight. The wind blew their black locks over their eyes and faces. Each carried a six-foot spear in his right hand. His left he extended before his face in a gesture not unlike a Roman salute. And as these wild desert warriors descended, their thousand voices chanted in rhythm with their march—a wild, monotonous wail that could be heard all across the city. But from their marching bare black feet, there came not the faintest sound.

This chanting, saluting, naked band, beneath a forest of spears, moved slow as a funeral march down to where I stood, and past. They were all ages from fourteen to seventy; all black, but more Arab than Negro in appearance; all tall, slender, fine-featured, thin-lipped; all fierce and cruel as hawks; and all smelling to high heaven of rancid mutton fat.

These were Somali warriors from the surrounding deserts, who had marched into town to pay homage to the Emperor before they left for the battle line. He had welcomed them at the steps of the palace, in the twilight, up on the top of the hill, and had given presents to their chiefs. Now, in the darkness, they were descending the great stairway in ceremonial procession, bearing with them, as a sacred flame to kindle their loyalty and their bravery, the blessing of their Great Chief.

I looked up and saw the figure of the Emperor, still standing on the top step, silhouetted against the palace lights, and I felt sure he must be admiring the dignity and primitive beauty of this savage company.

When I reached the gates of the palace, the Emperor had withdrawn to change his clothes, about which clung the mutton odor in which he had been steeped for the past hour. The general led me into the Hall of Audience, where I found, somewhat to my dismay, that I was to be the only guest. He introduced me to the Emperor's youngest son, the Duke of Harar, who had been sent to greet me.

The Duke was only eleven, but a more self-possessed and ingratiating youngster I've never met. His private tutor, a Frenchman, had taught him perfect French. Smiling politely, he greeted me, and I noticed how his large eyes shone in his pale brown face.

"My father sends you his apologies for being late to receive you. His Somalis kept him overlong," the boy said.

This polished little Prince—and those barbaric war-riors—they were such a contrast! What would the man who ruled the race that produced such divergent types,

himself be like? I remembered my interview with Ibn
Saud—six-feet-six, massive, bull-necked, tyrannical,
marrying and divorcing a new wife every third month, a
creature half man and half god from out the Arabian
mythology—would the Emperor of Ethiopia be anything like that? The pictures I had seen—one top-
hatted, another in a lion-mane cape—had only confused
my preconception.

"His Majesty is coming now," said the general in
broken French.

The double doors at the end of the room swung wide,
and the Emperor, the Conquering Lion of Judah,
walked into the Hall of Audience.

I received one of the most unexpected surprises of my
life. Haile Selassie was about as much like Ibn Saud
as a slim and tawny deer is like a buffalo. He was
younger by about thirteen years. I found him less than
medium height, delicately made, with small, artistic, almost fragile hands and feet. His face, curly-bearded,
thin-featured and light brown in color, was especially
striking for its keenly intelligent expression. His eyes
revealed eloquently a generous and sympathetic heart.
He melted and enchanted everyone who approached him,
and I was no exception.

Haile Selassie was dressed in a white satin, gold-em-
broidered cape and tight-fitting satin trousers, his in-
formal evening costume. I noticed he wore shoes. That
a king should be wearing shoes would be hardly worth
mentioning—except that he was one of the extremely

few Ethiopians I had seen not barefoot. My general, a distinguished officer of the highest rank, white-bearded, strewn with medals, had never adopted shoes.

And the Emperor of Ethiopia did *not* have fifty wives. He had just one, to whom he had been married twenty-one years. She entered the hall behind him, a plump, quiet, motherly woman, obviously not one who would take an interest in affairs of state. She was even more light-skinned than her husband, and she too wore a white satin cape. Whereas he spoke fluent French, she understood only Amharic, the local language, and was shy in the presence of a foreigner.

Behind the Queen came the Princess Royal, twenty years old. She was dressed in a European dinner-gown. Of all the family, hers was the most aristocratic face, although her hair, which she wore in a high pompadour, was somewhat kinky. She had spent her life in English and Swiss schools, spoke English, French and German without an accent, played Debussy on the piano, and had a graceful manner which would have distinguished her anywhere. She could not be called exactly beautiful, and yet her perfect complexion and alert eyes gave her face great charm. Unmistakably, and under all circumstances, she was a royal princess, conscious of the fact that she was descended straight from the Queen of Sheba. Her younger sister, not present that evening, had been married at thirteen, the usual age in Ethiopia. She herself had not yet been betrothed.

The origin of the royal family is still one of the proud legends of the country. The story is partly recorded in the Bible:

In the year 1000 B.C., King Solomon in all his wisdom and glory ruled in Jerusalem. At the same time, Ethiopia was ruled by the Queen of Sheba, the daughter of Ethiopia's great hero, who had rid the land of dragons and been crowned King by the grateful people.

Wishing to become acquainted with Solomon, the Queen sent presents ahead by ambassadors, crossed the Red Sea to Arabia, and traveled by camel to Jerusalem. And there she was welcomed with fitting ceremony by Solomon.

The Amharic version of the Bible completes the story with details that are familiar to all Ethiopian Sunday Schools:

The Queen, runs the story, feared that Solomon, with all his three hundred wives and seven hundred concubines, might try to add her to his list. But Solomon agreed to make no such overtures—so long as she neither ate nor drank anything which he did not offer her personally.

He then proceeded to banquet her on the saltiest possible food; and that night, sleeping in an apartment next to the King's, the Queen of Sheba was seized with a great thirst, and finding a pitcher of water on a table, drank from it.

The crafty Solomon was watching all the time. Sheba

had broken the contract, and promptly became wife Number Three Hundred and One.

A son was born to them, named Menelik. Later this same Prince, on a visit to his father in Jerusalem, stole the Ark of the Covenant and the original Ten Commandments. With these treasures he fled back to Ethiopia. There, in the city of Aksum, Sheba's capital, they were hidden in the rock, or so the priesthood claims; and there they remain to this day, guarded by the highest officials of the church, and defended carefully from the polluting gaze of any layman. *So* carefully, in fact, that from Menelik's time until now, no one has seen them!

Menelik inherited the throne of Ethiopia from his mother, and founded the royal line that continued for three thousand years—until the Italians came to overthrow it. And it is by right of this descent from Solomon that Haile Selassie bore the title, "The Conquering Lion of Judah."

Haile Selassie himself did not come to the throne peacefully. Few monarchs of Ethiopia have.

From 1889 to 1916, Ethiopia was ruled, gloriously, by Menelik II, the most despotic but the most vigorous ruler in the history of the country. He had no sons, only daughters. On his deathbed he designated his favorite grandson, Lidj Yasu, to be his successor, and made all the great chiefs swear fealty to the new ruler.

But no sooner had Lidj Yasu come to the throne, at nineteen, than he began to scandalize the country by his wild extravagances, heroic dissipations and his inclination toward the Moslem religion. In short order he was deposed (1916) by a congress of chiefs, and imprisoned in a remote stronghold where he still lives on, chained with a four-foot golden chain to his keeper.

In his place, the chiefs chose as ruler Menelik's daughter, Zauditu, and as regent Haile Selassie, a son of Menelik's cousin. There were other princes more directly in line, but he was the one best qualified to counsel, and later inherit, the throne. He had made a notably fine record as Ras (chief or baron) of a province, and is still called merely Ras Tafari—Baron Tafari— by many of his subjects.

In 1930, the Empress Zauditu's husband, wishing to rid the Empress of her over-progressive regent, made war against him and was defeated. The day after the defeat, Zauditu died with convenient suddenness. Automatically, Ras Tafari became King; and to his coronation, almost every country in the world sent important personages. The King of England was represented by one of his own sons. Rarely, even in Europe, has such a galaxy of princes been seen, as that which gathered at the savage little city of Addis Ababa to watch Haile Selassie become Emperor.

The entire nation rejoiced, for the new Emperor was the very symbol of progress. Under him Ethiopia would grow in riches and power. . . .

And then came the thunderbolt from Rome—Mussc- lini's promise to the Italians that he would give them more colonies, and that Ethiopia, independent for three thousand years, was first on the list.

This promise cast Italy into a state of war-expectancy, for most of the Italians not only coveted Ethiopian territory, but wished to settle an old score with that country as well.

Near the end of the nineteenth century, the Italians annexed the Red Sea coast of Ethiopia, now called Eritrea. Encouraged by this success, they penetrated deeper into the country, with the intention of turning all of it into a protectorate.

But Italy had not reckoned with King Menelik II. A violent, arrogant, unconquerable personality, Menelik roused his countrymen to defend themselves against invasion.   In 1896, at Aduwa, near the Eritrean border, he waited with eighty thousand tribesmen to meet the invading Italian Army of twenty-seven thousand trained soldiers.

Many of the Ethiopians had rifles; but when the battle began they flung away these unfamiliar weapons, stripped off their hot encumbering uniforms, seized their daggers, and yelling—and looking—like wild beasts, went after the heavily clothed and heavily armed enemy. The Italians tried to escape the terrifying assault which swept over them.   But they didn't know the way out; their maps were faulty.   They found themselves lost in untraversable country.   They probably put up a good fight, determined to sell their lives dearly; but they didn't have a chance.   Ten thousand Italians perished

outright; seven thousand more were captured and subjected to various horrors—in battle there is no limit to
Ethiopian cruelty. Ten thousand of the invaders struggled back to Eritrea. They had brought seventy pieces
of artillery—but they returned with none.

Menelik became the national hero, founded Addis
Ababa, and for twenty years, with an iron hand, ruled
the country he had saved.

The Italians, appalled by the disaster at Aduwa, decided not to annex Ethiopia that year. Not for forty
years did an Italian soldier dare set foot across the
frontier. Not until 1935. . . .

And if, on the night I sat down to dinner with His
Ethiopian Majesty, he looked (behind his charming social exterior) none too happy, it was because he knew
that at that moment, two hundred thousand Italian soldiers were massing at his frontiers to invade and crush
his country. He knew that hundreds of airplanes were
standing by, laden with bombs to drop on his villages
and his capital. He knew that slaughter and anguish
lay ahead for his people.

Dinner, a very excellent meal cooked by a French
chef and accompanied by the best champagne, was well
served. But I was too tense with interest in the Emperor's answers to my questions about the war, to take
much notice of the food.

During our first exchange of compliments, I had expressed, in my best French, my appreciation of the Emperor's invitation to the palace.

"I am always happy to meet any friends of your American Minister," he replied. "And because he has told me that you are a journalist, I am especially pleased that circumstances permitted this evening together. I feel that I really owe a debt to the representatives of the world press, especially the American press, for the sympathetic understanding with which they have championed Ethiopia's cause. The moral support we are receiving in every land is our greatest strength in the present crisis."

"Undoubtedly that is a considerable asset, sir," I answered. "But foreign observers report that your greatest advantage lies in the topography of your country."

"I am aware of that too," the Emperor said, smiling. "The ruggedness of Ethiopia's mountains and canyons will help us; and our deserts and heat and mosquitoes will help as well. The deeper into such natural defenses our enemies penetrate, the more exhausted and vulnerable they will become.

"But as for my own soldiers, they are at home in such surroundings. You saw a thousand of my tribesmen as you approached the palace. In a pitched battle, what could they do with their spears against tanks and poison gas? But in irregular guerrilla warfare those tribesmen are superb. They live on almost nothing—on a fraction of the water and food supply needed by an Italian— and yet they have extraordinary endurance. In their own element, the rocks, the burning desert, they are incomparable fighters.

"They have a contempt for death; and illiterate and simple-minded though they are, they realize the great danger that threatens them—the end of their freedom, the end of Ethiopia as an independent nation—and they will fight accordingly."

"Do the isolated little tribes in the hills understand the conception of Ethiopia as a single sovereign state?" I asked.

"Not in a modern political sense," Haile Selassie explained. "But they understand the immemorial tradition of unity which has kept their homeland independent. And the threat of Italian aggression has engendered such resentment among all ranks of my people, that if I showed the slightest sign of weakening in my policy of vigorous, determined, to-the-bitter-end defense—if my people feared that I would give in to Italian demands for territory rather than fight—I would be dethroned by a revolution."

In Ethiopia, it has been the custom from time immemorial for the Emperor, the Empress and the Abuna, the head of the church, to lead the army in person into every battle. All the battle-scenes painted by native artists for hundreds of years back show these three personages, shaded by umbrellas, riding on horseback in the midst of their troops. At the battle of Aduwa, the Ethiopian Army was led personally by Menelik, assisted by his wife and the Abuna.

So I asked Haile Selassie if he planned to continue this ancient custom. And I looked across at his plump matronly wife, and wondered how she would fare in a battle.

The Emperor smiled. "I cannot say," he replied. "The science of war has changed so completely. Now there is not just one battle-front, but several, all along the hundreds of miles of our Eritrea and Somaliland frontiers. I cannot be everywhere at once. So it may be best for me to remain in Addis Ababa, and hold all the lines that extend to the battlefields, and administer my country as a whole rather than direct single engagements. . . . But I am afraid," he added with another smile, " that those Somali soldiers I received before dinner will not have much use for me if I fail to lead them in every charge."

As the evening advanced and our conversation developed, I realized there was not a trick, psychological, international or military, that Haile Selassie did not understand and was not prepared to turn to Ethiopia's advantage. He had weighed the might of the forces beating against him, but he was undismayed, clear-sighted, grimly resolute.

Impressed by the Emperor's personal courage, I remembered that I had encountered the same spirit everywhere in Ethiopia, and remarked on the fact.

"It is true," he said. "Today every man, woman and child is aroused by the danger confronting us, and is ready to sacrifice everything, life included, to protect our freedom and our homes."

This sacrifice was made in vain. Three months later, the Italians, moving forward behind a curtain of airplane bombs and poison gas, entered Addis Ababa. The despairing, broken-hearted Emperor fled with his family to Djubiti. He has been living in Europe ever since.

CHAPTER XXXI

IN THE TRACKS OF HANNIBAL

THE monks living in the St. Bernard Monastery at the summit of the eight-thousand-foot St. Bernard Pass across the Alps have been sheltering travelers of every nationality and every station for nearly a thousand years. But it is unlikely that any guest will be remembered longer than one named Elysabethe Dalrymple.

Because Elysabethe Dalrymple was an elephant, the only elephant to cross the pass in over two thousand years.

When this extraordinary visitor drew up before the hospice door, she was not alone. Riding on her shoulders was an amateur mahout who seemed none too sure of his seat, for he held on to his mount's enormous ears with both hands.

The Prior of the monastery, when he recovered from his astonishment, invited this odd pair of travelers to come in and sign their names on the register. The elephant could get only part of one foot through the door. So the mahout had to dismount and sign for both, taking the elephant's dictation through the window.

For the elephant:

Name—"Elysabethe Dalrymple. But please add," said the elephant, "that everybody calls me 'Dally'— my real name is too silly."

Address—"Jardin d'Acclimatation, Bois de Boulogne, Paris."

Profession—"Generally a lady of leisure, admired and loved by the entire population of Paris; but at present suffering servitude to an eccentric——"

The mahout looked up, and hesitated to use such an adjective to describe himself. . . .

"Go on," exclaimed Dally. "Write it down. I said *eccentric* American—who is riding me over the Alps on the most harebrained adventure I've ever experienced in all my twelve years. The American thinks he's the reincarnation of Hannibal—but (if you want *my* opinion) he looks and acts about as much like Hannibal as I do."

The mahout made a wry face of chagrin on hearing his elephant talk about him so disrespectfully. But the elephant wouldn't let him change one word. So he gave up remonstrating and began to fill in his own registration blank:

Name—"Richard Halliburton."

Address—"Carthage." (The elephant snorted with disdain seeing the mahout write "Carthage." She knew his original home was Memphis, Tennessee.)

Profession—"Generally a respectable writer of books on travel and adventure, but at present occupied with the caprices of a temperamental elephant"— here the mahout gave Elysabethe Dalrymple a very superior look—"which I'm riding over the Alps in the tracks of the elephants ridden in 218 B.C. by that terror of Rome, that greatest of Carthaginians, that most famous elephant conductor in history— Hannibal!"

Back in Ethiopia, soon after my visit with Haile Selassie, I looked at the calendar and realized that the season had arrived—July—when I could again seriously consider my elephant expedition over the Alps. All during the months that had elapsed since Elysabethe Dalrymple ran away with me in Paris and since the snowstorm in the passes had prevented my making the trip with Big Bertha I'd not lost sight of the elephant-march project, nor had my enthusiasm for it faded. In fact, after the last few weeks in the broiling heat of Ethiopia the appeal of the Alps was stronger than ever.

So I sent a cable to Hanover, Germany, where the zoo director had agreed to rent Big Bertha to me the year before, asking if Bertha was still available for the same purpose and under the same conditions. He answered that Bertha had been leased to a circus and was no longer for rent.

But I had another idea. After all, there was no other elephant in Europe so well qualified for my particular needs as the Paris animal—that is, if her fear of motor noises could be overcome. I cabled the Paris zoo: "I still want Elysabethe Dalrymple for Alpine expedition. Can you start traffic-training immediately and have her ready in two weeks? If agreeable will return Paris at once."

Paris cabled an encouraging answer: "Will begin training today. Confident you can leave for Alps on your arrival."

And in two weeks, after making a non-stop journey by the Rhinoceros Express to Djibouti and by boat back up the Red Sea and through the Suez to Marseilles, I was in the Jardin d'Acclimatation, climbing aboard Dally's broad shoulders. To my delight and relief I learned that the elephant, once terrified by automobiles (how well I remember!), was now actually in love with them. Her trainer had gradually increased her daily dosage of traffic until she had become accustomed to all forms of motor mischief. The zoo director assured me that fire engines themselves wouldn't frighten her any more, and that we could depart at my convenience.

It was understood, of course, that I would take along Dally's trainer, Louis Harel, who always accompanied the elephant. This was highly agreeable to me for I saw at once that he would make an ideal assistant. He had been in charge of Dally from her infancy, and consequently they were mutually devoted and mutually trustful. A Norman countryman, he had found in his boyhood that he had a gift for training animals, and had followed this profession. He was now thirty-two years old, inexhaustibly energetic, happy-natured, resourceful, strong as a horse, and ready to conduct Dally across the Alps, or up to the moon, or anywhere else I wanted him to go. Without Harel I would have been helpless. With him I had every reason to hope for success.

Together we hired a small motor truck to accompany us and carry Dally's food, blankets, buckets and our own personal baggage. We also found a chauffeur to drive the truck. Lloyd's again insured us. Three days after I reached Paris, we were ready to depart.

This time, having learned my lesson the previous October, I preferred to cross Paris after midnight on our march to the freight yards . . . out of the Bois de Boulogne into the Place Maillot, down the Avenue

Grande Armée, around the Arc de Triomphe, along the Champs Élysées to the Place Concorde. Our truck filled with sweet-smelling hay moved slowly just ahead of Dally's long nose—a device that helped us guide her through the streets.

Crowds of taxicabs and motorists, seeing an elephant ambling down the boulevards at midnight, followed us in such increasing numbers that the police had to intervene in order to allow traffic to move at all.

Even so, despite the confusion, Dally consented to pose for flashlight photographs before the Arc de Triomphe and Notre Dame.

At the freight yard the elephant climbed unhesitatingly into her private boxcar—a heaven of straw, hay and sugar. Then, accompanied by Harel, she rode across France and along the borders of the Lake of Geneva into the upper Rhone Valley. At Martigny, where the motor road starts climbing over the mountain wall dividing Switzerland from Italy, I rejoined Mlle. Dalrymple, got aboard her back and prepared to start up the trail.

At last I was launched on an adventure the very thought of which had captivated me from the time when, as a boy, I'd first read the story of Hannibal's elephant ride across the Alps at the head of his army. It had seemed to me then that Hannibal had got hold of a fine idea—an idea which I would like to try myself some day. At the time, it combined for me all the allure of mountain-climbing, circus-riding and military exploits. I'd outgrown my other juvenile ambitions to be a locomotive engineer and an acrobat; but this one—this preposterous, extravagant dream of riding over the Alps on the back of an elephant like the great Carthaginian—had refused to die.

In the volume of ancient history which had introduced me to Hannibal there were two vivid full-page pictures of his African army on the march. One picture showed the thirty-seven elephants that accompanied the army, crossing the Rhone River near Avignon on enormous rafts. The other picture showed the same elephants, carrying officers, struggling in a long line over a steep, snow-covered, precipice-edged pass in the Alps. From above, the mountaineers were hurling huge boulders onto the elephants. And two of these giant beasts were plunging downward into the cloud-filled abyss.

The two pictures made an indelible impression on my young mind. Today, after more than twenty years, I can recall every detail. And from the first time I saw them, and read the story of the immortal march they illustrated, Hannibal has remained one of the towering figures in my galaxy of heroes.

Alexander, Cæsar, Napoleon, may have been as great generals as Hannibal. But they fought and won their battles riding on horses, or leading their troops on foot. *Here* was a leader who fought battles from the back of an elephant, who mounted his officers on other elephants, who rode his five-ton pachyderm from Spain into France, crossed the Rhone on those huge rafts, marched on into Switzerland, drove his monstrous beast up the skyscraping defiant slopes of the Alps into the regions of eternal snows, braving the freezing winds, the avalanches, the precipices, the showers of boulders, and descended, with what few elephants had survived, upon the backs of the Romans, to inflict the most terrible defeats ever suffered by their armies in their long military history.

Courage—audacity—imagination! Hannibal was the top!

And to relive this particular chapter from the past, to ride my own elephant over those same terrible Alps in Hannibal's tracks, seemed to me to be the top of adventures.

But reliving history was not my only reason for this elephant-ride. There was the sporting element too. Had Hannibal never existed, the idea of climbing those particular mountains on an elephant (had I ever thought of it) would have appealed to me as amusing sport. And I hoped it would prove as amusing to the people along the way as to myself.

As soon as I had announced, back in Paris, that I planned to cross the Alps via the Great St. Bernard Pass, I became the target of ponderous criticisms from earnest historians who observed that the route I had chosen was not the route followed by Hannibal. The Great St. Bernard, said my critics, was the one pass least likely to have been used by the Carthaginians who were marching from southern France. Why, these historians asked, would Hannibal, with winter upon him, have gone many miles out of his way, around to the north side of the Swiss Alps, to cross by the most notoriously difficult pass of all?—especially when the two passes leading directly from France into Italy, the Little St. Bernard and Mt. Cenis, were right in front of him? These two passes were more than a thousand feet lower, infinitely easier to traverse; were, in fact, the routes of two principal Roman highways leading into Gaul.

I quite agreed that these critics had some reason on their side. But obviously, they had not read with much imagination the original sources of Hannibalic history.

For the outstanding feature of all the reports of ancient historians about this, the Second Punic War, were the fearful difficulties encountered and the appalling casualties suffered by Hannibal on his mountain march . . . fifty per cent of his forces lost. One Roman writer tells a story (a tall story indeed) that at one point Hannibal found his path completely blocked by huge masses of rock. His men could climb over, but not his elephants. So, with wood fires, he heated the rocks till they were red hot. And then he poured onto them a barrel of vinegar . . . and behold!—the rocks split asunder, and the elephants crept through.

All this doesn't sound much like a principal Roman highway into Gaul!

But it does sound exactly like the Great St. Bernard which at that time was crossed only by a footpath. The very unlikeliness of this route may have caused the Romans to leave it unguarded—the best reason in the world for Hannibal to choose it.

It is also interesting to note that Livy, the Roman historian, writing two hundred years after the Second Punic War, states that the Great St. Bernard had acquired the name "Poenine Pass," presumably to commemorate a Phoenician (Carthaginian) invasion that crossed that way. However, there is little or no actual evidence one way or the other. The people living today along the Little St. Bernard and Mt. Cenis highroads firmly believe Hannibal came their way. The monks at the monastery at the summit of the Great St. Bernard insist the honor is theirs. So one guess is as good as another.

Obviously, then, since nobody could direct me with certainty, I was free to choose my own route. And since the sporting element was so strong in my undertaking, I decided to get the last possible ounce of flavor out of the exploit, and to choose the steepest, hardest, highest, snowiest, most challenging pass I could find. This, without question, was the Great St. Bernard.

For nine months in the year this route is completely closed to traffic by snowdrifts thirty feet deep. For only twenty days out of the three hundred and sixty-five is it free from frost. It has killed as many people, probably, as all the rest of the Alpine passes put together Its deadly nature caused St. Bernard, a thousand years ago, to found a hospice at the summit to provide security for travelers in distress.

And also, Hannibal or no Hannibal, the Great St. Bernard, for any explorer in the field of history, offers other names as famous and resounding as the Carthaginian's. Julius Cæsar several times came this way; and Charlemagne. In 1800, Napoleon marched past with an army of forty thousand men en route to Marengo in north Italy. And in between these great names one finds an endless procession of popes, kings, conquerors, scarcely less celebrated.

And then there was a final reason I chose the Great St. Bernard. I wanted to visit the monastery and call upon the famous dogs.

As for the elephant herself, she differed considerably from those used by Hannibal. His elephants were all African. (In Roman times these beasts were numerous in what is now Tunis, where the city of Carthage was situated.) But mine, a female, came from Sumatra, the East Indian island. She was born there in 1923, caught in a trap while still a baby, and brought to the Paris zoo. Hannibal's mounts probably weighed as much as five tons each; Dally weighed only three; and in contrast to the brutal discipline to which I suspect the Carthaginian animals were subjected, Dally had never received a harsh blow, scarcely even a harsh word, in her life.

In fact I cannot believe any captive elephant ever had a happier home than Elysabethe Dalrymple. In the Paris zoo she had known nothing but gentle treatment and affectionate friends. Her own amiable disposition and good manners made her the pet of the Garden, and a special favorite among the children who climbed on her back and rode her around the bridle paths of the Bois de Boulogne. The other five elephants in the zoo all had evil tricks. But Dally, never.

Her intelligence equaled her gentleness. She learned to stand up on her hind legs twice as quickly as her class-mates. In two lessons she could sit down quite grace-fully. On the harmonica, which she played by closing the end of her trunk about the instrument and blowing upon the keys, Dally was a virtuoso. Harel insisted she was the most precocious young elephant he had ever met.

And this was the docile and lovable creature on to whose great back I climbed at Martigny, to march across the Alps for a new conquest of Italy.

CHAPTER XXXII

UPHILL

"I hope you don't mind, but I've got an elephant out here."
Courtesy of Theodore Hall and The Washington Post.

THE moment Dally reached Martigny the news that an elephant had come to town, an elephant which was going to climb the Alps, had spread like wildfire. In ten minutes the entire population swarmed about us in such numbers we had difficulty getting Dally out of the boxcar and under way. The Chief of Police had to come to our rescue. In return for this favor he asked a favor of us: to visit the local children's hospital and let the patients, among whom was his own daughter, see the elephant.

I gladly complied. And in the courtyard, surrounded
by a ring of a thousand people, with every window above
filled with children's heads, Dally put on a show. She
sat upright on the flagstones, stood on her front feet,
and lifted Harel on her trunk high above her head.
When she played her harmonica the shrieks of laughter
from the spectators in the sick wards could be heard for
blocks. In fact Dally outdid herself, seeming to know
that she was giving an extraordinary amount of
pleasure.

By the time we got clear from Martigny darkness
had set in. However that was my plan, for there would
be less traffic and less heat for our first day's march.
Our little truck, loaded down with hay and meal, went
ahead to warn approaching motorists. The warning had
to be repeated at least three times before they grasped
the fact that there was an *elephant* coming up the road.
A hundred boys on bicycles offered sufficient protection from behind.

But there was, at first, no warning for the Swiss peasants along the way. They looked up from their cottage
doors to half-see, in the darkness, the shadow of an enormous, unearthly beast hurrying past—the first elephant
most of them ever had beheld. Some of the women
and children screamed and fled. Some of the men stood
in their tracks too astonished to move or to speak. No
elephant had come this way since Hannibal's herd of
thirty-seven struggled up this same road more than
twenty-one hundred years ago.

Soon word that we were on the road began to flash
ahead of us. At each village, though it was well past
bedtime, we found the entire population standing tense

and staring, waiting for the monster to approach. Had it been a brontosaurus or a dinosaur I rode, the excitement we caused could not have been greater.

We quartered Dally that night in an ancient stone stable used in the old days for pack-mules, at the little town of Orsières, eighteen kilometers from Martigny. Again every human being in the place, and all the cats and dogs, flocked to see the elephant; and numbers of them sat till dawn, whispering and wondering, around the stable where Dally slept.

Next day we covered another fifteen kilometers, climbing up the writhing road alongside a roaring torrent, into rarer and rarer air. We passed through heavy showers of rain, and through bursts of blazing summer sunshine. The ice-armored peaks above and ahead glittered for a moment against the blue, and then were swept from view by a wave of clouds. We let Dally set her own pace, and stopped to rest whenever she liked. I continued to ride on her shoulders, close behind her head, while Harel, whenever there was a crowded passenger bus or bridge or dangerous ledge-road to pass, walked beside her to give her confidence. The buses were our greatest trials, for they were almost as wide as the highway, and each time they passed, thundering and lurching and pressing us against the parapet or the mountain wall, I wondered if Dally was going to take fright and run away again as she had eight months before on the Paris boulevard. But her traffic-training seemed to have been thorough. The buses, even the loudest and reddest ones, no longer alarmed her. And for that I was profoundly grateful, for had she been thrown into a panic here on this dan-

gerous, sometimes crowded mountain road, had she become unmanageable and plunged through the congestion of people and automobiles, there is hardly a chance
that we could have avoided fatal consequences.

One complication arose which neither Harel nor I
had anticipated—horses. Every horse that caught sight
of the elephant shook with terror, reared and fled. As
a precautionary measure we secured a big cloth sack
with which Harel ran ahead, whenever we saw a horse
approaching, to put over the animal's eyes till the elephant could get past. Livy, describing Hannibal's first
big battle in northern Italy against the Romans, tells
the same story: "Hannibal's elephants, looming large
on the outer extremities of the wings, gave rise to such
a panic, particularly among the horses, not only by their
strange appearance but also by their unfamiliar smell,
as to bring about a general rout."

The second afternoon we reached St. Pierre, the last
village before the summit. By now the entire countryside was in a fever of excitement. All day the crowds
of mountaineers following at Dally's heels had increased
continually in number. Now at St. Pierre they packed
the village's single street and little square. They came
running down the mountain side, or up from the banks
of the tumbling river, breathless and amazed. Some
brought their hay rakes and scythes. Some carried their
babies, holding them carefully out of reach of Dally's
inquisitive snout.

But generally a great wave of sympathy flowed from
the mountain people to the elephant. Dally, despite
her colossal size, inspired immediate affection from
almost everyone. Women called her pet names, ca-

ressed her thick hide and bombarded her with sugar, peanuts and carrots. The children, almost beside themselves with joy over the visit of the marvelous beast, swarmed about her and over her in dense and shrieking mobs. At every opportunity I lifted a child or two upon the elephant's back to sit tight behind me. And nothing the rest of their lives will ever be for them such a memorable adventure. Without planning it I found myself in possession of the magic power of the Pied Piper. (I only hoped for Dally's sake that we would attract no rats.)

And curiously enough, once these mountaineers had got over their first shock, they began to laugh at the sight of my good-natured monster. It was a special kind of laughter—the kind aroused by a clumsy, woolly, affectionate collie puppy who runs up to greet us. Dally amused not the mountaineers' sense of humor, but their hearts. Strange, I thought, that the same human emotion which makes us love diminutive animals like puppies and kittens and monklets, makes us love the biggest animal of all.

A hundred times on our expedition I was struck with this extraordinary good-will toward herself that Dally stimulated. Had I been riding a giraffe or a rhinoceros up the Great St. Bernard we might have attracted crowds as large and staring as those Dally gathered. But they would have been merely curious, aloof, ready-to-run crowds. No other beast could have reduced the entire countryside to the childlike state which Dally brought to pass.

And my amiable elephant played her rôle of friendly ambassador from the animal kingdom, to per-

fection. When her admiring public was largest and
densest she would ask Harel for her pocket harmonica,
which she adored to play, and give a demonstration that
made everyone who heard it shout with merriment. Or
she would seek the village fountain and bathe skilfully
and methodically by shooting water over her back and
sides with her trunk—a trick that was sure fire with
the gallery. Personally I never thought much of this
self-shower business, for several times on the march,
when my attention was occupied elsewhere, Dally, passing a pool or stream, would suck up a gallon of melted
snow and spray an icy bath back upon me, to be followed, like as not, by a blast of sand and mud. To protect myself against these dousings I had to wear my
trench-coat continually.

St. Pierre, once the first fury of its elephant-fever
died down, seemed to me a village well worth noting.
Two hundred years after Hannibal the Romans, who
used the pass in summer, built here the twenty-third
rest-station for soldiers marching from Rome over the
Alps. Roman mile-posts are still found round about.
And past this village in May, 1800, Napoleon, planning his audacious surprise attack upon the Austrians
gathered in northern Italy, dragged forty thousand
French soldiers on over the Great St. Bernard. In
May the pass was still buried in snow (it is not open
to regular traffic till the end of June), but the French
managed somehow to plow their way through.

Exhausted and half-frozen, Napoleon himself reached
St. Pierre at noon and stopped at the town's only hotel
for food and rest. The moment he departed a rope was
drawn across the door of his room, and from that day

to this, nothing in that room has been changed or touched. The hotel is now called "Déjeuner de Napoleon"—Hotel of Napoleon's Lunch.

This is still the only place in town where travelers can sleep. And into the same stone stable where Napoleon's saddle-mule was sheltered, Harel and I, assisted by every inhabitant of the village capable of standing on two legs, led Dally.

Next day was Sunday. Services in the thousand-year-old church were scheduled to take place as usual at nine o'clock. But at nine o'clock Dally was back in the square standing before the public fountain, giving herself her morning beauty-treatment of ice water and dust; and every member of the congregation stood gazing, too fascinated by the spectacle to think about church.

The summon-to-prayer bells clanged impatiently; the priest stood waiting at the door. Still the villagers did not turn their enchanted eyes away from the elephant even long enough to glance in his direction. The good man was in despair. Driven to it, he approached and asked me *please* to remove my demoralizing elephant until the church hour was passed. So I locked Dally out of sight, and then, at the priest's further request, myself led his wayward flock into their pews.

Services over, we left St. Pierre and struck out again toward the summit, now only thirteen kilometers beyond. Not less than five hundred people, including all the church congregation, followed us. As usual I had lifted three small children on behind me, and the rest of the childhood of this particular valley danced

and shouted all around, elated by the rare experience
being enjoyed by three of their tribe.

We were favored with a morning of brilliant clarity.
The woods and fields had put on their brightest, greenest
dress. The streams dashed downhill alongside the road,
and above, rank after rank, the white fangs of the Alps
hung over us and walled us in. Dally, rested and fed
(like Napoleon), and stimulated by the freshness in the
air, paced along up the twisting road faster than Harel
could walk.

But not for long. The altitude began to affect her.

We were not especially high, as mountains go—about
sixty-five hundred feet. Neither Harel nor I was in-
convenienced by the rarity of the air, nor did we expect
to be, below nine or ten thousand. But Dally was not
so constituted. She had never been above sea-level before in her life. From the Sumatra lowlands and the
Paris zoo she now found herself elevated a mile and a
quarter. Her huge heart quickened. Her lungs had
to work faster. So we let her rest as often and as long
as she liked.

These rest periods came at shorter and shorter inter-
vals as we continued to ascend. I began to be apprehensive lest the eight-thousand-foot summit was going
to be too high for Dally's strength. Hannibal's elephants, I remembered, had suffered numerous casualties in climbing this (or some lower) pass. . . . I hoped
it had been the shower of boulders, not the altitude.

The continual procession of Sunday autobuses and
motorcars, grinding past us, did not help the situation.
The news of the elephant's presence in the pass had by

now spread far and wide, and motorists by the dozen, from Geneva, Lausanne, Bern, and from the Italian side, came to witness the unprecedented sight (since two millenniums) of an elephant climbing the Great St. Bernard.

I did my best to persuade them to speed on and leave Dally in peace. But my pleas were ignored. Every bus and motorcar would stop just ahead or behind and disgorge Sunday tourists by the score, who planted themselves in our path and frantically photographed each other beside the elephant.

These elephant-fanciers and their parked cars caused a complete blockade of traffic. Those coming down the pass couldn't get through. Those climbing up were halted. Motor horns blasted and screamed with impatience.

To make matters worse the brilliant morning sunshine suddenly deserted us; a blanket of fog descended, and a sharp and icy wind, sweeping down from the glaciers, chilled to the bone both the animal and her crew.

We couldn't see—or be seen—fifty feet ahead, so the traffic confusion became indescribable.

Dally was becoming more and more unhappy. I walked from time to time, in order to lighten her burden as much as possible. But even that did not help much. Not content to stop for rest periods of fifteen minutes at a stretch, she now took to sitting down in the middle of the road (had Harel not taught her how?) . . . and autobuses could just wait and take out their knitting till Dally felt like getting up and unblocking the highway again.

Harel, as unaccustomed to the mountains as Dally, became thoroughly alarmed over Dally's increasing lassitude. But I had done enough climbing to realize that she was merely exhausted by the thin air, and with a brief rest she would be quickly restored. Any mountaineer knows that in high altitudes one tires quickly but, if allowed a few moments of complete relaxation, recuperates with equal speed. And that's just what happened to Dally.

In Paris I had bought two heavy tarpaulin "overcoats" for the elephant, in order to be prepared for such emergencies as this. We now took these from the truck and gave her their protection. And every half-hour we fed her a washtubful of moistened meal, and two pounds of sugar.

Fed, rested, warmed, the brave and patient beast would slowly make up her mind to plod on.

My admiration for the elephant, already high, increased anew as I watched her behavior under these trying circumstances. She kept her poise and her good nature through everything. She did not balk or surrender, but only asked that we let her take her time. She seemed to say: "I'll go with you to the top of the highest mountain in the world . . . if you just won't press me. . . . Give me plenty of rest; I have to get accustomed to this thin air. . . . But don't worry—I'm sure we'll make the grade."

Dally's courage and determination seem all the more remarkable when we remember that she was only twelve years old, and would not even be adolescent for another six years!

This very immaturity gave rise to another one of

Dally's traits that I must mention—her passionate devotion to Harel. As I have explained, ever since Dally came to Paris, Harel and no one but Harel had taken care of her, fed, trained, washed and nursed her, taught her to stand on her hands and play the harmonica. The language he used with the elephant was a curious jargon of Norman patois, and she seemed to understand every word he said. At least she always obeyed. Whenever he came to greet her in the morning she flapped her great ears and bobbed her head up and down from sheer joy at seeing him again. And when he left her at night there was no mistaking her expression of distress. Harel, a Hercules of a man, had a way of talking baby-talk to his three-ton pet, in a singsong voice such as we ourselves use in speaking to puppies or canary birds. And when she heard herself being called his "little cabbage" and his "little sweetheart" she would come lumbering over to him, wrap her trunk adoringly around his neck, and sway back and forth on her great legs in a sort of ecstatic dance.

Harel's frequent recourse to the use of "little cabbage," more than anything else, encouraged our elephant to continue the struggle.

We had left St. Pierre at ten o'clock in the morning. It was now two in the afternoon, and we still had another thousand feet, and the last long mile, to climb. But happily at this point we broke through the layer of clouds that hung over the valley, and found ourselves once more in blazing sunshine.

All around, the shining pinnacles obscured since morning, now sprang up again closer than ever and rose another seven thousand feet above. Mont Blanc loomed in the distance. We had passed the timber-line, so the mountain sides were barren of vegetation but strewn with banks of snow. Below, the great blanket of fog still hid the valley we had left behind.

But now, just ahead, Harel and I saw a new obstacle 'hat promised trouble. We were approaching a defile (was it the same in which the Carthaginian elephants, according to Livy, were attacked so savagely by the mountaineers?) into which ice during the previous winter had piled forty feet deep and formed a small glacier.

This ice-bank, athwart the road, had not melted with the advance of summer. Consequently it had been necessary for the St. Bernard monks to dig a tunnel, six hundred feet long, right through the ice in order to make the road traversable. This tunnel had been made high enough for motorbuses to pass. But was it high enough for Dally? We could not hope to go round since either side was still blocked by snow banks high as a house.

We approached cautiously, I again on the elephant's shoulders. I feared Dally might hesitate even to try to enter this gleaming icy cylinder.

But she showed no fear, and marched straight into it. To our great relief we found that there was just enough ceiling, if I dismounted, to give her clearance. The tunnel dripped with icicles, and from them a steady slow shower of ice-water dropped down. This freezing bath none of us enjoyed, so we hurried to the far end and out into the sun again.

And there, at the tunnel exit, we found half a dozen St. Bernard monks and three of their famous dogs, come down the pass to meet us. Were we in trouble?

Did we need assistance? Could they bring food or blankets for the elephant? We thanked them; but their kind services, fortunately, were not needed.

The dogs were more astonished at the sight of Dally than the mountaineers had been. At first, growling and mystified, they refused to go near this extraordinary monster which confronted them. By coaxing and lugging we finally persuaded the biggest of the dogs to meet the lady. He sniffed cautiously at Dally's feet but remained taut and ready to spring away if she made an unfriendly move. Definitely he did not like her strange smell, nor her size and shape. He presently shrank off, and at a safe distance stood and barked defiantly at the incomprehensible giant. Dally, on the other hand, took no more notice of the dog than she would have taken of a turtle.

Led forward by the monks, we plodded on, zigzagging up the final reaches of the pass, with Dally stopping to rest every hundred yards, perhaps to sit down in the road, to eat another washtub of meal, to advance another fraction of a kilometer.

The monastery came in sight. Two thousand people were waiting for our arrival. Seeing us at last on the road just below, they ran down to greet us, making a lane through which we could pass. Dally, realizing this was her moment of glory (and that she was being photographed by a battery of cameramen from half a dozen news-reel companies), refused to rest again. She ambled on, still carrying me on her shoulders, right up to the front door of the monastery—at the topmost point of the Great St. Bernard.

The elephant! The elephant! *Such* a heroine as Dally

was that day! The fifteen monks stood about wide-
eyed; the dogs, barking and excited, looked on bewil-
dered. People climbed to the roof, hung from the windows. Several came running out of the café across the
road from the monastery, carrying glasses of cognac
and steins of beer to drink to the health of Mademoiselle
Dally.

The elephant stood unperturbed in the midst of this
mob-scene, and calmly accepted all the adulation. But
Harel and I felt it was only right that she should thank
her admiring public for the reception. So we got the
Swiss border-police (the Italian frontier is close by)
to clear a round space before the monastery's front
door. We lined the circle with the monks and as many
dogs as we could corral.

Then Dally, at the summit of the pass, eight thousand,
one hundred and twenty feet high, hemmed in by the
snow-covered Alps, on the spot where Hannibal probably pitched his camp, and surrounded by a crush of
two thousand people, made her bow. At Harel's command she rose up on her hind legs, raised her trunk as
high as possible, and blew a mighty blast on her harmonica.

That was all. She was too tired to put on the other
acts of her show.

The monks led her into a clean new garage, used to
shelter the monastery's supply·truck. And there, half-
buried in warm, sweet hay, and wrapped in blankets,
Dally for thirty-six hours enjoyed the rest and comfort
she so magnificently deserved.

But the last of our two thousand visitors did not depart till late that night. When at length the final auto·

mobile-load had been sped on its way by the Prior, this patient and merciful man sank down exhausted, in his armchair.

"What a day!" he exclaimed wearily to me. "That Dally of yours has brought more excitement and more visitors to this monastery than we have known since we entertained Napoleon."

CHAPTER XXXIII

HALF-WAY TO HEAVEN

THE monks at the St. Bernard Monastery are living half-way to Heaven. Their good works should certainly get them the rest of the way. For a thousand years they have dedicated themselves to the service of travelers struggling over the Alps. For a thousand years they have fed the hungry, sheltered the weary, dug away the snowdrifts that bury the trail for nine months out of the twelve, rescued the perishing, and prayed for those who have died before rescue could come.

These monks ask nothing in return. The traveler leaves a donation with the hospice if he is so inclined. But the majority express their gratitude only with words.

It is natural that the monastery should be celebrated in Europe, for it is located dramatically at the top of a pass over which climbs one of the great highways of the continent. But the fame of this hospice is not limited to Europe; it is world wide. Who in America, or South Africa, or Australia, has not heard of the St. Bernard? Yet it is not because Hannibal and Cæsar and Napoleon led their armies by this pass across the Alps that the monastery is famous abroad; nor because of the long and colorful history of the Bernardine brotherhood. It is because of the wonderful dogs who rescue travelers in the snow.

It is likely that every person who reads this page, at some time in his childhood, has seen a picture of a St. Bernard dog, with a flask of brandy attached to its collar, bringing aid to a snow-bound wayfarer. The details may vary; the dog may be carrying the unconscious traveler on his back, or dragging him out of a snowdrift, or barking over his prostrate form to attract the attention of the monks. But whatever the illustration, the idea has struck the imagination of us all and made the St. Bernard dog a universal nursery symbol of heroism and fidelity.

Up until the tenth century there was no form of shelter for Christians at the summit of the St. Bernard. Yet during the few weeks in summer when the trail was open, travelers preferred to cross the mountains by this route as it was the most direct from France into Italy. Pilgrims especially, en route to Rome, chose to come this way.

At that time the Italian and Swiss valleys leading to the pass were infested with heathen idol-worshipers who robbed and killed the pilgrims. The natives had built a temple to Jove at the crest (the ruins are still there) and resented the profanation of their shrine by the Christians.

Distressed by this situation, a young Italian monk named Bernard (born in what is now the French province of Savoy) received the assistance of the Pope in building a fortress-monastery at the pass, to be used as a military headquarters for pacifying and converting the heathen mountaineers, and as a hospice to shelter wayfarers.

The news of its existence spread quickly across Europe, and in a few years the number of travelers using this route quadrupled, because from having been the most dangerous route, as far as human enemies went, it had now become the safest.

Bernard's monastery housed only about thirty monks, yet hundreds applied for admission—a strange fact, since in no other monastery in the world was life quite so grim. During May, June, October and November, the monks were continually out in the snow searching for exhausted travelers who were trying to cross the pass before the trail was open or after it had closed. Then in July, August and September they were deluged with visitors, twenty thousand a season, whom they had to feed, clothe, and often nurse to health.

And at the same time, while the weather permitted, they must drag up to their hospice all the provisions and equipment required during their long imprisonment, when the snow piled thirty feet deep around them.

In 1560 the demands upon St. Bernard's original building became so great that it had to be torn down to make way for a more commodious one. The new building, austere as its surroundings, contained one hundred rooms and four hundred beds. Its walls were six feet thick to keep out the cold.

This was the building I saw when, having climbed eight thousand feet and forty miles up the Swiss side of the pass, aboard Elysabethe Dalrymple, I turned the corner of the last steep switchback on the trail and approached the crest.

St. Bernard, when he founded the monastery in 950, certainly made no provision for the care and feeding of elephants at his hospice. But the present-day monks are daunted by nothing. Though Dally was the first elephant that had ever come to call since Hannibal passed by, she was taken in and fed and cared for skilfully.

Once my big beast was warm and secure, I was shown to a room in the monastery (accompanied by two of the friendly dogs) and invited by the Prior to take my meals with the monks.

I found my quarters by no means uncomfortable. The monastery has long been a favorite charity with rich travelers who enjoyed its hospitality. Queen Victoria was once a guest and made a generous donation. King Edward VII, when Prince of Wales, came by and later sent (of all things!) a piano to the monks. The Kaiser traveled past in 1883 and left behind a substantial check. Today the King and Queen of Italy, who are frequent visitors, see to it that the monks lack nothing.

Consequently, in this solid, somber building, constructed during the reign of Queen Elizabeth, one finds central heating, a power house for electricity, a radio, telephones and a well-equipped garage.

Where once there were thirty monks, one now finds only fifteen, since the Simplon tunnel and the motor age have greatly simplified trans-Alpine travel. As many people as before visit the monastery, but ninetenths of them come by automobile, so that the chief assistance the monks render during the summer is to run a model filling station! In the snow-blockaded months, most travelers take the train *under* the Alps, and reach Italy from Switzerland in two hours instead of two weeks as previously.

The Prior turned out to be a great student of history, with a particular interest in Hannibal and the Punic Wars. And to my delight he staunchly defended my claim that Hannibal crossed the Alps with his ele· phant herd via the Great St. Bernard.

"It took Hannibal nine days," remarked the Prior, "to ascend the pass, so much opposition did he encounter from the mountaineers, and from the wildness and ruggedness of the country. If he'd used the Little St. Bernard with its paved Roman highway he'd have been up and over in two or three days instead of nine. In my opinion our hospice is built on the very spot where Hannibal, on reaching the top, pitched his camp in order to rest his men, wait for stragglers, and forage for food."

I could well believe that Hannibal's *elephants* were in need of rest. I had seen how my own Dally without howdah or baggage, constantly fed and carefully covered with blankets, still was able to move at no more than a snail's pace up the pass, because of the altitude.

But Hannibal's beasts were saddled with heavy howdahs carrying four to six armed soldiers. And food, according to Livy, was almost non-existent. For three days and nights, blocked by masses of rock and cut off from the main army by a wedge of hostile mountaineers who had broken through the long line of march, the elephants had to stand unprotected in the snow without so much as a blade of grass to eat. No wonder the casualties were so heavy.

I was curious, of course, to know all about the famous dogs, and the Prior, who was very proud of them, was perfectly willing to enlighten me.

They were first introduced in the sixteenth century, he told me, and have no relationship to the Newfoundland breed with which they are commonly confused. The St. Bernard is a cross between a bulldog and a sheepdog. Its face and head and chest have a decided bulldog quality. It has the strength, character and toughness of a bulldog but the intelligence of a sheep-dog.

Accustomed to cold weather for generations, the St. Bernards are as much at home in the snow as Arctic huskies. They have their kennel outdoors, and only in the bitterest winter storms do they prefer to come inside.

Before the days of the telephone, the monks made it a practise, once the snow season had begun, to start out each morning on skis, accompanied by their dogs, to look for travelers in distress. And many and many a half-dead traveler, buried by snow or avalanche, would have been overlooked but for the keen-scented dogs. Today when anyone starts up the pass out of season, the monks are telephoned and go to meet him.

In snowstorms, when all sense of direction is lost, a St. Bernard unerringly leads the way. And stranger still, the monks insist that when unexpected travelers, approaching the monastery, are overwhelmed by cold and snow and in desperate need of help, the dogs sense the fact, bark to be released, plow through the drifts to find their man, and rush back to lead the monks to his rescue.

One dog is always called "Barry" in memory of an especially clever and courageous St. Bernard who, toward the end of the nineteenth century, saved so many lives that he became famous all over Europe. His body is now preserved in the Museum at Berne. His son, "Barry, Jr.," had a career only little less heroic than the sire's. The son's body, also carefully mounted, is on display at the monastery.

Despite the strenuous efforts made to safeguard the pass, lives are lost each year—two in 1934, three in 1926, five in 1917. During the past century a dozen monks themselves and not a few dogs have perished in their efforts to save others, or died from the results of exposure and exhaustion.

The monks who die while serving at the monastery are laid in coffins and entombed in a rock vault. But the unclaimed bodies of laymen are merely wrapped in a shroud, or in their own storm coats, and placed uncovered on the floor of a windowless charnel house where the coldness and rareness of the air mummify the corpses and prevent decomposition.

The Prior took me out to show me this strange morgue. Inside, he said, were forty-five bodies, some standing up against the wall, some reduced to bones and dust. The door, the only opening, was kept sealed tight with masonry, so that each time a new corpse was admitted the door had to be broken down with sledge hammers, and then built up again. The oldest mummy had been there since 1620. The newest was only one year old.

Elysabethe Dalrymple, Harel, the baggage truck and chauffeur, and I, spent two days and nights as guests of the monastery. I would have liked to remain longer, but having reached the top of the Alps successfully, I decided to continue on in the tracks of Hannibal (as long as the elephant-march amused me, and Dally herself seemed willing) toward Rome.

So I climbed aboard the elephant's shoulders, and Harel took his place, on foot, by her side. Blown by the cold morning wind from the glaciers, I rode to the crest of the ridge and looked back down the trail that led up from Switzerland—and forward into Italy. Before me stretched a road that would continue on to the River Po, on to Turin, and Genoa, and Pisa, and Florence, and, I hoped, the capital itself.

And sitting there I recalled that of the thirty-seven elephants with which Hannibal began his ascent of the Alps, only one reached the heart of Italy. And even this one perished long before the Carthaginians, fighting every step of the way, arrived at the walls of the imperial city they had come to destroy.

For Dally's sake I prayed that I'd have better luck.

The entire company of monks and dogs came out to bid us God-speed. Dally raised her trunk to salute our hosts, and we started down the southern slopes, paused at the statue of St. Bernard to pay our respects to the founder of the hospice, turned across the Italian frontier, and descended into the valley that led on to the plains.

CHAPTER XXXIV

THE ELEFANTESSA

WITH every step forward into lower altitudes, Dally's spirits rose. Only for the first hour did the rarefied air make our progress slow. After that Dally no longer stopped to get her breath, but scampered along downhill in the Alpine sunshine, ready, apparently, to break all records on her march to Rome. With the crest of the mountains behind us, Harel, who ran beside the elephant, and I, who bounced on her shoulders, were in a gay mood. No more freezing winds, no more mountain sickness, only sunshine and wine and singing days ahead. We let Dally have her beloved harmonica, and the valley rang with happy elephant music.

But we gave ourselves over to rejoicing too soon. At about five thousand feet we rounded a curve and ran head-on into the mountain maneuvers of the Italian Army of Northern Italy. Forty thousand soldiers sprang up all around us. The slopes and woods suddenly swarmed with them; they filled the road, they and their military trucks, and their artillery, and their tanks and cavalry.

The Roman legions were as surprised to see us as we were to see them. Most of the soldiers were youngsters, who stood in astonishment at the sudden appearance, right in the midst of their war-game, of an *elephant*—especially an elephant playing a harmonica. Discipline went to pieces. Whole companies came running up from all sides with shouts of, *"L'elefantessa! l'elefantessa!"* as we lumbered by. Some of them no doubt thought we were the Abyssinians attacking from the rear.

Through this military scene we had plowed our way on down the road for perhaps half a mile, when disaster fell upon us. The heavy artillery, firing real shells at an imaginary enemy in a government range across the valley, suddenly let go full blast with six or eight guns from a hidden battery not two hundred yards away.

The concussion coming so unexpectedly was earsplitting. The whole earth shook, and the very air, caught between two mountain walls, vibrated with the echo.

Poor Dally! The bombardment had found her weak spot. Being a musician she had a horror of blasting noises. An especially raucous motor-horn had been the cause of her runaway down the Paris boulevard. This fear I thought she had outgrown. But I was wrong. It was only *automobile* noises she had become used to— not artillery-fire. When this terrifying, deafening explosion went off just ahead, the startled elephant rose on her hind legs, her eyes wild with fear, trumpeted frantically, wheeled about in a flash, and dashed back up the congested road in an even more uncontrollable panic than that which had seized her in Paris.

This paroxysm had come so suddenly neither Harel nor I was prepared. I was thrown from the elephant's back as she wheeled, and landed clumsily in the dust.

The guide-rope which Harel used to lead her through the masses of troops and baggage trains was jerked from his hands, trod upon and ripped to shreds, as the three-ton animated tank charged the armies of Rome.

Shouting and pleading, Harel and I rushed after her, fearful not only of the havoc she might bring to the soldiers, but also of the damage she could do to herself.

Fortunately the wild yelling from all sides, as Dally plunged up the road, gave warning to those ahead. The soldiers fell off into the ditch as the Juggernaut rushed by. Again it was fortunate that all the trucks and gun-carriages were strewn along the right half of the road, leaving the left half open. And by a miracle, at that particular moment no other motorcars were coming down the mountain out of line. Consequently, despite the blindness of her flight, Dally avoided any serious collision.

The elephant had passed through most of the military congestion and was slowing down. . . . Harel and I were almost up to her again . . . when a *second* discharge of the guns from the same battery gave new wings to her heels and caused her to dash forward in fresh terror and with redoubled energy. Once more we were left behind.

But thank heaven she did not veer off the twisting road which wound back, higher and higher, into ever rarer air. And the altitude accomplished what Harel and I could never have done--it presently exhausted the elephant's colossal strength. Panting for breath and completely winded, she was physically unable to run another step. We were able at last to get the chains around her legs again, with the assistance of a score of soldiers and every mountaineer in sight.

But we soon found that her terror had not yet subsided. We attached the chain to a two-thousand-pound boulder until she could rest and calm down. She pulled the boulder out of its bed as though it had been papiermâché. We shackled the chain to a four-inch tree, the biggest in the neighborhood. She tore it up by the roots and dragged it about. Her power, so quiet and docile heretofore, was now on a rampage and nothing could curb it.

Nothing but a stream of water. Having run full speed two kilometers up a sun-baked mountain road, Dally had become fearfully hot and thirsty. Now, seeing a small stream near by, she waded in and began to drink and to shower herself luxuriously. This gave us a chance to bring up the truck and get hold of the food buckets and feed her five gallons of her favorite meal—a form of pacification that worked successfully.

For three hours we rested by the stream, waiting for the soldiers with their damned pop-guns to leave for their camp in the valley below. Then we tried once more to travel on toward Aosta. But Dally, with that famous elephant memory, refused, positively, to go back along the highroad where she had encountered that terrifying noise. And nothing could budge her. I fetched a heavy military truck and tied her to it, hoping this would be a forceful persuasion. She sat down in the road, planted both feet before her, and defied the truck to move.

A shepherd boy solved our problem. He showed us a cow-path paralleling the road, but fifty feet farther down the slope, leading to the next village just ·as the highroad did. Dally had no objections to ·using the path.

Once more sweet as an angel, she followed Harel along this narrow trail, not realizing she was passing within fifty feet of the spot where she had been almost blasted off the road and frightened out of her skin, a place to which she would *never* knowingly have returned.

We had lost half a day, thanks to our encounter with the big guns. It was midnight when we reached Aosta at the foot of the Alps. And there, once more assisted by every citizen in the town, we put a very weary elephant to bed.

Compared with our exciting descent from the St. Bernard, the next few days were uneventful (except for the motorist who was so astonished at seeing an elephant in his path he ran his automobile into a tree). We marched on south in the direction of Turin, followed by the same mobs of shrieking children we had collected in Switzerland, and causing the same kind of tumult in every town we entered. The number of children was larger in Italy and the tumult greater only because the towns were bigger.

At every step now we were accompanied by reporters and photographers. The word "Hannibal" had upset everybody, for his conquest is still remembered in northern Italy where, strange to say, thousands of men are named for him. Our expedition was being followed on the front page by every newspaper in the country, from the Alps to Sicily. For the moment even the Ethiopian war had taken a back seat in public interest. People came in bus-loads from Milan and Genoa to look at the famous *elefantessa*. The editors of papers in Rome and Naples telephoned long distance every evening to our rest-stations, to ask for a report of our adventures of the day. Paris, London, Berlin phoned in as well each night. The-elephant-that-had-crossed-the-Alps-in-the-tracks-of-Hannibal was the talk of Europe.

And this circus-parade spirit increased in intensity as we drew near Turin. Progress became increasingly difficult, till we learned to dodge part of the crowds by leaving our hotel at four o'clock in the morning.

Despite the unprecedented and unexpected commotion we were causing, my elephant-ride was going well enough. But a serious menace to our advance now threatened. Harel, after one of his daily examinations of Dally's feet, announced that they were beginning to be bruised and blistered, and that the elephant must be given a complete rest for at least a week.

A week—and did this mean that we must cut our day's march of twenty miles in half, and, considering the hotness and hardness of Italy's stone roads, travel perhaps only every other day?

Harel believed it meant just that. Dally had stood in a comfortable zoo all her young life. Her pads, which would have been hard as hoofs if she had been left to roam the jungles, were soft after ten years of captivity, and had not, as we had hoped, toughened with use.

So I had to face the fact that instead of reaching Rome in three weeks, as was my schedule, it would possibly take three months—if we ever got there at all.

And then, just when I was in a quandary over this bruised-foot situation, Harel, driving ahead in our truck to examine the road into Turin, collided with a speed demon in a racing car and was driven off the road. The truck did two complete roll-overs down a twenty-foot embankment and landed at the bottom, smashed beyond repair.

Harel's right arm was driven through the shattered windshield and lacerated so badly that he would have to carry it in bandages several days. The truck's regular chauffeur, riding beside Harel, suffered injuries that put him also completely out of commission. Our baggage was demolished. How Harel and the chauffeur escaped being killed outright is hard to understand.

I soon reached the scene of the disaster with an ambulance. Once the two victims were in the hands of a doctor and resting comfortably, I was able to survey the wreckage of my expedition . . . no trainer, no chauffeur, no truck, no baggage, and Dally herself *hors de combat* with damaged feet.

I had to stop and consider what to do. Playing Hannibal had been, as I hoped it would be, an amusing adventure—up to a certain point. But I certainly did not plan for my devoted "army" to suffer casualties. Harel's misfortune distressed me deeply. I cursed the motor age which had dogged every mile of our journey— a menace the Carthaginians never dreamed of. And I knew that as for my march to Rome, I would have to admit defeat. For obviously there was no hope of going on, without delays which I could not afford. Harel and I faced the collapse of our plans with as good grace as possible, and prepared to retreat to Paris.

After a rest of several days we were able to hobble the last ten miles into Turin. There five thousand people—and a brass band ordered by the Fiat company—met us. It was a blaze of glory for Dally, who bowed her thanks for such a reception to the crowds that lined her path. Rome itself could not have capitulated more completely.

Three days later, back in Paris, I went to say goodby to Dally. She was again in the Jardin d'Acclimatation, back in her old stall, munching at her hay as complacently as if she had never been away, had never gone places no other elephant had gone since the time of Hannibal. To look at her calm, detached countenance, one would not have suspected that she had climbed the Alps, defied the cold and altitude, sent two score towns and villages into a frenzy of excitement, demoralized the Army of Northern Italy, brought reporters and cameramen speeding to her side from almost every big newspaper and movie company in Europe, and been the most photographed, admired, discussed, described, beloved elephant in history.

Nor did I realize until that hour of parting how deeply attached I had become to the brave beast that had carried me uncomplainingly for so many difficult miles. I went inside her stall, put my arms around her trunk, scratched her ears, and fed her the two pounds of sugar I'd brought along. She leaned against me and with her snozzle searched my pockets for more sweets. She made me feel I was losing the most affectionate and most lovable comrade I'd ever known, and that I must reward her magnificently for her fidelity and her good sportsmanship.

And so I did. I brought forth my farewell gift, a

shining new harmonica, extra large. Dally, seizing it eagerly in her trunk, blew vociferously upon its keys. And as I walked away, with a lump in my throat, I still heard fading behind me the whine of the harmonica, and I felt sure that though she may have been foot-sore and travel-weary, Elysabethe Dalrymple, besides being at that moment the most famous elephant in the world, was the happiest.

THE END

Some of the other titles in the AdventureTravel Classic series published by The Long Riders' Guild Press. We are constantly adding to our collection, so for an up-to-date list please visit our website: **www.thelongridersguild.com**

The Rob Roy on the Jordan	John MacGregor
In the Forbidden Land	Henry Savage Landor
From Paris to New York by Land	Harry de Windt
My Life as an Explorer	Sven Hedin
Elephant Bill	Lt.-Col. J. H. Williams
Fifty Years below Zero	Charles Brower
Quest for the Lost City	Dana and Ginger Lamb
Enchanted Vagabonds	Dana Lamb
Seven League Boots	Richard Halliburton
The Flying Carpet	Richard Halliburton
New Worlds to Conquer	Richard Halliburton
The Glorious Adventure	Richard Halliburton
The Royal Road to Romance	Richard Halliburton
My Khyber Marriage	Morag Murray Abdullah
Khyber Caravan	Gordon Sinclair
Servant of Sahibs	Rassul Galwan
Beyond Khyber Pass	Lowell Thomas
True Stories of Modern Explorers	B. Webster Smith
Call to Adventure	Robert Spiers Benjamin
Heroes of Modern Adventure	T. C. Bridges
Death by Moonlight	Robert Henriques
To Lhasa in Disguise	William McGovern
The Lives of a Bengal Lancer	Francis Yeats-Brown
Twenty Thousand Miles in a Flying Boat	Sir Alan Cobham
The Secret of the Sahara: Kufara	Rosita Forbes
Forbidden Road: Kabul to Samarkand	Rosita Forbes
I Married Adventure	Osa Johnson
Grey Maiden	Arthur Howden Smith
Sufferings in Africa	Captain James Riley
Tex O'Reilly – Born to Raise Hell	Tex O'Reilly and Lowell Thomas

The Long Riders' Guild
The world's leading source of information regarding equestrian exploration!
www.thelongridersguild.com

Printed in the United States
1268400003B/48